Alan Mitchell is a business writer, a contributing editor to *Marketing Week* and columnist for a number of other marketing, retailing and new media publications. He has tracked the unfolding revolution in marketing over many years, as a former marketing correspondent of *The Times*, editor of *Marketing* magazine, and author of the *Financial Times* report 'Brand Strategies in the Information Age'. He can be contacted by e-mail at asmitchell@aol.com.

Right Side Up

Building Brands in
the Age of the
Organized Consumer

ALAN MITCHELL

HarperCollinsBusiness
An Imprint of HarperCollins*Publishers*

HarperCollinsBusiness
An Imprint of HarperCollins*Publishers*
77–85 Fulham Palace Road,
Hammersmith, London W6 8JB

www.**fire**and**water**.com/business

Published by HarperCollinsBusiness 2002
1 3 5 7 9 8 6 4 2

First published in Great Britain by
HarperCollinsBusiness 2001

ISBN 0 00 6531962

Set in New Century Schoolbook

Printed and bound in Great Britain by
Clays Ltd, St Ives plc

To Dad

ACKNOWLEDGEMENTS

Three people have particularly influenced the development of this book. Barry Hill first set me on this track back in 1996 with his brave (but failed) infomediary experiment Request. He is currently UK Managing Director of Transnational. The thinking of Philip Evans (Boston Consulting Group) and John Hagel (McKinsey & Co) was also extremely influential. Each of them has kindly taken time to talk to me about his ideas.

I have drawn on hundreds of other conversations with other people in various chapters, but the following were particularly helpful in clarifying my thoughts – though they may be horrified at some of the conclusions I have drawn! I list them below in alphabetical order (with the job titles pertaining at the time of our conversations).

Dave Allen (Chief Executive, Enterprise IG), Jan Andreae (President, Albert Heijn and member of the Royal Ahold board), Graham Booth (Supply Chain Development Director, Tesco), Ralph Drayer (Vice President, product supply and customer business development, Procter and Gamble), Martin Glenn (Chief Executive, Walkers Snack Foods), Simon Gulliford (marketing consultant), John Foster (General Secretary, National Union of Journalists), Anthony Freeling (Principal, McKinsey & Co.), Jan Hall (partner, Spencer Stuart), Dan Jones (Director of the Lean Enterprise Centre at Cardiff Business School), Simon Knox (Professor of brand management, Cranfield Management School), Chris Macrae (World Class Branding Network), Stan Maklan (consultant, CSC Index), Regis McKenna (consultant), Joseph Pine (consultant), Martha Rogers and Don Peppers (consultants), Paul Polman (Head of global fabric care, Procter & Gamble), Ian Ryder (Vice President of brand and communications, Unisys), Doc Searles (*Cluetrain Manifesto*), Peter Simpson (Commercial Director, First Direct), Mike Saylor (CEO, Microstrategy), Enrico Toja (Vice President, Johnson and Johnson International), Sandra Vandermerwe (Chair of Management and Professor of international marketing, Imperial College), Heinz Wiezorek (Chairman of the management board, Coca-Cola Germany), Sergio Zyman (former Chief Marketing Officer, Coca-Cola).

PREFACE

Over the past decade I've conducted in the region of 5000 interviews about marketing: with practitioners, consultants, academics – experts all. In that time there has been one question I could never find a satisfactory answer to.

Marketers display incredible insight and deep expertise when applying core precepts of marketing such as 'find out what the customer wants and give it to him' to their organizations' products and services. But why don't they practice what they preach when it comes to their own activities? Why is it that companies never seem to think that their marketing in its broadest sense – how they go to market – should add as much value to the consumer and be as 'worth buying' as their products and services?

What follows flows from my attempt to answer this question. The end result is part critique, part crusade, and part (I hope) a cold, clinical analysis of the forces and trends which are helping to turn the world of business and marketing – you've guessed it – Right Side Up.

Traditionalists may find some of what follows infuriating. Good. It is meant to provoke. If it doesn't prompt you to think again about unquestioned assumptions and practices in business today, it will have failed. On the other hand, I hope, it might just help point a way to a better alternative.

contents

introduction: marketing turned right side up

> *In the coming decade marketing will be reengineered from A to Z. There is little doubt that markets and marketing will operate on quite different principles in the early years of the twenty-first century.* Philip Kotler[1]

For its first hundred years, marketing – and business itself – has revolved around a single driving imperative: helping sellers to sell. With the dawn of an information age, however, this world is being turned upside down. Or to be more precise, Right Side Up.

We are entering a new era where the most influential businesses organize demand rather than supply; where the dominant form of marketing revolves around helping buyers to buy, rather than helping sellers to sell. Where business and marketing is done by, for, or on behalf of consumers or buyers, rather than by sellers for sellers; where Mohammed no longer has to go to the mountain. But where the business mountain has to come to the consumer Mohammed.

No marketing concept, tool, technique or assumption – no

business entity or brand – will escape the effects of this tectonic shift. This book explains why, and what it means for buyers and sellers alike.

CALM BEFORE THE STORM?

It would be difficult to portray the last few roller-coaster years of Internet and e-commerce frenzy as a period of relative calm. Never has there been so much excitement, activity and hype in the business world. Yet, looking back, we'll see this period as just a prelude to a much deeper revolution.

This first phase began to draw to a close as great expectations – especially for business-to-consumer e-commerce – began to make way for great disappointment. Somehow, somewhere along the line, the promise seemed to evaporate.

But why? What went wrong? During the first phase of the great connectivity revolution, we mouthed the phrase 'the Internet changes everything' but even as we did so we naturally and unconsciously took with us the assumptions of a previous era – an industrial, seller-centric era when business was all about helping sellers to sell.

Don't knock it. Information is creating huge potential here. But it's still only half of the picture, and it's the other half that really changes everything.

As new information age capabilities and opportunities – such as plummeting transaction costs and new flows of information which rise 'upwards' from buyer to seller and burst sideways from consumer to consumer – mature they create the conditions for completely new types of business to flourish. Not traditional business-to-consumer businesses, but consumer-to-business and consumer-to-consumer businesses. And among these new types of business we discover a critically important catalyst of change: the organized consumer and his agents.

Now consumer agents are set to transform the very nature of our economic, and marketing, system. To make it buyer-centric, rather than seller-centric. To turn it Right Side Up.

INTRODUCING BUYER-CENTRIC MARKETING

Buyer-centric, rather than seller-centric, business marketing? What, exactly, does this mean? As Philip Kotler said, it means markets and marketing are beginning to operate according to quite different principles.

Take **marketing communications**. Today's world of marketing communications is entirely seller-centric. It is done by sellers, for sellers. Advertising, direct marketing, public relations and so on all present the information sellers want to present, in the form they want to present it, to the people they want to present it to, to achieve their purposes: to shepherd targeted buyers to 'my offer' and persuade them to choose 'my offer' in preference to that of my rivals.

Right Side Up, buyer-centric communications, on the other hand, shift the centre of gravity towards the dissemination of information that helps buyers reach their objectives: to buy the best quality product or service, that's most appropriate to their needs and circumstances, at the lowest possible price. From the buyer's point of view, seller-centric communications are partial, biased and self-interested, whereas buyer-centric information is impartial, objective, comprehensive, relevant and useful.

Today's **distribution channels** create seller-centric forms of marketplace: designed to work in a way that helps sellers to sell. The tied dealership is a classic example. It creates an environment where everything is controlled by the seller: what is stocked, how it is presented, what information is made available, what sort of incentives and promotions are offered, and so on. It restricts consumer choice to the products of one or a few selected seller(s), thereby discouraging 'shopping around'. And it hands control over price to the seller, with devices such as recommended retail price.

Buyer-centric channels and marketplaces, on the other hand, are constructed to help buyers search out the items they want, make informed comparisons and decisions, and get the best possible deal. Independent retailers, who place competing items next to each other on the same shelf and stock what sells, rather than what suppliers want to push, represent a halfway house. But their prime role is still to act as a selling rather than a buying channel. In fact, retailers tend to be consummate sellers and a key part of a selling system.

Fully fledged buying channels, on the other hand, are constructed in such a way that they help buyers buy. Reverse-auctions, for example, 'rig' the system so that sellers bid against each other for a buyer's custom. While recommended retail price puts the seller in charge, reverse auctions create a pricing system that puts the buyer in charge.

Today's definitions of **value** are also seller-centric. They follow the inner industrial age logic of 'what do I make and how can I sell it?'. Seller-centric marketers make a tremendous fuss about focusing on, and meeting the needs of, the consumer. But this focus on the consumer is just a means to an end: to sell their particular product or service more effectively.

A soap powder brand – the classic icon of traditional marketing – is a good example of seller-centric value. The value is defined by what is convenient for me the producer to make in my factories, not what is convenient for you the consumer to achieve in your life. Having brought this value to market, I expect you, the consumer, to come searching for it, and to organize your life – the things you have to do to realize its value such as washing and ironing – around it.

A buyer-centric approach to value, on the other hand, doesn't start with the value the producer wants to sell, but with the value consumers want to realize in their lives: in this case, fresh clean clothes, ironed and ready to wear. It points, in other words, to the design of completely different business systems.

INTRODUCING AGENTS

Today's **businesses** – modern corporations – are also entirely seller-centric. The modern corporation arranges *the supply* of goods and services in an organized, disciplined, professional manner. It makes its money by creating offers which it brings to market, to sell. In the unfolding information age, new breeds of consumer agent organize *demand* in a disciplined, professional manner. They make their money by sourcing the best offers and constructing the best outcomes at the best prices on behalf of their consumer clients. Agents come in many forms. Numerous types of **buying agent**, which act for buyers within markets, are emerging. Buying clubs, which aggregate consumer buyer power, are one example. Infomediaries, which gather information to help buyers make the best comparisons and choices and negotiate the best deals, are another. There are also **solution agents**, which construct complete solutions on behalf of their clients. And **transformation agents**, which work with their clients to help them to reach important goals. And **passion brands**, which organize people around the pursuit of common interests and causes.

The ideal consumer agent is a cross between a solicitor, a trusted expert adviser who I pay to be on my side and who will hopefully save or secure me far more than I pay him; a butler, who is worth his weight in gold because he takes on the chores I don't want to do; and a mass-market retailer whose operational efficiencies, sourcing skills and buying power means I get the best possible deal from suppliers at the lowest possible cost.

The potential permutations and combinations of these roles are endless. But they were never possible as combinations in an industrial age where personal service and expert advice were too expensive for the ordinary individual, and where the latest technologies and economies of scale were owned and controlled by sellers rather than buyers. Agents seize the potential of the information age to change all that.

A new breed of superbrand is emerging. It is sparking a revolution at the heart of capitalism itself.

Over time – they are still young and it will be some time before they mature – they will come to dominate entire realms of commerce such as home replenishment, home management, personal financial management, health and personal transport, seizing the high-points of industrial age marketing – its brands and offers – and turning them into the raw material of new types of business.

Whereas the traditional corporation represents organized capital, the agent represents the organized consumer. The pivotal commercial institution of the industrial age was the joint-stock company. It rose to prominence because of its ability to realize the potential of that era's new technologies. These technologies required massive investment in infrastructure such as plant, machinery, mines, railroads and factories. Only joint-stock companies could make such investment, because only they could raise enough capital: the critical bottleneck resource of that time. Today, the joint-stock corporation is the undisputed centre of commercial gravity, strutting the globe as the world's dominant economic actor.

Consumer agents, however, represent a new type of institution. Let's call it the joint-info-stock company. It is designed to realize the full potential of the critical technologies of our era, which revolve around information processing. It gathers, aggregates and deploys the critical bottleneck resource of our time: information from and about consumers – about demand. Whereas the joint-stock company's key source of capital was money from investors, the joint-info-stock company's key source of capital is information from consumers and customers. And to gain access to this capital it must maximize the return it generates for these investor/consumers. In other words, it must act as the consumer's agent, rather like the modern board of directors acts as the shareholder's agent.

In the early days of the industrial age, there was huge pent-up demand for goods and services and hardly any organized supply. As a result, suppliers called the shots. Today, however, thanks to the incredible wealth creating capacity of the industrial age, we have an abundance of capital and a relative dearth of sales: saturated markets and overcapacity. Instead of having too little supply meeting too much demand, we have too much supply chasing too little demand. The boot is on the other foot.

That is how, by putting the buyer in the driving seat not only operationally, but financially and economically too, Right Side Up represents the beginning of a revolution in the institutional heart of capitalism itself.

A NEW MARKETING SYSTEM

Right Side Up heralds the dawn of a completely new marketing system. As Kotler predicted, it penetrates deep – very deep – into the *principles* by which markets and marketing work. As we shed light on this emerging system, we not only find fundamental building blocks such as marketing communications, distribution channels, forms of value and business institutions turning upside down. We also find ourselves questioning many of the long-standing, deep-seated and unquestioned assumptions that underpin our notions of marketing itself – assumptions about what marketing is, who does marketing, and who for.

We discover, for example, that the core, generic functions of **marketing** – matching supply to demand, and connecting buyers to sellers – can be undertaken by anybody: sellers, buyers or independent third parties. We find sellers losing their one-hundred-year-old monopoly on marketing as an organized, professional process. And we see the rise of market-*ing* (going to market) as an organized, professional process that is carried out for, and on behalf of, buyers and consumers.

We realize that '**the consumer**' is an artefact – and relic – of the industrial age. Consumers are human beings. But industrial age marketers invented 'the consumer' by stripping people of all their human attributes except the ones they cared about: the attributes that contributed to their role as a unit of demand for sellers' products or services. Look again, however, and we can see that 'the consumer' has a lot more to trade than just money. He is also an investor and seller of other assets such as information, time, attention and commitment.

This paves the way for our next discovery: that '**the market**' is not the final arbiter and clearing house of value, as we tend to think it is. Markets as we know them are cold, hard, instrumental mechanisms designed to facilitate a very particular – industrial age – form of exchange: the one-dimensional exchange of money for goods or services. Real, human exchange is much richer. It is multi-dimensional, encompassing the sharing and exchange of those other forms of value: information and ideas, of time and attention, of goals and objectives, of values, passions and emotions. Compared to the potential of real human exchange, market exchange is thin gruel indeed.

And we discover that **brands** as we know them, the apparent high point of modern marketing, are nothing of the sort. They are, in fact, the high point of seller-centric narcissism. My brand is built by me – the seller – to represent my attributes in the best possible light in order to make you – the 'consumer' – want me and be 'loyal' to me. The process of brand building is me telling you how wonderful I am. Now we are seeing the emergence of a new breed of buyer-centric brand which organizes and represents consumers rather than producers.

IT'S ALL ABOUT WIN-WIN

That doesn't mean that traditional markets, brands, selling, sellers, marketing or marketers are about to disappear, decline or 'die'. The rise of an industrial age didn't mean the end of farming. We still had to eat. It did, however, mean that the key players of the previous era – such as landlords – lost their central, critical importance to make way for new stars of the economic stage.

Likewise, the rise of an information age doesn't mean we stop producing and selling. We still need products and services. But it does mean that the business and marketing strategies that made sellers' brands powerful yesterday won't necessarily keep them powerful tomorrow.

'Win-win' lies at the heart of it. Every successful business relationship or transaction creates a superior win-win outcome. If it's not a win for both sides, one side or the other will see no reason to pursue the relationship, or close the transaction. If it's not a *superior* win-win, one side or the other will find a good reason to go elsewhere.

Industrial age win-wins were constructed on the foundations of ever-improving economies of scale in matter processing, we were able to share the benefits of our ever-improving ability to make better quality things at lower prices. The new information age win-wins are driven by ever more efficient information processing. This shifts the win-win focus from *making* to *marketing* – ever better quality *marketing* at ever lower cost.

Marketing's core tasks of matching supply to demand and connecting buyers to sellers are highly information intensive. They're also hugely expensive: as we'll see later, they now account for about a half of all economic activity. But by going Right Side Up – by moving from a 'push' marketing system driven by sellers to a 'pull' marketing system controlled by buyers, for example – vast swathes of these costs can be eliminated. At the same time, an ever richer exchange of information between buyers and sellers opens up huge new opportunities for a more finely tuned – and more efficient – matching of supply to demand.

Such things are easily said, but very difficult to do. Win-win marketing means, for example, that marketing activities and investments must add as much value to the buyer as they do to the seller: marketing must be 'worth buying' in its own right. And richer exchanges of information are not possible in traditional one-dimensional markets concerned only with the exchange of money for goods. They require human exchange: the multi-dimensional exchanges that take place not in 'markets' but in 'communities'.

We'll end up using the insulting term 'the consumer' throughout this book. But make no mistake. Right Side Up heralds the end of 'the consumer' and the re-emergence of human-centred wealth creation – that involves people not only as 'consumers' but also as investors, sellers, producers and as partners in the whole process – to mutual benefit. And the processes and mindset of seller-centric marketing positively hamper our progress towards this goal.

Buyer-centric win-wins point to a new acid test of business success: the ability to create wealth or add value 'in my life' – to maximize *the buyer's* profit or return, rather than the seller's. In a Right Side Up world, shareholders don't necessarily lose. Win-wins remain crucial. But maximizing *shareholder* value isn't necessarily the ultimate or underlying purpose of every business.

> *Agents represent the organized consumer. They change who marketing is for.*

Buyer-centric win-wins also transform the brandscape. Brands tend to represent the pinnacles of win-win value creation. As the win-wins change, so does the brand pecking order, with the rise of a new breed of buyer-centric superbrand.

STORM WARNING

Over its first hundred years, marketing has weathered many a tumultuous storm. It rode the waves of change from press to radio to TV. It seized upon the enormous potential of the database. It spawned an ever-growing range of disciplines and sub-disciplines: advertising, direct marketing, public relations, sponsorship and design. It invented ever more sophisticated tools and concepts such as one-to-one marketing, relationship marketing and permission marketing.

Within the profession, there were long and stormy arguments about which of these media, disciplines, tools and concepts was most important. But compared to the storm that's now brewing, each one of these developments and debates was just a minor squall. Each and every one of these squalls raged within the same tea cup. They were all about how to help sellers sell more, more efficiently, more effectively, more profitably.

Right Side Up, however, is the first storm to shake every element of marketing to its core – to change the very nature of the beast itself. As we've seen, this transformation encompasses who does marketing and who marketing is for; fundamental changes to the forms of business and market; the means by which we create value and build brands; the content of our communications.

As with all revolutions, the slogans are simple but the processes of change will become very messy, as sellers struggle to adjust to an increasingly buyer-centric marketing environment. Some will continue to focus on driving traditional industrial age win-wins forward. (These win-win outcomes are not subsiding evenly, and will never disappear completely.) Some will *pretend* to be agents, adopting an agency 'positioning' in order to make old-fashioned selling strategies seem more palatable to buyers. Many more will seek to head off the agent threat by incorporating elements of buyer-centric marketing into their strategies: by doing things which *have the effect of* helping buyers to buy even when the overall strategy is seller-centric. Others will positively welcome and work with agents to reengineer go-to-market costs: to build completely new forms of win-win with agents and their customers. Yet others – especially in the fields of retailing, financial services and media – will seek to become agents themselves, seeing the agency role as their heaven-sent opportunity to reinvent themselves to become twenty-first-century superbrands.

Seller-centric marketing as we know it has survived and flourished for one hundred years already. Why should it not survive and flourish just as well for the next hundred years? The answer doesn't lie simply in the fact that Right Side Up is desirable. Or even that, thanks to the information age, it has become possible. Or even that a deepening crisis within industrial age marketing is making a root-and-branch overhaul of marketing theories and practices necessary. The answer lies in the fact that all three – the possibility of change, the necessity of change, and the desirability of change – are fusing to create a moment of huge potential and possibility. That moment is Now.

PART 1

from offer to agent

Wings on the elephant

Industrial age marketing is the greatest win-win commercial system ever invented. It powered the most amazing wealth creation for over a hundred years. But it has begun to run out of steam. And as it does so, its flaws and weaknesses are coming to the fore.

At the same time, however, we are entering a new information age, which is spawning a new marketing system. Marketing as we have known it for the last hundred years has been all about helping sellers to sell. Now a new and very different win-win system of buyer-centric marketing is emerging.

the agency revolution

> *Selling focuses on the needs of the seller, marketing on the needs of the buyer.*   Ted Levitt[1]
>
> *We are creating a new type of market: a special power of attorney of the consumer. We are unionizing them all.*   Mike Saylor, CEO Microstrategy[2]
>
> *What companies don't realize is that customer relationship management is a different business.*   Barry Hill, Managing Director Transnational UK[3]

COWBOY KILLER

It's February 2000, and for the UK, the weather is unseasonably mild. People's thoughts are naturally turning to spring: spring cleaning, gardening, home improvements. For the thousands of hard-working horny-handed sons of toil knee-deep in mud, digging foundations and drains, the warmer weather is a real boost. There's a house price boom under way and home owners' demand for home improvement projects is strong. Business this year should be good. But if anyone was to tell them that the Internet was about to transform their working lives, that would seem far fetched. 'OK. I've heard a lot about the Internet. But what has it got to do with the intensely physical task of digging foundations and manhandling bits of bricks and mortar?'

On St Valentine's day, in London, a new 'dot-com' company was launched. And if its dreams come true, the UK home improvement market will never be the same again. The new venture's name is HomePro.com, and it is using one of the things the Internet is very good at – connecting people to other people and to information quickly and efficiently – to kill the cowboy builder.

HomePro.com recruits only pre-vetted, reputable building contractors to be listed on its website, so any consumer seeking a contractor via the site has an immediate reassurance that 'this particular contractor is not a cowboy who is going to rip me off'.

HomePro.com doesn't just take the contractor's word for it. Each company's track record is inspected. The vetting process not only includes standard checks of county court and bankruptcy judgements. It also involves choosing ten previous customers at random from the contractor's invoice book and personally visiting them. That way, the contractor cannot choose people who'll only say nice things about him, or prime them before the visit. Of those who dare volunteer for the inspection, enough skeletons are found in their cupboards for 40 per cent to be rejected straight away.

HomePro.com makes it quite clear that any contractor found guilty of bad practice will be immediately removed from the list. Plus, the work of any contractor hired through the site is insured, just in case the contractor goes out of business and can't put things right. The consumer can't lose.

This is one corner of the traditional economy which proved itself immune to industrial age marketing. In such a small scale domestic jobbing market, there were few economies of scale to be realized. So no big companies with big brands and reputations to protect emerged.

Instead, all the incentives of the market favoured the rip-off artist; the cowboy. Contacts between individual home owners and specific contractors are so few and far between (mostly for 'one-off' jobs), that few contractors face the prospect of winning repeat business by 'delighting their customers'. And because so many home owners are desperate, and/or ignorant about the technicalities, it is very easy for unscrupulous cowboys to 'blind them with science', do shoddy work and charge exorbitant prices. They could get away with it, because they never had to do business with the customer again. The way this particular market worked, it positively incentivized villainous behaviour.

HomePro.com creates a new type of marketplace, however, where 'at last, the good guy has somewhere to plant his flag', as founder and director Kim Rehfeld puts it. Here, all the incentives are reversed. Good guys have an incentive to register with the website because it lowers their customer acquisition costs and they know that fearful consumers will flock to the site in search of the peace of mind it offers. Once registered, they have a positive incentive to do a good job because HomePro.com keeps a tag on consumers' assessments of their work – and those contractors receiving the best ratings from the customers automatically go to the top of the list for new business. So they get to pick and choose the jobs they want to do.

HomePro.com also has an incentive to make sure that every deal it brokers works out well, because that's how it makes its money: by taking a fee from contractors for every lead generated and every contract signed. The more satisfied customers use its site, the more money it earns. In other words, by using the capabilities of the information age HomePro.com has crafted a win-win-win solution (for consumers, 'good guy' contractors and itself) out of a running sore of a win-lose set of relationships.

Yet as far as HomePro.com is concerned, that's just the beginning – it is not just a virtual exchange electronically connecting buyers to sellers. It is also a buying club, and an excellent source of information. It uses the feedback generated by the interactions and transactions to transform its market's workings.

HomePro.com will know, for example, that this month there are, say, orders for 500 conservatories going through its system. It can then collate the contractors working on these conservatories into a buying club to negotiate special bulk discounts with suppliers. Result: lower prices for contractors plus lower go-to-market costs for suppliers.

But there's more. Taking advantage of the potential of modern IT, HomePro.com is creating 'personal folders' for each customer, which give those customers the tools to plan their work in detail, online, and transmit these details to the contractors concerned. Soon, it hopes, it will have perfected a system that allows home owners to take a digital photograph of the four walls of a room, reconstruct the room or home digitally in their personal folder, and then use a special tool-box to experiment with the changes they want.

This is a real service for the customer – and a lot more. It means that HomePro.com not only knows that consumers X and Y have a dream to transform their homes, it also has a near perfect idea of the detailed content of that dream – a long time before any of those decisions are actually realized via purchases in the marketplace.

> *When consumers start to realize their real value they will exercise power.*

Using its personal folder service, HomePro.com is developing an online, real-time sensor of the home improvement market: what projects people are going for, which design styles are most popular, which colour schemes, and so on.

Materials and decorating suppliers would die for such information: if they could get hold of it. They would be round there like a shot, perhaps with a mail drop, or a phone call. Information like this would allow them to preempt the market's traditional forms of competition. HomePro.com offers them this opportunity: but with a twist.

It doesn't just sell the names and addresses as a typical list broker would. It doesn't make money by selling information about customers to other companies. It uses this information to make money *for* its customers. It does this by selling sales leads to sellers – not names and addresses, just the fact that 'we have a customer who is looking for this'. And it then lets sellers 'bid' for this business by offering these customers special deals, via HomePro.com's website.

So the customer doesn't get any old special offer or blanket promotion. The content of each offer is customized – specifically to fit the needs of each particular customer as detailed in his design specification. For the customer this is a real benefit. He gets, say, a 30 per cent discount on exactly the items he is looking for, at the exactly the time he is looking for them. And he's got this benefit in return for handing over information to HomePro.com. The supplier gets to close a sale. And he effectively pays the customer (in the form of a special discount) for giving him the information that helped him close this sale and reduce his go-to-market costs. Once more HomePro.com takes a cut on the transaction.

If HomePro.com succeeds – it's early days yet – it will be one of the first of many consumer agents which are helping to turn marketing Right Side Up. That is how it sees itself. That is its mission.

'Our role,' explains Rehfeld, 'is to act as the consumer agent – an infomediary. The fundamentals of the model – and this applies to various sectors – is the consumer movement. Consumers vote with their feet. They can, in numbers, change the decisions of businesses. They can vote bad offerings out. Also the Internet allows consumers' voices to be compounded through their numbers. This is what the Internet is strong at: bringing consumers together.

'The consumer is the most important part of any production chain,' Rehfeld continues. 'When consumers start to realize their real value – the value of their information – they will exercise power. At the moment that information is solely used by marketers to spam consumers with messages. We want to turn it around. We want to use private information, and to categorize it for you, so that you start seeing us as a trusted agent. We give value back to the consumer in the end.'

CATALYST OF CHANGE

The actual notion of agency isn't new at all. Agents have always existed. Doctors and solicitors earn their living by deploying their expert knowledge on behalf of their clients. 'My solicitor' is my agent within the legal system, acting on my behalf, representing my interests. 'My doctor' is my agent within the health system, helping to sort out my health problems for me. Consumer cooperatives, mutual building societies and mutual life assurance companies have acted for their members within markets, aggregating their buying power and sharing the resulting benefits. Consumer-oriented pressure groups such as the Consumers Association in the UK and the Good Housekeeping Institute in America have sought to gather and use information about products and services to help buyers (rather than sellers) to make more informed choices.

But ultimately, these various forms of agent have remained on the margins of industrial age consumer markets. Expert advice and personal services have always been too expensive to become mass market brands. Pressure groups have always been constrained by a lack of funds. Cooperatives and mutuals have made significant inroads in sectors such as the mortgage and life assurance markets, but in competition with their full-blooded capitalist competitors they have often been hamstrung by their mutual status. Decision making has either been too slow or has lacked the ruthlessness of rival profit-oriented concerns, or they have found themselves either with too little capital or too much – and prey to 'carpetbaggers'.

But now, thanks to the information age a whole new zoo of agent-based business models are developing. They use new information age capabilities to fulfil all of the functions of their industrial age predecessors – expert and impartial advice and information, aggregated buying power, personal service – and a lot more. They are moving from the periphery to the heart of modern commerce.

Agents are the catalysts of the Right Side Up marketing revolution. Their change-triggering abilities boil down to three simple factors. First, agents turn the tables on a hundred years of marketing. Agents take the side of the buyer. In doing so, they turn the old marketing system upside down. Or, to be more precise, Right Side Up.

Second, agents are quintessential information age businesses. They only exist because technological developments make them possible. Most marketers are embracing the opportunities presented by the Internet, the data warehouse, and so on, to *make the old system work better*. This is perfectly legitimate. Those who succeed in this will create a tremendous amount of value. But agents go one step further. They use the same technologies to *change the way the system works*: to lead a value revolution on behalf of consumers.

Agents use plummeting transaction and interaction costs, for example, not to help sellers send out more selling information at a lower cost, but to access and process information to help buyers buy more efficiently and effectively. They use new information flows to aggregate information from and about consumers to fully utilize their power within the marketplace. They deploy ever richer data content, not to 'target' sales prospects ever more efficiently, but to help their clients find the deals that are just right for them: they put the database (and all the whizz-bang technologies that surround it such as data warehousing and datamining) at the disposal of the customer rather than the supplier.

Third, agents not only put the tools of marketing at the disposal of the buyer; in order to help buyers buy they actually change the way markets themselves work; how they are constructed. A reverse auction, for example, where sellers bid for a buyer's custom, is a completely different type of marketplace.

Agents which help 'customers' seek out and extract value from 'vendors' are now emerging in most consumer markets. That's one reason for picking HomePro.com as an example: you would think there was no way that the Internet could change the home improvements business as plumbing, for example, is not an information intensive process. But the *market* for plumbers is an information intensive process, as *all* markets are.

So no sector and no brand is immune. Cars, household durables, groceries, financial services, transport, health, leisure, everything to do with creating and managing a house and a home: every commercial concern serving every aspect of the modern consumer's life will find itself being sucked through the mangle as agents turn the market (and marketing) upside down. Or Right Side Up.

HOW, THEN, DO AGENTS CREATE VALUE?

Agents also represent a completely different sort of business model. Traditionally, sellers invest in assets such as factories or shops, and use these assets to generate offers. If they can earn enough money from these offers – a margin – they can cover their costs and make a profit.

The agent's core asset is the customer: his money, his information. Agents add economic value by gathering these assets up, aggregating them and using them on behalf of their clients, within the marketplace; by revolutionizing the processes needed to match and connect offers to buyers. The very way they go about their business means that they make markets and marketing work according to the 'quite different principles' Kotler talked about.

Using the example of HomePro.Com shows how this adds value for consumers. In essence, the way agents earn their keep is by taking 'a cut' of this value for themselves. Economically speaking, the sources of this value come from:

- gathering more, better quality information from consumers to create better, more sophisticated matches between demand and supply – connecting exactly the right seller to exactly the right buyer far more efficiently; opening the way for consumers to say, 'This is exactly what I want.'.
- drastically cutting the costs to both buyers and sellers in communicating, interacting and closing transactions.
- using aggregated information from and about customers to reap new economies of scale, from the combined buying power of the consumers, to identify market trends, segments and opportunities in real time, as they unfold.
- eliminating waste from industrial age matching and connecting processes by reversing the flow of information, so that it flows from buyers to sellers, as well as from sellers to buyers.
- using new information processing capabilities to minimize the time and money spent planning, coordinating, organizing and administering routine functions.

Traditionally companies make money on their margin – i.e. the difference between cost of product and price. Agents' sources of income are different. Agents are experimenting with an enormous range of business models and income streams including transaction fees; commission generated on connecting buyer to seller or on sales generated; 'selling attention' (by charging sellers who want to get in touch with buyers who are interested in their offers), selling aggregated information about market trends to suppliers, subscription and membership fees and professional fees (payments for expertise and advice).

Sometimes, the actual money that changes hands comes from sellers rather than buyers, and for this reason, it's easy to conclude that, in reality, agents are just another 'channel to market' for sellers. But a closer look at the fundamental economics reveals something very different – and this difference goes right to the heart of the shift from an industrial to an information age.

First, one of the reasons why sellers are prepared to pay agents is because agents reduce sellers' go-to-market costs. They are genuinely adding value. But second – and this is crucial – economically speaking, *the prime source of agents' income is the information they gather from consumers*. No information, no agent. *Consumers effectively 'pay' agents with information* about themselves, and agents are then charged with the task of maximizing the value of this information – for the customer. If agents fail to use this information to create value for the customer, the customer withdraws from the relationship. No agency services, no information, no agent.

Thus, if HomePro.com recommends a dodgy contractor because it has been paid to do so, it quickly jeopardizes the real source of this 'income' – which is not the payment, but its customers' trust. For this reason, HomePro.com specifically and deliberately bars suppliers from using enhanced commission payments or other incentives to encourage it to favour one supplier over another. For example, unlike many websites, it does not receive a payment for putting a supplier on its 'recommended list'. Likewise, it refuses to sign any 'exclusive' deals with any particular suppliers.

> *In the information age the price of consumer information is agency services.*

It also makes its commission terms transparent to customers, who are in a position to see and understand the process – so that they can be reassured that there is never any incentive for HomePro.com to favour one supplier over another.

Many previous attempts at the agency concept have foundered as sellers used sales incentives to 'subvert' the agent's role. For example, so-called 'independent financial advisers' (IFAs) were supposed to be unconnected to sellers, giving their clients impartial 'best advice' about investments. But the system was subverted by seller commissions: the higher the commission, the more incentive the agent had to persuade his client to buy a particular product. Most IFAs were effectively 'captured' by sellers. They became just another sales channel. Most non-agent dot-coms are the same: they are sales channels for sellers, not consumer agents. But the new breeds of agent are different because they seize a development which is fundamentally transforming the marketing environment.

THE HUMPS OF THE CAMEL

Right at the very heart of industrial age markets and marketing there lurks a bizarre irony.

As every business person knows, information drives every business. Without timely, accurate, relevant information about the nature and shape of market demand, companies cannot help but end up making the wrong things (which fail to sell), failing to make the right things (thereby losing sales opportunities), making too much of one thing that's left, taking up space (and cash) in warehouses, or making too little of another (thereby frustrating customers).

Similarly, without timely, accurate, relevant information it's impossible to go to market efficiently. How can you sell your product or service if you don't know which customers are likely to be interested and how to get in touch with them? These two functions of matching supply to demand and connecting sellers to buyers form the generic heart of marketing, and they are both driven by information. Gathering information from the market, i.e. discovering from customers what sorts of things they want, and who is and isn't interested in buying what – is the fuel that powers all marketing.

Yet that is the one thing industrial age marketers lacked. Consumers were anonymous buyers of products, not named customers. Transactions and interactions were conducted on a remote arm's length basis, usually via intermediaries such as retailers and the media. Transactions involved only an exchange of money for goods, and nothing more – no additional information changed hands. In addition, the system of wealth creation that revolved around mass production, distribution and advertising positively resisted variations from the standardized average. Variations from the average created cost and complexity and disrupted crucial economies of scale. So there was no effective mechanism, or incentive, for consumers to say, 'Here I am, this is what I want.'

Classic industrial age markets are therefore like a closed book.

They give nothing way. There is precisely zero flow of information from the customer to the supplier, from the buyer to the seller. The only information 'sent' from the buyer to the seller comes after the event, indirectly and in aggregate – in the form of market data as to whether the item sold, or failed to sell. By which time all the crucial investment decisions had already been made, long ago.

The entire construction of modern marketing, including its core concepts and devices, was built around this information hole – to compensate for its defects. Precisely because there was no information flowing upwards from the customer, marketers had to invent a complete array of compensatory devices – such as market research, advertising and brands – to fill the information hole. The customer was unable to say, 'Here I am, this is what I want,' so marketers were forced to take on sole responsibility for marketing as an organized, professional process. They had to build a marketing system that focused exclusively on the message, 'Here we are, this is what we have to offer,' instead. All of the information flowed one way.

If we look back at the history of marketing, we can see that each one of its major innovations has been driven by a sustained – and brilliant – attempt to fill this hole at the heart of marketing.

Industrial age markets were remote and impersonal. So marketers invented brands as a surrogate for the relationships that were once the norm in smaller, closer markets and communities. They invented advertising as a surrogate for dialogue – the mutual exchanges of information – that naturally take place in relationships. Market research was a surrogate for the learning that takes place through such a dialogue.

A traveller stuck in a desert and dependent upon a camel to take him to his destination is fully justified in marvelling at the camel's prowess. Our traveller would not survive without the camel's ability to travel for days without nourishment. Every one of nature's adaptations has its own kind of beauty, of course. But the fact is, the humps of the camel are the product of its past, its evolutionary origins in a nourishment and refreshment desert.

Today, marketers worship at the feet of things like brands, advertising and market research, which they see as the stuff of marketing. But like the camel's humps these devices are simply the remains of the age which bore them. They are the products of marketing's past in an information desert. Today, however, the industrial age information desert is turning into an information sea. Consumers can say, 'Here I am, this is what I want,' for the first time in an organized, professional way; they can break the seller monopoly on marketing, turning supply chains into demand chains, thereby short circuiting, bypassing, sidelining and rendering redundant vast swathes of yesterday's industrial age marketing machinery.

But by tapping, gathering and collecting information from and about consumers at source, and passing it back up the chain to suppliers, agents do more than fill the information hole, they also emerge as potential successors to the traditional joint-stock company. The joint-stock company was the catalyst that helped the industrial age reach critical mass. The joint-info-stock company will be the catalyst that helps the information age reach critical mass. For a simple reason. Information age technologies need to be fed by information, just as industrial age technologies needed to be fed by capital. But increasingly consumers will not divulge their precious knowledge without earning a return on their investment. Increasingly, the price of customer information will be agency services.

THE BUILDING BLOCKS OF AGENCY

Consumer agents are still crude, unrefined, full of glitches, and their influence on long established markets is still small. Of the 500 would-be car makers that set up in the industry's early days in the US, only three survived to become mega-successful. Likewise, most agency experiments will fall by the wayside. But that's part of the process of learning and consolidation. Today the core concept's viability is being tested to destruction – and proved – as agents explore different building blocks of information-driven value creation. These include:

▓ using rich data sources to take the core marketing processes of matching and connecting to new levels, both of efficiency *and* effectiveness – ever-finer tuned, personalized, customized matching of supply to desires
▓ demand aggregation: collecting and leveraging consumer buying power

▓ reverse auctions: organizing markets so that instead of consumers having to search out the deal that's best for them, suppliers have to bid against each other for custom.

▓ solution synergies: slicing out costs and unleashing value by finding new and better ways to assemble separate ingredients into complete, valued solutions.

The most powerful agents will do all of these things, and more – such as exploiting the huge potential of virtual exchanges and communities of interest.

Infomediaries

The core of the infomediary service is the gathering and use of information from, about and for their customers; to help them achieve whatever objective they have in mind. The crudest form of infomediary service is simply a piece of search agent software that helps buyers search for the best deal. Some are getting quite sophisticated. As soon as you click on an item on a website, RUsure.com, for example, automatically searches the Net for alternative, cheaper sources for the same item. Most infomediaries, however, use such software as the core of more complex services.

An early example was compare.net (now part of Microsoft's MSN), which enables consumers to research and comparison-shop 40,000 automotive, electronics, home and garden, home office, and sports and leisure items. As its websites boasted, 'Because all product comparisons are factual not editorial, you can make your own decisions without bias or influence from pushy sales people.' Likewise, productopia.com promises to 'pick the best products without influence from manufacturers or advertisers' – using experts to assess different products features.

Others, like epinions.com, collect users' experiences and opinions of suppliers to help guide other buyers in their decision-making. They effectively 'qualify leads', not for sellers, but for buyers. Shoppinglist.com, meanwhile, gathers real-time information about special offers and discounts to guide bargain hunters to the best deal. Yet others, such as Planetfeedback.com, collect up consumer comments about companies and pass these on, not only to the companies themselves but to pressure groups and politicians – 'to raise the stakes for companies to respond to their customers'.

Another key infomediary function is to use information from consumers to match and connect the right buyers to the right sellers in more efficient ways. Ybag.com sends out messages to suppliers from consumers who want a particular item and aggregates the responses, thereby reducing the consumer's 'search and compare' tasks.

In the future, infomediaries will also reverse the flow of marketing communications, so that consumers can specify which suppliers they are willing to accept messages from, about what, when. Strategy.com is currently developing the technologies for this kind of service. The potential: to eliminate the waste involved in communicating to people who are not in the market for your product or service. Sellers are obviously prepared to pay good money for the chance to make offers to buyers who have specifically signalled interest in their product or service. One way consumers can be 'paid' for this is in the form of special, personally-targeted offers.

> *Agents reverse the flow of information at the heart of the marketing system.*

Buying agents

While infomediaries use information to help purchasers make better, more informed decisions, buying agents actively intervene in the process 'on the buyer's side'. The simplest, clearest forms of buying agent are:

- buying clubs, or demand aggregators, who gather together purchasers of a particular item to force down the price
- reverse auctions, which solicit demand for a particular product or service from customers, and then solicit 'bids' for the contract from suppliers

Mercata.com and Letsbuyit.com are prominent examples of the buying club concept. Mercata aims to bring 'large groups of consumers together so they can achieve tremendous buying efficiency that results in lower prices for everybody'. Its 'we-commerce' system has the twin aim of delivering consumers greater discounts – 'the kind usually reserved for big chain retailers' – while benefiting manufacturers by allowing them to sell products in larger quantities, at lower cost. It boasts, 'In the not-too-distant future Mercata will be the place to shop for anything, anytime, anywhere, anyhow' (including over high-bandwidth electronic media such as cable TV).

Priceline.com is a pioneer of a particular form of reverse auction. In a typical auction, a company puts a product up for sale, and would-be customers bid up the price for it. In Priceline.com's 'buyer-driven commerce' system, the opposite happens. Customers name their own price – the price they are prepared to pay – and companies then decide whether they are prepared to do business at that price. Priceline.com started out selling unsold airline tickets, but has since branched out into hotel rooms, new cars, mortgages and loans, insurance, telecommunications, cruises, rental cars and credit cards.

Solution agents

But pure information processing can only go so far. There are still many walks of life where neither the industrial age's ability to automate matter processing, nor the information age's ability to automate knowledge processing, have yet made significant inroads. Washing and ironing clothes is a classic example. Buying agents and solution agents occur where product marketing and service marketing meet buyer-centric Right Side Up marketing.

These agencies use new information age efficiencies in tasks such as ordering, communicating, administering and coordinating to create completely new bundles of service which combine good old-fashioned labour with new information processing economies to enhance their clients' personal productivity. Solution agents will take many forms, including:

▓ *outsourcers* which take on complete tasks their clients do not want to bother with. The *principle* is illustrated easily by the example of a home-delivery pizza parlour. It delivers a piping hot pizza to the door, ready to eat, thereby freeing the client of the need to do shopping, cooking etc. Solution agents take the same principle and extend it much, much further: to take on the complete management of a client's financial affairs, for example. Outsourcing has grown to be a huge element of business-to-business relationships. It is set to become equally big in business-to-consumer relationships.

▓ *solution assemblers*, which assemble a range of disparate products and services into a complete package. To run a car, for example, I need to purchase it, service and maintain it, make repairs, insure it etc. A solution agent combines all of these into a single package – and then goes further. Do you really want to own one particular car, or would you prefer to have access to a range of different cars, depending on the occasion and circumstance? Solution agents construct complete personal mobility solutions. By doing so, they reconstruct the way entire industries function.

▓ *transformation agents*, which work with their clients to reach their customers' personal goals – goals to change themselves. Counsellors and psychotherapists, fitness trainers, educators and teachers, career advisers potentially all fit this role. They can rarely draw upon new information processing economies to create new value, but they are a part of the agency *Zeitgeist*: the emerging consumer mood that says, 'If I can afford to, I will pay an agent to help me reach my goals in life.'

Agency facilitators

Closely linked to these various forms of agent are other information age entities such as communities of interest and virtual exchanges. Strictly speaking, they are not agents. They are independent, third party players. But they do provide matching and connecting services which help buyers buy. And the boundaries between these different beasts have a natural inclination to blur.

Communities of interest take two main forms:

▓ *communities of content* organize people around their members' shared fascination or interest in a subject, whatever it happens to be. They flourish via the exchange of information. (They are a perfect information age entity.) But they are also natural trading forums: they facilitate not only the exchange of news and views but the buying and selling of information, products and services related to the particular area of fascination. Once a community of interest forms it may quickly find itself taking on more explicit agency roles by becoming a buying club or reverse auction.

▓ *communities of purpose* organize people to achieve a particular end. A community of purpose may take the form of a buying club (a narrow, specific instrumental purpose, in other words) or a passion partner (where people come together to advance a particular cause or belief).

Virtual exchanges

These, on the other hand, are designed specifically to act as independent third party intermediaries designed to connect buyers and sellers efficiently. Simply by gathering together many different offers from many different suppliers – as a traditional retailer does in physical stores – virtual exchanges can help buyers find better bargains, while upping the ante between suppliers. There has been a veritable explosion of these exchanges in every conceivable business to business commodity area from motor components to vegetables. But they are moving to the consumer arena too. House buying and the job market are two obvious examples.

A particularly fascinating form of virtual exchange is in consumer-to-consumer *auctions*. Auction sites like e-bay.com are opening the way for new forms of consumer-to-consumer marketplace which enable consumers to trade whatever they have with one another: skills, second-hand cars, baby-sitting services, whatever. Such consumer-to-consumer marketplaces often work best within relatively confined localities, to become community builders as well as useful trading forums. Priceline.com is experimenting with this concept with its town-based 'Perfect Yardsale' concept: 'Tell us what you want to buy and we'll find it for you. Or tell us what you want to sell and we'll find you a buyer.'

THE NEW SUPERBRANDS

What effects will such an explosion of agents have on traditional markets and brands? The answer is: a complete and fundamental shake-up. This shake-up revolves around four key areas, each of which transforms the way brands need to compete. They are:

- the race for affiliation: to be 'on the customer's side'.
- the consumer's marketing department: doing marketing for and on behalf of the consumer in an organized and professional way (thereby breaking sellers' traditional monopoly on marketing).
- trumping traditional sources of value: saying 'my job is to get you the best product at the best price' is very different from claiming 'my offer is the best on the market (but it's up to you to find out whether that's true or not)'. Agents use the end product of seller-centric marketing – sellers' offers and brands – into their raw material.
- meta- or super-branding: agents rise above the world of offer marketing to pick and choose, and to assemble what's best for their clients.

Under Right Side Up marketing, the focus of competition migrates to whether you are 'on my side' or not, and if so, how efficient, effective and enthusiastic you are at acting on my behalf. As Boston Consulting Group's Philip Evans notes, this is creating a new race to 'affiliate to the customer' where affiliation is defined as 'how closely do I match your interests?' The challenge to the status quo is fundamental. The race to affiliate creates 'a very different basis of competitive advantage,' Evans points out, 'because I, as a customer, would rather deal with that kind of navigator [agent].'4

Those words sum up the agent's catalytic role. If there is one thing industrial age marketers have strived to achieve over the last hundred years it is to become the kind of brand or company that 'I, as a customer, would rather deal with'. Brand preference is what it's all about. But the very way seller-centric marketers go about trying to achieve this, by persuading consumers to give preference to their particular brand, puts them at a compelling disadvantage when faced with an agent who is on the customer's side.

Agents do this by acting as the consumer's marketing department, taking over – and transforming – functions once regarded as a seller's monopoly. Matching supply to demand by researching the market and deciding what products to develop has always been a key marketing task. But when agents advise clients on potential purchases they take on a similar function. Instead of this function being carried out by the offer-producer on a general, aggregated basis, however, the advising agent brings this matching function inside the customer's life, to make it personal and specific. 'What are my particular needs and how can they be best met?'

Perhaps even more importantly, the agent's stance is to stand with the consumer, on the 'inside' of the consumer's life, looking out.

Offer-based marketers start with their assets. Their starting point is outside the consumer's life. Which means that they always have to 'reach in' from the outside to achieve their goals. They 'reach in' to research consumers' needs and wants. They 'reach in' again to try and grab the consumer's attention and influence purchasing decisions and behaviour. Marketers like to pretend that getting close to, and understanding, customers is the eternal key to success. But it's not really a solution at all. It's an expression of their essential condition. They can never really get close to their customers because they are always on the outside, looking in.

> *Marketers want to get close to the consumers. But they are stuck on the outside looking in.*

Agents on the other hand are already 'inside' the consumer's life, helping the consumer to 'reach out'. Microstrategy.com Chief Executive Mike Saylor likes to talk of 'earning permissions' to act on the consumer's behalf. There are hundreds of permissions consumers can decide to grant, from permission to wake them up in the mornings to permission to arbitrage their equity, he notes. One of the key permissions agents seek from their clients is to help them to get the best out of their dealings with the world outside, including other brands.

Agencies also trump offer marketing, turning traditional offer-brands into the raw material of their service. They stand on the shoulders of what industrial age marketing has produced – a cacophony of offers – to glide across its surface picking, choosing, connecting, assembling on behalf of the buyer. As such they represent a completely new 'layer' of service, doing a different business, which follows a different logic.

By doing this, they become a new form of super-brand, or meta-brand – a brand that helps its clients get the most out of other brands. This not only destabilizes existing brands' relationships with their customers. It also creates a new and desperate race to be one of the tiny handful of agents 'invited in' to the consumer's life. Not many will make it. Just as most of us don't have more than a handful of close friends, most of us will probably choose to build close relationships with only a few agents who play an especially important, trusted role in our lives. Probably not more than five. Almost certainly less than ten.

THE NEW GOLDRUSH

So who are these agents likely to be? The answer is that the field remains wide open. Pure-play dot-coms were the first into the fray for all the traditional reasons – they weren't held back by 'legacy' systems, assets, mindsets or revenue streams. But whenever organizations gather large amounts of information from and about their customers, they have the opportunity to deploy that information on their customers' behalf, rather than use it for traditional operational and cross-selling purposes.

Every day, for example, traditional bricks and mortar retailers aggregate consumer demand to create buying power. But there is a big difference between using this buying power as an internal operational tool – to help you buy cheap and sell dear – and using this buying power as an upfront customer service: to source the things your customers tell you they want to buy.

Credit card companies have huge amounts of data about their customers' purchasing behaviour. Why not use this information for, and on behalf of these customers, within the marketplace? Likewise, insurance companies gather vast amounts of data about the things their customers own, where they go wrong, the prices at which they can be replaced, and so on. Again, why not deploy this information for and on behalf of their customers, rather than simply using it for internal operations?

When it comes to specialist areas such as holidays, motoring and personal finance, media companies already offer valued, impartial information that helps buyers buy – information that is valued by their readers and viewers. At the same time, they are in thrall to advertisers, who are their real customers and pay their bills. But what's more valuable to them in the long term? The ability to build readers' and viewers' trust and to evolve into an added-value conduit to market for these customers? Or their continued ability to deliver audiences to advertisers?

The same goes for new Internet brands such as AOL or Yahoo! Does their real future lie as forms of 'Internet service provider' or as online media companies? Or could they deploy their customer relationships and information to act for their subscribers in reaching out to the online world?

The consumer agent role represents a huge 'white space' of opportunity within the commercial arena, and a whole range of businesses – both new and old – are well placed to converge on different parts of it. To reach this destination, however, they will have to embrace the 'quite different principles' that Kotler talked about.

on the shoulders of giants

> *If I have seen further, it is by standing on the shoulders of giants.*
> Isaac Newton

PAY HOMAGE TO A WORK OF GENIUS

Procter & Gamble, Unilever, Coca-Cola: icons of marketing and branding like these are universally admired for their marketing skills. People see them as universities of brand management. They didn't just 'do' marketing better. They were not just brand *builders*. They *invented* marketing and branding. They were *system* builders. Before companies like these came along, the classic packaged goods marketing system that came to inform and dominate modern marketing thinking didn't exist.

The system they helped construct, along with other companies such as Ford and General Motors, was a work of genius, powering the most dramatic period of wealth creation mankind has yet seen.

The industrial age's big secret was the way it managed to weave a wide range of different parties with different (and often conflicting) interests into a system that delivered huge benefits to all of them. The glue that held it together was its win-win nature.

The mass marketing system worked like this. Companies invested in research, development and productive capacity to produce new, better goods at lower cost. In order to guarantee a market for these 'New! Improved!' products, they researched the needs of target buyers and advertised the benefits of the new products to them. Consumers, appreciating the obvious benefits of these products and made aware of them by manufacturers' advertising campaigns, went to their local stores to buy them. And retailers, keen to see increased footfall and sales, were only too happy to stock them – thereby feeding demand back to the manufacturer.

This wasn't just a win-win marketing system. It was a win-win-win-win marketing system. Mass advertising and distribution created for manufacturers the confidence and the demand that enabled them to invest even more in research, development and productive capacity. These investments created powerful economies of scale which meant ever lower unit costs.

The secret of industrial age marketing's success was its win-win nature, not its tools or techniques.

These ever-increasing economies of scale – along with the fruits of nonstop research and development – delivered consumers a double whammy of benefits. First, their lives were made easier by better, cheaper products of incredible value compared to older, handicraft-based methods of production and distribution. Second, they also benefited from an increasing range of good quality news and entertainment at a heavily subsidized rate – subsidized by the advertising that powered the growth of new media from national newspapers and magazines through radio to broadcast television.

Media owners benefited hugely, because this advertising made rapid expansion of their business possible. And so did retailers, who benefited from the demand created by advertising, and the excitement of a never-ending stream of new products, promotions, offers etc.

Within this system, marketing played a pivotal role. It aligned what the corporation produced and offered to what consumers needed and wanted: an absolutely critical task. If a company invests in producing things it cannot sell it fritters away its precious resources, and dies. If a company fails to make the things its consumers want, it throws away a huge opportunity. By connecting production to need, marketing acts as the ON switch of wealth creation, unleashing the energy of economic activity, to the benefit of both producer and consumer.

Then, of course, mass advertising delivered the awareness that turned potential into real demand – actual sales. So much so, that advertising soon seemed to be as important to the process of wealth creation as production itself. As Seth Godin, former Vice President of direct marketing at Yahoo!, observes: 'The big surprise is that it wasn't factories or the car that caused the big increase in corporate profitability. It was advertising. The economies that came from establishing a product as the leading brand, the huge premiums that were derived by charging for a trusted name, dwarfed the savings in production. Marketing rapidly became the most profitable part of the enterprise.'[1]

BRANDS AS A VEHICLE OF WIN-WIN

Branding played a critical role in completing the win-win circle. Mass markets create a huge – potentially crippling – drawback to effective, efficient exchange. Mass markets are anonymous and transactions within them are one-off arm's length affairs. And as game theorists (who try to model interactions between different players in different circumstances) point out, conditions like this positively militate against the building of long term, trust-based relationships. As Douglass North, the Nobel Prize-winning economist, puts it, 'Cooperation is difficult to sustain when the game is not repeated . . . when information on the other players is lacking, and when there are large numbers of players.'[2] Enter the brand: an easily recognized package of information and promises that fills the information void and encourages the transaction to be repeated.

Like the marketing system itself, brands were a brilliant win-win invention. Brand manufacturers could use the brand as a highly efficient and effective tool for achieving the alignment that saved them from wasting precious investment. Through brands, manufacturers could target particular 'New! Improved!' products at particular market segments or groups of consumers – and communicate with them in the most appropriate fashion. If marketing was the ON switch of wealth creation – it was brands that actually flicked the switch to create the connection.

Brands also helped deliver win-win solutions in another crucial way. They not only delivered the most appropriate bundles of value to consumers. They did so consistently, which gave the consumer another huge benefit. Suddenly, the risks of making the wrong purchase were greatly reduced. And the process of searching for the right product was greatly simplified: the brand's immediate recognizability and universal availability made sure of that. Through the ingenious devices of brand names and logos, colour cues and pack designs, brands became an extremely efficient means of communicating complex sets of promises in nanoseconds: the time it takes to recognize the familiar logo on the shelf. Compared to pre-industrial days, when non-packaged goods of questionable quality placed a great onus on the shopper to shop around to ensure the right specification at the right quality at an affordable price, the instant recognizability of brands provided significant benefits to the shopper as well as the consumer. They helped the shopper shop.

This, in turn, delivered a further benefit to the manufacturer. Once a consumer knew that a chosen brand delivered its promise, it was safe to choose it again and again. This 'brand loyalty' turned a one-off transaction into a constant flow of income, thereby minimizing the risk involved in investing in its creation and production, and maximizing the return on this investment.

SYSTEM SUPERIORITY

At every level in every way, therefore, the industrial age marketing and branding system truly was a work of win-win genius.

This system didn't need any external *Gauleiter* to corral different players, such as manufacturers or retailers or media owners, into playing their part. They were only too happy to, because it suited their own commercial interest. Here we can see 'the hidden hand' of the free market working at its best.

No wonder this system swept all before it. Packaged goods are hardly the biggest sector of the economy. There are all sorts of other business beasts out there: law firms, the extraction industries, utilities, travel agents, charities, and so on. But this model, and all its tools, techniques and methodologies, became *the* paradigm. Everyone looked to it for a lead.

The system itself was also extremely flexible. As it matured it sustained severe shocks such as wars and oil crises. And it was also (potentially) disrupted by waves of technological and business innovation. In media, marketers rode the waves of change from print to radio to TV with consummate skill, for example. Manufacturers also learned how to adjust to far-reaching changes in retail structures, such as the decline of department stores or the move to out-of-town 'discount' retailing. In fact, over the decades it has seemed so flexible and so robust that for many marketers the notion that the system itself may be collapsing is unthinkable.

It was the marketing *system* as a whole, not just isolated ingredients such as market research or advertising, that made the industrial age so successful, so when the system itself begins to unravel – as it is now – there is no way that any one isolated ingredient can save it.

the great incubus

> *Many dynamical systems . . . [are] eventually driven to extinction, despite their own best efforts, by the collective behaviour of the system as a whole.*
>
> Stuart Kauffman[1]

> *If somebody asked me, rather than one of my distinguished predecessors, which half of my advertising was wasted, I would probably say 90 per cent of my advertising was wasted but I don't know which 90 per cent. Our marketing, advertising and marketing support budget is over £4 billion. It is by far the biggest element of cost in this business.*
>
> Niall Fitzgerald, Unilever Co-Chairman[2]

If the win-wins that powered industrial age marketing through to its post-war heyday were still operational today, a Right Side Up marketing revolution wouldn't be necessary. Unfortunately, the win-win dynamics that have energized marketing for the last hundred years are collapsing into their opposite. A win-win system is sinking into win-lose or lose-lose. Yesterday's virtuous spiral is fast becoming a vicious circle.

MASS PRODUCTION

The economies of scale generated by mass production lie at the heart of industrial age win-win marketing. But as the system matures it has an inherent tendency to flip over into its opposite. Each individual producer has an incentive to expand capacity to reduce unit costs and increase market share. But the sum of many such individually rational decisions is collective irrationality: endemic overcapacity in market after market, industry after industry, category after category. Yesterday, firms couldn't make enough of what they sold. Now they cannot sell enough of what they can make. Whereas yesterday investment in production helped to lower unit costs, today every per cent of unused capacity adds cost to the system.

> *Industrial age marketing's win-wins are collapsing, turning a virtuous spiral into a vicious circle.*

For example, the worldwide auto industry can make 20 million more cars and trucks than it can sell. Every car plant in the US could be shut and still there would be worldwide overcapacity. In Europe, overcapacity is around 20 per cent. In 1999, Ford's manufacturing capability was 2.25 million cars: it sold 1.7 million. Result: deflation has set in. Car prices are falling and how to cut capacity is now one of manufacturers' top priorities.

Excess capacity has its knock-on effect on other parts of the system, such as advertising effectiveness. In the system's heyday when markets were growing, advertising helped generate measurable incremental demand, sales and revenues. But as markets mature advertising becomes part of increasingly expensive trench warfare between established brands for market share: more a matter of running as fast as you can, simply to stand still; a zero-sum game; a cost of remaining in business.

'NEW! IMPROVED!'

In many a marketer's mind, the crisis of overcapacity has made effective innovation doubly important: the one magic bullet that can spur renewed demand, generating incremental sales.

Wherever innovation leads to genuinely 'New! Improved!' products this is, of course, true. The great post-war consumer boom is a result of such innovation. From the 1950s through to the 1980s lives, lifestyles, consumption patterns and shopping were transformed as refrigerators, washing machines, freezers, microwaves, motor cars, TVs etc. became mass market commodities – driving demand for all manner of secondary products such as washing powders and convenience foods. Most of today's big consumer brands are the product of this wave of technology-driven creativity. At the same time, marketers' power and influence were boosted time and time again by 'New! Improved!' communications technologies such as TV.

But innovation isn't a universal panacea. It, too, experiences diminishing returns. Organisms, technologies and industries rarely evolve smoothly and continually, growing ever more sophisticated through little, gradual refinements and innovations. Rather, they burst upon the scene with a revolutionary and fundamental design breakthrough; they then spend a period of time exploring the potential of this breakthrough, before entering a longer period of relative stagnation – when all the best, most fruitful avenues have already been explored and when innovation has been reduced to variations on a theme. As complexity theorist Stuart Kauffman observes, 'Soon after a major innovation, discovery of profoundly different variations is easy. Later innovation is limited to modest improvements on increasingly optimized designs.'[3]

We can see this process occurring in most of the consumer markets that drove the post-war marketing system so far and so fast. As the ability to come up with fundamental breakthrough conceptual innovation declines, so does the nature and scope of the marketing strategies built around 'New! Improved!' products. In mature western economies the things that generated so much excitement generations ago – such as fridges and washing machines – are now necessities. And they're not changing much either. The big new idea in white goods recently, for example, has been not a breakthrough in washing or refrigeration technologies, but in not painting them white. Hence the comment nowadays that most products are at functional parity: an explicit admission that for these marketers 'New! Improved!' is running out of steam.

Another constraint on innovation is that within any one market there is likely to be one optimum answer that best tackles the problems it is supposed to solve – and which acts as a magnet for all competitors, bringing them closer and closer together. A perfect washing powder, for example, would remove all stains, make clothes feel and smell lovely and fresh, not fade bright colours, and be 'kind' to fabrics. Every washing powder wants to achieve these things, and so every competing brand converges on the same sweet spot – or 'fitness peak', as Kauffman would call it.

Problem: the closer different competitors get to this fitness peak, the less room they have to experiment with genuinely 'New! Improved!' concepts. Which explains why industrial age marketers are so obsessed with differentiation. The faster marketers converge on these fitness peaks the more similar their offerings become, the harder the job of standing out from the crowd, and the more intense the pressure to 'invent' differences rather than create and bring genuine differences to market.[4]

Like overcapacity in the area of production, this collapse of 'New! Improved!' is creating lose-lose situations out of former win-wins. In Europe, an amazing 525,000 new products were launched over a thirteen month period. Yet 90 per cent of them failed. And most of these so-called 'new products' weren't really new at all. According to the researchers a tiny 2.2 per cent could be truly classified as innovative, while 76.7 per cent were line extensions. Glen Cox, Senior Vice President of ACNielsen European Marketing, commented, 'Innovation is critical but rare in new product introductions.'[5]

Increasingly, in other words, 'New! Improved!' is no longer really helping to make exciting new and valuable products available to the consumer. Instead it is turning into innoflation: a welter of gimmickry – bells and whistles often invented largely out of desperation to seem different. This leads to spiralling costs, as producers find themselves spending ever more for ever lower returns. In the US, for example, packaged goods companies are now spending $2 billion a year on new product launches – and that's not counting the development costs.[6]

This problem is not confined to packaged goods. Dell Computer's

CEO Michael Dell dismisses the traditional approach to computer making and selling as 'a lose-lose proposition. Much of the technology that was created was never purchased. And customers hungry for technology were forced to order from a fixed menu of items, whether they liked it or not, in addition to assuming the high costs associated with funding all sorts of creations.'[7]

And as ever, as one part of the system starts going wrong, it generates new problems elsewhere. Whereas once 'New! Improved!' helped lower costs as rising sales led to reduced unit costs, the proliferation of such ersatz products and me-toos does the opposite. It creates massive complexity and cost in both production and distribution, as companies try to make and sell ever smaller amounts of ever more variants of basic themes. The role of advertising is transformed too. Increasingly, new product development revolves around the hunt for something fresh to say in the ad campaign. Surprise, surprise! Marketers are now complaining that ads aren't as effective as they once were.

Increasingly marketing is adding more cost than value to producers and consumers alike.

Consumers also lose out once innoflation takes hold. Where once, 'New! Improved!' offered genuine added value to the consumer, now it's more likely to add stress and confusion as product lines proliferate. In 1975 a typical supermarket sold 5000 lines. Twenty years later, this number had quadrupled to 20,000, and has been growing ever since. In the US, the number of lines is closer to 35,000, with more than 2,500 new products on the shelves vying for attention each month. 'Choice' – that magic word of marketing – is being transformed from a liberation to a chore.

MASS DISTRIBUTION

Mass production doesn't flourish without mass distribution, but here too, diminishing returns have set in. In the early days of the system, retailers were a mere 'channel to market'. Their job was simply to sell what manufacturers made as efficiently and effectively as possible. The core job hasn't changed, but the relationship between the two sides has.

As retailing has evolved, the most advanced retailers (in areas such as packaged goods) have become the closest thing to the industrial age forerunner of the consumer agent. Because retailers sell a range of different products (unlike manufacturers their prosperity does not depend on pushing a particular product) they can afford to offer impartial advice about products. Because retailers are dealing directly with buyers, they can 'get closer' to them, gleaning more information about their needs and desires – and using this information to bargain with suppliers. As retailers' buying power increases, they force down supplier prices, both to increase their own margins, and to fight their own market share battles.

The net effect of this rise of retailer power is simple but devastating. Whereas the retailer was once a channel to market, nowadays he's just as likely to be a hurdle, an obstacle course or a barrier.

MEDIA

The same can be said of the media. The media was once merely a communications channel. Increasingly, though, it too is an obstacle course and a barrier for the marketer. A key factor in this development has been the double-edged sword of media fragmentation. It offers marketers the chance to target specific groups ever more effectively. However, it also makes mass communication ever more expensive.

And like the rest of the industrial age system, the media itself is now plagued by overcapacity. Fifty years ago newspapers, magazines and TV programmes were a relative novelty. Choice was limited. Today, the media has moved from a situation of content scarcity to content overload. Consumer attention is becoming scarce, and editors and broadcasters find themselves caught in a vicious circle. On one hand, they're finding it ever harder to grab and keep audiences' attention. On the other hand, competitive dynamics demands that they pump out more and more 'content'. Yet most of this proliferating content is aimed at fewer and fewer consumers, and fails.

One result is a mad scramble among advertisers for 'quality' content and audiences. This in turn leads to primetime media inflation and (like relationships between retailers and manufacturers) increasing tensions between media owners and advertisers. US advertisers are furious, for example, that in just four years, the cost of a thirty-second spot in the primetime show *ER* soared from $180,000 to $478,000. Likewise, in the UK, the cost of TV airtime ballooned by 21 per cent in three years – way ahead of the retail price increase of 8.9 per cent.

This, in turn, makes marketing communications – a critical link in the old system's win-win chain – too expensive to do. Thus, explains Unilever Co-Chairman Niall Fitzgerald:

> In the 1960s you could reach 80 per cent of women in the US between the ages of 18 and 49, which is our main target audience, with three minutes of network television per week. And you got your three minutes largely by buying cheap airtime during the day. If you wanted to replicate that coverage today, you would have to buy 250 advertising spots at various times of the day at astronomical cost, and at least 40 per cent of them would have to be at primetime.[8]

Traditional advertisers therefore find themselves caught in a vicious circle. As Seth Godin comments, the end result is 'Catch 22: the more they spend, the less it works. The less it works, the more they spend.'[9]

WASTE, WASTE, WASTE – JUST IN CASE

In this way, because of the very dynamics of the system itself, each of the links in the industrial win-win chain are dissolving while the costs only escalate. The way the system works has created layer after layer of incremental cost, which makes it ever harder to earn returns. One compelling reason for the agency revolution is its ability to strip away these layers of cost.

Right at the centre of this onion of marketing cost lies the information hole we talked about in Chapter 2. Because there was no efficient, effective mechanism for consumers to say, 'Here I am, this is what I want,' suppliers never knew exactly what to make or how much of it to make. This is the first, most intractable and probably the biggest area of waste created by the old marketing system. It is a 'just in case' rather than a 'just in time' system: the marketer makes his product 'just in case' customers might want to buy it. He makes his product available everywhere he can, 'just in case' these customers might want to buy the product from that outlet. And he advertises it to everyone, 'just in case' they might be moved, or persuaded to buy it.

These just-in-case processes are laborious, roundabout, wasteful, hit-and-miss affairs. Take production. Companies research the market, develop new products and launch them on the market in the hope that they will sell well. If their research and development process hits the right spots the product succeeds and customers buy it. If not, the product fails. And most do. Making the right product (or service), the thing the customer actually wants, is a massive challenge under the old system.

Having decided what to produce without any input from the customer, the old system's marketer must then decide how much to produce. This is another source of tremendous waste, because invariably, companies end up producing either too much – which they can't sell, and which therefore eats up precious resources – or too little, which means they lose revenue opportunities and undermine customer relationships. Usually, companies err on the 'optimistic' side – that they will sell more than they do – partly because of internal pressures to meet optimistic internal forecasts and budgets, but partly because producing too much is seen as the lesser of two evils.

Distribution follows the same wasteful logic. Take books. In the US 30 per cent of the books that are printed commonly end up being pulped. Just in case someone wants to buy them, books sit on the shelf, gathering dust and costing money: money to print, money to transport, money to display in a prime retail site – and then, yet further money to transport once more, and to pulp. To survive, publishers have to load these costs into the prices book buyers have to pay.

The same just-in-case waste pervades the entire marketing communications industry. Most television ads have nothing relevant to say to most consumers – most of the time, simply because those consumers are not 'in the market' for that particular product or service. But they might be interested. So the ad is broadcast anyway: to catch the few that might be, just in case. Likewise, a response rate of 1 per cent on direct mail campaigns underlines just how irrelevant most so-called direct marketing is to the 'target' consumer. But the 99 per cent of consumers who did not respond still had to be mailed, just in case they might be interested.

This just-in-case system creates waste in trying to reach the right people. It also generates waste by failing to reach people at the right time. Sitting relaxing in front of the TV, or rushing to get to work when the mail arrives: these are not times when most consumers are thinking about, or conducting, purchases. Their attention is on other things. But advertisers want to grab their attention on these occasions, to embed the memory of their brand in consumers' minds, just in case they might be in the market at some later date. Compared to sending the right message to the right person at the right time – which becomes possible if we reverse the flow of information – these brand and marketing strategies are massive monuments to waste.

The first layer of the marketing onion, then, is the waste created by the very nature of the just-in-case marketing system. The second layer is the extra costs incurred in trying to reduce the waste created by this system: market research to reduce the risk of making the wrong products or appealing to the wrong people, forecasting and supply chain projects to reduce the amount of just-in-case stock in the system, and so on.

GOOD MONEY AFTER BAD

The third layer of costs is incurred by companies' attempts to compensate for their inevitable failure to eliminate these sources of waste. The best laid plans, the most insightful research, the most creative advertising can never create order in a chaotic marketplace. Companies finding themselves with extra stock lying around in warehouses end up organizing sales, running price promotions and so on in order to shift that stock. These promotions themselves add cost: the cost of planning them, organizing them, advertising their existence and so on. In fact, so regular are these costs that in many companies they are embedded and institutionalized within the organization's annual budgets as a 'normal' activity.

Layer four of the marketing onion is a knock-on from layer three. Once a system of 'push' promotions becomes embedded in the way a market works, it begins to create 'noise' within the marketplace. A classic example of 'noise' goes like this. A manufacturer produces too much stock, so he organizes a promotion. Thanks to the promotion, orders fly sky high. In response to booming orders, he ratchets up production, thereby flooding the market with new stock – only to find himself exactly where he started: with too much stock left sitting in the warehouse.[10] As lean manufacturing experts James Womack and Dan Jones note, a very high proportion of perceived marketplace chaos or volatility in most industries 'is in fact self-induced, the inevitable consequence of the long lead times and large inventories in the traditional world of batch-and-queue overlaid with relatively flat demand and the promotional activities which producers employ in response.'[11]

THE PEACOCK'S TAIL

Yet still, the marketing onion has more layers. Layer number five is the simple fact that all these activities take place in a competitive environment. Every marketer is trying to do the same thing: to grab the consumer's attention and win his preference. And as they battle it out, they tend to cancel out each other's efforts, while raising the costs of doing business in the process. 'Brand wars' are a classic example. Brand A launches a campaign to draw attention to itself and its qualities. So Brand B fights back with its own campaign. The costs for both sides escalate as each side throws ever more men and troops into the battle to 'cut through the clutter' to win the war for customer attention and preference.

Set-to fights such as Coke versus Pepsi and Nike versus Reebok versus Adidas are the stuff of marketing mythology. But in all honesty the real focus of this battle is not the consumer, but the competition. The aim is not to use this massive resource to improve the value *received* by the consumer. The aim is to beat off the competition to gain a greater share of revenue streams *from* the consumer.

Like most wars, brand wars of this sort are lose-lose exercises. Often the winner is simply the one with the deepest pockets – the one who can take the pain for longer. To this degree, traditional brand wars are like the peacock's tail: a magnificent sight to behold but, at root, just a deliberate display of waste for the purposes of establishing superiority.

The peacock with the biggest and best display must be extremely fit if he can sustain the enormous costs of carrying that tail around. That signal of fitness helps the peacock win mates. Likewise with brand wars. Only those with the biggest budgets dare enter the fray. And the very size of the budget – the amount you are prepared to throw down the drain to win – has become a competitive weapon. Yet unlike the peacock who pays for the costs of his own tail, brand wars are ultimately paid for by consumers, not producers. It is the consumers who stump up the final cost of extravagant marketing campaigns in the prices they pay for the products or services concerned.

Seller-push marketing creates layer upon layer of extra cost. These costs are itching to be peeled away.

Layer six of the marketing onion relates to who these costs are actually incurred for. Sometimes marketers need to invest large sums to make consumers aware of 'New! Improved!' products or to educate them about the potential of a new technology. But often in mature markets, the marketing campaign has a very different purpose: to pump up the brand's imagery, to justify a price premium; to persuade the customer that it's worthwhile paying more. Such activities (and costs) are not incurred to add value for the buyer. They are incurred in order to take value *from* the buyer – even as they are conducted *at the expense of* the buyer.

With six heavy layers of unnecessary cost to carry, the old marketing system is indeed burdened. What would happen if a new system came along? A system capable of slicing these layers of cost away? That, of course, is what Right Side Up marketing is about: creating a better alternative.

The camel's hump is a worthwhile investment if you live in a desert. The peacock's tail is a worthwhile investment if the only way you can get a mate is by ostentatious display. They are both the price of survival within certain conditions: conditions created by an environment where consumers cannot say, 'Here I am, this is what I want,' and it's left to marketers to say, 'Here we are, this is what we have to offer.'

But what happens if you are no longer living in a desert? What happens if you can get a mate without having to bother with that ridiculous tail? Then, suddenly, these things become unnecessary. Instead they become something very different – a costly burden.

THE GREAT MARKETING INCUBUS

None of what has been noted above is in any way new. In fact, the real shame is the opposite: that it's all so familiar that we simply accept it as a given. Yesterday, marketing was all about seizing the enormous opportunities created by the biggest and most powerful win-win economic system the world has ever seen. Practitioners didn't need to worry about the big picture because by pursuing their specialism – by fulfilling their chosen tasks ever more efficiently and effectively – they were making the system work better. They were its engine room. They added to its energy, its zing.

Today, marketing has become a massive, sclerotic machine whose embedded infrastructures, processes and procedures increasingly absorb most of the energy and resources invested in it simply *to keep it ticking over*. The focus of the marketing debate nowadays – indeed the entire mindset – revolves around fighting fires and solving problems rather than seizing opportunities. How to maintain sustainable product differentiation? How to contend with media inflation? How to cut through the clutter – within the media, on the retailer's shelves? How to prove that your efforts have had any measurable effect on market share or profits? How to market marketing?[12]

As a result astonishing revelations begin to appear, such as the internal Procter & Gamble memo that admitted: 'We can't afford to continue spending about a quarter of net sales on marketing support . . . we are at the point where marketing support spending is the biggest area of cost disadvantage vs. private label. We have to eliminate unproductive marketing costs.'[13] With this memo, P&G was effectively admitting that the cost of its marketing was in danger of becoming a competitive disadvantage, rather than a source of competitive advantage.

Peter Sealey, a University of California professor, summed up the prevailing mood when he wrote the following:

> Over the past 20 years annual advertising spending in the United States has quadrupled in current dollars to more than $200 billion. The budgets of some major brands now sound like the GDPs of smaller nations: Sears – $664 million; Chevrolet – $656 million; McDonald's – $580 million. Total non-advertising expenditures, such as promotions, trade allowances, coupons, sweepstakes, and sponsorships, exceed even those amounts. But the results have been disappointing . . .
>
> Manufacturing companies have taken impressive steps to increase efficiency while improving quality . . . [But] marketing hasn't realized any great advances in decades. At a time when productivity in manufacturing is rising steadily, marketing seems to be getting more expensive and less effective. It is little wonder that marketing has become the subject of much debate.[14]

The great incubus grew to its current massive size because, at one stage in its history, it delivered massive benefits. Today, its costs rise inexorably while the benefits fall equally relentlessly, transforming the marketing agenda.

BEYOND PIECEMEAL SOLUTIONS

This crisis has been widely discussed, of course. Over the past few decades, declared McKinsey consultants John Brady and Ian Davis in an influential article, 'marketing departments have generated few new ideas'. Marketers, they continued, 'are simply not picking up the right signals any more' and have become 'tremendously averse to risk', failing to deliver on all counts: innovation, brand share, growth, and in terms of advertising and promotion effectiveness. So much so that 'many consumer goods CEOs are beginning to think that marketing is no longer delivering'.[15]

But in one important sense, such criticisms miss the point. Of course, the quest for accountability and effectiveness is always important, but as Peter Senge points out, 'Either the larger system works, or your position will not work.'[16] That's the source of the real problem: not in marketing departments themselves, but in the increasingly dysfunctional marketing system they struggle to work within. But this system is not only dysfunctional because its costs are getting out of kilter with its benefits. Its problems reach deep into the modern marketing mindset itself.

wanted: 'new! improved!' marketing

> *Changing times, ancient reasons, that turn to lies. Throw them all away!*
> Neil Young, *New Mama*

> *It is impossible to talk about mass marketing without thinking of customers and marketers as adversaries ... Your customers know that their own interests are in direct conflict with yours.*
> Don Peppers and Martha Rogers[1]

Marketing as we know it is not just a technical tool-box – a set of specialist techniques for getting certain tasks done. It's also an ideology; an instinctive way of thinking about things. As old industrial age win-wins begin to founder, the marketing system spawned by that age has begun to compound – rather than alleviate – its crisis. Right Side Up doesn't only involve *doing* marketing differently, to strip away accumulated – and increasingly unnecessary – layers of cost. It also involves *thinking* differently.

THE TRANSACTION FOCUS

For sellers, closing transactions is as much a necessity as breathing air is for a mammal. If your business can't close transactions, money stops coming in, and you die. Closing sales (profitably) is the ultimate test of success for seller-centric marketing.

But this obsession with closing transactions brings its own baggage. We've already seen how it led marketers to invent the dehumanizing concept of 'the consumer' – a person whose only purpose in life is to consume. And we'll see later how the same transaction focus creates an adversarial relationship between buyers and sellers, while blinding marketers to opportunities elsewhere – opportunities which do not depend on the direct exchange of money for goods and services.

> *For sellers, closing transactions is as much a necessity as breathing air is for a mammal.*

The same obsession with closing sales has also led marketers to conjure up a series of euphemisms which are fundamentally misleading and ultimately counterproductive. Take customer focus. A focus on the transaction is not the same as a focus on the customer, but modern marketing rhetoric deliberately elides the two. Marketers talk a lot about 'customer focus' and 'getting closer to the customer' but this is just a means to end, which is to close the transaction. 'Everybody says we are close to the customer, our job is to solve customer problems and help the customer to find what he or she wants,' notes Boston Consulting Group's Philip Evans. However: 'The truth of the matter is that you are not selling the product to help the customer. You get closer to the customer in order to sell the product. We are in the business of selling our product.'[2]

Even as marketers attempt to distance themselves from this transaction obsession they end up reinforcing it. Take the current fascination with building relationships. Truth is, most companies see these relationships as just another means to the same end: to close more sales, more efficiently. Likewise, the restless search for brand loyalty. This marketing nirvana consists of the consumer closing the same transaction, again and again, ad infinitum.

The use of warm, human words like loyalty, relationships, closeness and understanding is no accident. It's a way of dressing up and softening the cold, instrumental reality of transaction-obsessed marketing. But it has never rung true. It just creates a credibility gap instead.

ALWAYS REMOTE

Traditional marketing talks 'customer closeness' but lives and breathes remoteness from its purchasers. Partly, this is the simple product of physical, operational facts. The consumer goods brands that pioneered marketing were made in factories far away from where they were consumed. To reach their customers marketers had to rely on intermediaries such as retailers to get the physical product to the consumer, and the media to get messages about that product to the consumer. There was no direct contact. No touch. And there was no feedback either. It was all one way.

As the system evolved, this remoteness slowly became embedded in the core processes of marketing – its operational processes *and* its thought processes. 'The consumer' as a unit of demand for my products is a nameless, faceless, abstract, averaged, anonymous entity. And a company which thinks and plans around an abstract, averaged entity called 'the consumer' generates a different internal culture and mindset to one which thinks in terms of recruiting members and supporters, or acting on behalf of clients. As James Milojkovic, CEO of KnowledgePassion.com, points out (paraphrasing the philosopher Martin Buber), one revolves around an impersonal 'I–it' relationship, the other around a personal 'I–thou' relationship. 'I–it' relationships never progress very far, because the 'it' side doesn't usually like being treated as an 'it'.[3]

The operational remoteness that characterized the old system also created brand management as *mask management*. Brands are the masks companies invent to present their offers in the best possible light to buyers – they are easy to hide behind. A brand (name, logo, packaging design, colours, personality etc.) is invented by a brand manager to appeal to a particular (remote) target audience. Marketing then revolves around presenting the benefits of this brand to the audience. In order to do this, the brand manager projects a certain carefully chosen set of messages and images to the audience via a chosen medium. Meanwhile, the author of these images hides behind the brand screen, pulling the strings but remaining invisible, uncontactable, unknowable.

These images may sometimes be very powerful and very influential. But they do not create a relationship between people. The 'relationship', if there is one, is between a human being and a carefully constructed façade. Marketers like to think that they are using the media to connect with – and get close to – their customers. In some ways that may be true. But their very dependence on the media underlies the reality of their situation. The media is by definition a *medium*. It comes *in between* the parties. It creates and reinforces their separation. The very thing marketers rely on to 'get close to the consumers' is also the thing that keeps them apart.[4]

Brand management as mask management is now under severe pressure. It is media dependent, and that dependency becomes a great burden if media costs rise inexorably. It works best with relatively unsophisticated consumers who can be excited and bedazzled by smoke and mirrors. But modern, sophisticated purchasers are aware that there is a person behind the mask and they want to see him. And, of course, brand management as mask management makes another modern buzz-word – dialogue – impossible.

STIMULUS-RESPONSE

Brand management as mask management was built for a stimulus-response marketing system. In the absence of information flowing directly 'up' from the customer stimulus-response marketing was the only thing companies could do: send out a stimulus in the form of an advertisement or promotion and hope for a favourable response.

Stimulus-response meshed perfectly with the prevailing scientific ideology of the time: its obsession with 'objectivity'; of the white coated scientist who, through carefully conducted experiments, gets to know the inner workings of the world – the better to change it. Marketers uncritically (though quite understandably) adopted this ideology lock, stock and barrel. Through assiduous market research they sought to study the inner workings of their consumers – their needs, their desires, their motivations – the better to change their behaviour. If you could deliver the right stimuli then you could achieve the right response – consumers would buy your brand and not your rival's.

This stimulus-response methodology is a *control* methodology; an approach which perfectly fitted the prevailing command-and-control management mindset of the industrial age firm.

The brand as mind cuckoo

This stimulus-response control mindset also created the brand as a mind-cuckoo: a packet of information lodged into the consumers' minds to influence their behaviour at the crucial point – feeding time. The cuckoo inserts its egg into another bird's nest to dislodge any other eggs, and to get that bird to feed its baby. Marketers insert the brand – recognition, associations, imagery – into consumers' heads, to dislodge other brands, to get the purchasers to feed their brand by giving it preference in the marketplace.

The mind-cuckoo theory of branding was most powerfully captured by advertising genius Stephen King nearly thirty years ago when he commented that 'products are made in factories. Brands are made (and exist) solely in the consumer's head.' King's insight underlines the vital importance of information, communication, fame, recognition, awareness, understanding and emotional associations – all the things that make brands so powerful and important in society today. But it also displays the cybernetic engineering mindset of that era. The mental model is to construct the right tool (such as advertising) to reach inside the purchaser's mental machine to change the way it works (to make it do what you want it to do), just as an engineer uses his tools to reach inside the machine and fix it.

Under the old system, marketers are the active ones who do things *to* consumers, who are the passive ones. That is why stimulus-response phrases like 'pressing the right buttons', 'pulling the right triggers' and 'finding the right emotional hooks' (along with all the military metaphors such as 'targeting', 'campaign', 'scattergun' versus 'rifle shot' approaches, etc.) found their way into the day-to-day marketing lexicon. They were not trivial coincidences. They are symptoms of a complete mindset.

There is nothing wrong with trying to be scientific about marketing; in trying to understand cause and effect. And stimulus-response marketing has chalked up many successes. Nevertheless, it now faces rapidly diminishing returns. Consumers are becoming 'marketing literate'. They know they are being stimulated and are developing a resistance to these stimuli, even learning how to turn the tables. Consumers increasingly refuse to buy at full price, for example, knowing that a sale is just around the corner. They have fun 'deconstructing' advertisements. The observed has started playing games with the observer. Buyers are starting to use the system for their own purposes, just as marketers attempted to use it for theirs.

AN EXTRACTION MENTALITY

Stimulus-response marketing is inextricably linked to the old model's fourth fatal operational flaw: the relationship between marketer and consumer is inherently and fundamentally adversarial. Buyers naturally want to buy cheap, and sellers naturally want to sell dear. And each such transaction therefore inevitably sets buyer and seller head-to-head in a marketplace confrontation over price. But marketing's extraction mentality goes deeper than that. Once again, it is a product of its time. When marketing was being perfected, 'green' thinking – which sees man as being a part of nature and underlines the need to work *with* nature – was the preserve of a tiny band of nutcases on the fringes of society. The dominant ideology of the era was to tame nature, control it and use it for man's purposes. The job of industry was to extract wealth from nature: from the straightforward extraction industries of mining and forestry, and through know-how – learning how to turn crude raw materials into valuable products.

The industrial age marketer's approach to marketing is no different. The market, like 'nature', is a given – something that lies 'out there', waiting to yield up its riches to those clever enough to unlock the secrets of wealth extraction (the secrets so carefully teased out and exploited by sophisticated market research and marketing programmes).

Two things follow from this notion of 'the market'. The first is that it is deeply impersonal. 'The market' is not a group of people with whom you enter into a relationship, but an economic force to be grappled with, tamed and channelled. 'The market' is a *thing* to extract as much wealth as possible, usually by 'charging what the market will bear'. Secondly, you do this for your own purposes. The market has no purposes of its own.

Industrial age firms got to 'know' the inner workings of their raw materials so that they could use these raw materials for their own purposes: they wanted to understand iron so that they could turn it into steel, into cars. Likewise, the marketer wants to understand the inner workings of his raw material 'the consumer' so that he can bend the consumer's behaviour to his own purposes. Again, it's all about control for the purposes of value extraction.

Thus, talking about the importance of what they call 'strategic control points' – such as brands, patents, copyrights, control of distribution etc. – Adrian Slywotzky and David Morrison of Mercer Management Consulting write: 'The purpose of a strategic control point is to protect the profit stream that the business design has created against the corrosive effects of competition *and customer power*' (my italics). This, they add, is critical – forcing itself 'to the top of the priority list' – because of 'the rapid growth of customer power in the past decade and a half'. Thus, for Slywotzky and Morrison, strategic control is just as much about beating your customer as it is about beating your competitor.[5]

CHOICE: THE SAVING GRACE?

A narrow transaction focus, an essential remoteness, stimulus-response methodologies and attitudes; a value extraction mentality that creates a fundamentally adversarial relationship between buyer and seller: attributes like these don't add up to a pretty picture.

But the industrial age marketing system has a trump card: consumer choice. Industrial age markets can be huge and complex, but at root, they are not very different to a medieval market stall. Sellers bring their wares to market and display them to best effect. Buyers come to market and inspect, compare – and choose.

Compared to this single exercise of power, the many inherent flaws of the old system seem almost irrelevant. Marketers may do everything they can to stimulate the consumer to act in this way or that, but in the end the consumer faces many competing stimuli, and chooses from amongst them. Marketers may be doing their best to extract as much value as they can, but consumer choice means that they can never push their prices too high.

> *Buyers come to market and inspect, compare – and choose.*

Marketers may be transaction obsessed – approaching the whole business in a fundamentally cold, instrumental way – but then purchasers are acting in exactly the same self-interested way when they exercise choice. And choice also introduces a win-win element into even the most adversarial relationship. After all, if you have freedom of choice you don't enter into any transaction which doesn't benefit you.

The ideology of the offer

Choice is therefore the magic ingredient which sweeps everything – including the fatal flaws discussed in this chapter – before it. It's the saving grace that makes the rogue lovable after all. It's how seller-centric marketing sells itself.

Many marketing practices have been subject to devastating critiques – but no matter how compelling the criticism, 'consumer choice' has been the marketer's clinching trump-card.

We'll see later how agents trump this trump-card. But for now, note this: 'consumer choice' and fatal flaws such as the extraction mentality are just different manifestations of the same system. They are both built around marketers saying 'here we are, this is what we have to offer'.

This explains why marketers are so obsessed with the need to 'focus on' and 'get close to' consumers. When politicians talk of the pressing need for unity, you know their party is divided. When marketers talk of the need to 'get close' to their customers, you know there's a huge gulf between the two sides. Exhortations like this are not a part of the solution, as well-intentioned preachers intend them to be. They are a symptom of the problem.

But surely marketers can choose 'choice' and say 'no thanks' to the fatal flaws? Some people believe the breakthrough has already been made. New technologies such as the Internet have made dialogue and relationship building possible, they argue. The flaws we've discussed in this chapter are now history. They are to do with technology, not the nature of the system itself. But are they?

two false dawns

Even if your product isn't that different, better or special, it's the job of the marketer to make people think that it's different, better and special.   Sergio Zyman, former Chief Marketing Officer, Coca-Cola[1]

Direct marketing is like prodding rats through a maze.

Herschell Gordon Lewis

In the last three chapters we have explored the strengths and weaknesses of the standard seller-centric model of marketing: the incredible power of its core win-wins and the mechanisms of consumer choice; the terrible consequences of the collapse of those win-wins and the flaws which both define its obsessions and explain why they are never resolved.

What dominates practitioners in their day-to-day working lives, however, is not aspects of the system they have little power to change, but how to gain competitive advantage *within* the system – by building strong brands and making their marketing ever more efficient and effective. How do these central activities fit within a Right Side Up scheme of things?

A NEW ERA DAWNS

Database marketing has the promise a new dawn within it. *Business Week* rightly captured its importance when it described the database as the biggest thing to hit marketing since 'New! Improved!'.

By filling the information hole at the heart of the marketing system the database promised, at last, to liberate marketing from its many constraints. A database turns anonymous entities called 'consumers' into identified named customers. It transforms the exhortation 'know your customer' from an exercise in statistically-based, averaged research into real knowledge about real people. It moves marketers from remoteness to closeness.

It allows marketers to move beyond one-size-fits-all offers to personalized, customized products, services and communications. It creates the opportunity to move beyond one-way stimulus-response communications and offers interactivity and dialogue instead. It allows marketers to ease their traditional obsession with the transaction – closing the sale – to build longer term, mutually beneficial relationships. And in this way, the database points the way to a whole new world of win-wins.

The database creates the opportunity for dialogue. Dialogue leads to improved understanding. Improved understanding leads to ever better alignment of product, service and communication to need. Better results for both sides leads to a deeper dialogue. Improved dialogue in turn broadens the exchange between the two sides. The exchange expands into a new dimension: exchanging money not only for goods but for valuable information too. This exchange of knowledge, in turn, creates a relationship, which improves customer retention. Increased customer retention, in turn, leads to lower customer acquisition costs and therefore improved profits and/or lower prices. And so on.

These are different win-wins to the ones opened up by industrial age marketing, but they are immensely powerful all the same. They revolve around customization rather than standardization; deaveraging rather than averaging; closeness rather than remoteness. These win-wins lie at the heart of Right Side Up marketing. That's the plus side: a potential that will never be lost. But there is a downside, too.

SLUG TRAIL MARKETING AND CUSTOMER STALKING

Every transaction generates information. Like a slug and its trail, we each create a history of transactions as we buy the things we want and need. Historically, most of this information was lost. When you walk into a shop and pay cash for something, for example, no record is kept of your involvement in that transaction.

But now, thanks to new techniques and technologies such as the barcode scanner and the loyalty scheme and the computer cookie on the Internet, these information slug trails are being made visible. Companies can follow these trails, tracking the customer's every move and purchase, building up an ever more detailed profile.

> *Marketers say they want to get close to their customers. But is this as a friend, or as a stalker?*

For marketers, it's incredibly exciting. They can use these new sources of data to recognize, respond to, and anticipate changes in customer behaviour, sometimes on a one-to-one basis. Once-invisible patterns of behaviour and pathways of change can be discovered – and acted upon. Marketers can get to 'know' and 'understand' their customers better than ever before.

But it's mostly being done within the old model. And, bolted on to a transaction-obsessed, remote, stimulus-response, extraction-mentality-driven approach to marketing, it simply takes these attributes to their furthest extremes.

Modern direct and database marketing treats the consumer like a laboratory rat, using even more data collected *about* the consumer to discover which stimuli will prod the consumer into making the 'right' response. Despite the terminology, most data-intensive programmes are just rocket-powered stimulus-response. The marketer tries to 'build a relationship' with his customer, not to genuinely enter a win-win virtuous spiral, but to suck even more information and value from him: most customer relationship marketing programmes are little more than cross-selling exercises wrapped up in fancy jargon. The *language* is that of relationship and dialogue but the *content* is still all one way and instrumental. The company is still doing the marketing *to* and *at* the customer, who knows little, if anything, of it.

What most of these relationship marketing programmes miss is that it takes two to build a relationship. Gathering up ever more information *about* the consumer, to direct ever more finely targeted stimuli *at* the consumer, has got nothing to do with building a relationship. Nor is it an attempt to create a 'dialogue' if the other side isn't interested. Like an unattractive suitor pestering a pretty girl at a party – always trying to 'get closer' – such approaches can become a downright nuisance. And the fact is, most consumers do not want to build relationships with most marketing companies. Comments EMAP Marketing advisor Simon Gulliford:

> I have yet to come across any market research, ever, where the consumer uses the word 'relationship' to describe the relationship they have either with a brand or an organisation. The only time they use the word relationship is when they talk about people. This notion of relationship talked about by marketing directors is a complete myth. I don't have a relationship with a credit card *at all*. None whatsoever. And yet they behave as though they are my best friend.

At worst, this frenzied attempt to gather ever more information about customers becomes a form of customer stalking. You get close to someone in a relationship. But stalkers also want to 'get close' to their targets. The difference is, the stalker gathers ever more information about his target and tries to 'get close' entirely for his own purposes, regardless of the feelings and wishes of the person he is targeting. As one-to-one marketing pioneer Martha Rogers notes, too many database marketing programmes have become nothing more than 'technology enhanced customer harassment'.[2]

Customer relationship management is 'an oxymoron', notes James Milojkovic, CEO of KnowledgePassion.com. 'You cannot manage a relationship. A relationship is something you negotiate. It is a *social* contract. Relationships live in conversation. Human beings live in language. But marketers who are still thinking of customers as "its" are still thinking of "managing relationships" as a form of "how do I manipulate people to do the things I want them to do?".'

Not surprisingly, far from actually building closer relationships with consumers, database marketing exercises often have precisely the opposite result. 'The net effect is a consumer who is more likely to view companies as enemies, not allies,' says Harvard Business School researcher Susan Fournier. 'Consumers don't welcome our advances. They arm themselves to fight back.'[3]

That is why 'privacy' is becoming such an issue; why privacy law suits against database marketing companies are becoming common in less regulated societies such as the US. Fear of Big Brother corporations and governments has its part to play. But at heart the issue is much simpler. There is all this technology and information out there. It has wonderful potential. But who is it being used *for*?[4]

PERMISSION MARKETING AND PERMISSION PESTERING

The most sophisticated marketers have realized the dangers of this one-sided approach to relationship marketing. The customer has to have some say in what's going on; in how the relationship is unfolding. These insights are gathered together under the banner of permission marketing.

Just as dialogue and relationship and one-to-one personalized communications lie at the heart of Right Side Up marketing, so does this notion of permission. The consumer or customer is in control: it is up to him to give permission or not. '"What's in it for me?" is the question that has to be answered at every step,' explains Seth Godin.[5] 'Permission marketing offers the consumer an opportunity to volunteer to be marketed to. By only talking to volunteers, Permission marketing guarantees that consumers pay more attention to the marketing message ... It serves both consumers and marketers in a symbiotic exchange.'[6]

But once again, we discover that the ideals of permission marketing are subverted by the seller-centric 'what do I make, how can I sell it?' nature of the old marketing machine. It's just a matter of using bait rather than prods to do the job.

Here's the permission process as described by Godin. The marketer signals his interest in a relationship, usually by making some sort of offer, such as a free sample. If the consumer responds to the offer, he is assumed to be signalling his willingness to find out more. The marketer replies with yet another, bigger offer – thereby focusing promotional spend on the most valuable prospects until, at last, 'over time, the marketer leverages the permission to change consumer behaviour and turn it into profit.'[7]

To illustrate this process, Godin draws an analogy with dating. For a girl to say yes to a date, the guy has to offer something that's interesting enough for her to spend her time with him, he suggests. And if the guy tries to have sex with her on the first date she'll probably run a mile. So he has to build the relationship up over time, making small advances to keep her interested, until, at last, she is prepared to 'go all the way'.[8]

But this permission marketer doesn't want to earn the girl's permission because he loves her. He wants her permission to have sex with her: to change her behaviour for his benefit. Like every low-down dirty testosterone-driven male chauvinist before him, this 'permission' marketer still wants to use her for his own ends. And to achieve those ends he resorts to stimulus-response methodologies, the only difference being that they are more sophisticated ones. If 'one night stand' stimulus-response marketing doesn't work any more, replace it with 'New! Improved!' *iterative* stimulus-response marketing instead.

Of course, this is not real permission marketing at all. It's permission pestering. And once the girl has had experience of being used in this way, chances are she'll hate the pesterer. Indeed, in time, if permission marketing is applied in this way it could soon earn an even worse reputation among consumers than junk mail.

There's a big buzz in the Internet world right now about 'opt-in' e-mail. If the customer can opt in to receiving e-mails, he'll be more likely to pay attention to the messages he receives, the argument goes. It's true. Opt-in e-mail is one of the core technological platforms of the consumer agent. But, yet again, in nine cases out of ten, it's not being used that way. It's not being used to elicit a view from the customer as to what he would like; to respond better to that customer's needs. It's simply messages about the things I want to sell, delivered in a cheaper, more targeted way. That's a huge benefit to the marketer. But it's not really permission marketing. It's permission selling.

GOODBYE MR GRADGRIND

The second truly great breakthrough made by industrial age marketers was the recognition that all exchange and all consumption has, at some level or other, important emotional significance. With this insight marketers demolished the myth of *homo economicus:* man, the narrow, instrumental, purely logical, selfish, benefits-calculating machine dreamed up by the Mr Gradgrind school of classical economics.

Unphased by impressive bodies of economic theory expounding this fallacy, marketers pointed to the simple facts: wherever there are people, purely 'rational' buying and exchange decisions (as defined by the economists) don't happen. People are boiling cauldrons of non-rational and irrational drives, lusts, instincts, reflexes, emotions, passions, values, sensibilities and yearnings. They are people, not convenient one-dimensional elements in a neat economic theory. The decisions they make, the things they do, reflect this fact. At some level or other, all meaningful exchange takes place between people, and such exchanges both create and express meaning.

> *If businesses and markets seem like soulless machines it is because people make them so.*

This fundamentally important insight recognizes that all businesses, all marketplaces and all transactions have an emotional as well as a rational content. Businesses are communities through which people relate to people; markets are places where people exchange value with people. If businesses and markets seem like soul-less machines it is because people make them so. The ramifications are immense. For our purposes, however, the critical observation is this: even the most mundane day-to-day activities and products can be pregnant with social significance and meaning. Any act, from cleaning the toilet, to feeding the family, to wearing clothes, to saving for retirement is replete with emotional connotations: about order, control, safety, giving, protecting, nurturing, saying who I am, expressing membership of a group, dreaming dreams and wrestling with fears and worries.

The human, emotional connotations of brands are not 'invented' by marketers. Since the year dot, humans have invested things with deep emotional significance whether they are cowrie shells, beads, feathers, paintings, little statuettes of Christ on the cross, whatever. As US advertising commentator and academic James Twitchell remarks: 'Stand in the shampoo aisle for a minute and you will appreciate the deep magical meaning of hair.'[9]

Even a 'purely' rational, scientific demonstration of functional product superiority is a deeply emotional act, evoking reactions related to authority, reassurance, trust, etc. Ditto with purely rational price offers, which bristle with connotations such as greed, the love of a bargain or 'getting something for nothing', the excitement of the chase (to get the best bargain), a preference for no-nonsense, honest value, even superiority: really smart buyers go for the best deal.

It follows that any marketer worth his or her salt must recognize these emotional connotations and address them. These aspects of the brand are not separate from the physiological or functional need. They are part of the *whole* need and marketers most learn to address the whole need in their product or service development, and in the way they communicate its benefits. An advertising campaign that speaks to me in such a way that it fails to recognize how and why I use this product and what it means to me, tells me that the advertiser is insensitive to my needs. It becomes a positive turn-off. A failure to address the emotional attributes of brands *is*, therefore, a failure to earn a consumer's preference.

PROMISE BECOMES HOKUM

The road to hell is paved with good intentions, and the best of reasons often end up hiding the worst of intellectual slipping and sliding.

Recognizing that humans sometimes inject enormous emotional significance into the most trivial of material things does not necessarily mean that this emotional significance is created by marketers, can be created by marketers, or should be created by marketers. But that's what marketers began to do: to invent complete 'personalities'; to dream up a battery of 'emotional attributes' to wrap around a base, meaningless product, in order to make it sell more effectively. We no longer purchased soap powder to clean our clothes; we bought Persil if we wanted to be a good mother. As authors Simon Knox and Stan Maklan observe: 'The soap makers jettisoned "washes whiter" advertising and instead went for cuddly teddy bears, caring mothers, puppies and fairy tale princesses. At Unilever, brand psychologists replaced scientists as the drivers of added value.'[10]

This was the stimulus-response mentality at work again, except this time it was a matter of finding the right emotional buttons to press, the right emotional triggers to pull: all to get consumers to do what marketers wanted them to do – buy more, at a higher price. The consumer was still just a rat, but a complex rat, whose behaviour could be controlled by the right emotional stimuli.

That was the essence of Vance Packard's diatribe against marketers in the late 1950s in his exposé *The Hidden Persuaders*. It was influential because it struck a nerve.[11] Packard is often laughed at now. But his mistake was not that he misunderstood what marketers were *trying* to achieve, but that he assumed (along with the people he was criticizing) that they knew enough about human psychology to actually do it.

If the 'depth approach' described by Packard seems naive today, son-of-depth-approach is still alive and well. Thus, James Twitchell notes that when a woman buys a lipstick, 'what is being bought is place, prestige, comfort, security, confidence, purpose and meaning. Forget the lipstick; what you apply is the brand.' Advertising guru David Ogilvy's comment that 'the consumer is no fool, she is your wife' just doesn't wash, he suggests. The evidence 'indicates that P.T. Barnum's "a fool born every minute" is more appropriate'.[12]

Even more dangerous was the growing belief that 'the brand' as opposed to 'the product' was the thing that 'really' added value. When marketers first latched onto the importance of the emotional attributes of brands they still believed that they were creating value in their factory (or via their service infrastructure): the emotional overlay was just an additional, 'tie-breaking' inducement to buy. The next slippery step was to take Stephen King's brilliant argument that brands are 'made' in consumers' minds one stage further: to argue that not only is the brand 'made' in the consumer's mind *but so is the value*. What consumers buy – what they actually pay for – are not the functional attributes created in the factory, but the emotional attributes created by marketing communications. In this way marketing communication was elevated into the primary source of added value. Consumers no longer bought the product *per se*, but its marketing.

In some cases (these things are never black and white) it's actually true. For some categories, emotional reasons to buy do go beyond *supplementing* core functionality, to *become* the core functionality. For example, in categories such as luxury goods and fashion, where the brand image enables the consumer to make a public statement about himself in terms of status or prestige, affiliation to a particular group or a set of values, he ends up 'buying' the marketing communications as much as the product itself. The communications become a core part of the product.

But these are the exceptions, not the norm. And applying theories of 'emotional added value' to the norm quickly becomes an excuse for a retreat from genuine attempts to add value. It's often argued, for example, that in modern markets products and services have reached 'functional parity' and that therefore emotional added values have become the only meaningful differentiator. Thus, declares John Bartle, joint Chief Executive of advertising agency Bartle Bogle Hegarty, the old marketing's USP (unique selling point) is 'fast disappearing'. 'Then what becomes correspondingly more important is what we call ESP – the emotional selling point – and this is preeminently the business of advertising and advertising agencies.'[13]

Likewise, says John Periss, chairman of Zenith Media, as products become 'ever more similar in performance, so the key differentiator between one product or another, or one service or another, increasingly becomes its perceived value rather than its absolute value.'[14]

Here we have leading spokesmen of an imploding marketing system in open and public admission of defeat: we can no longer gain competitive edge by creating real incremental value, so we'll just pretend instead, by manipulating perceptions. In this way branding stops being an integral part of a dynamic, win-win system that's forever offering 'New! Improved!' value and becomes the complete opposite: a device, powered by advertising, to manipulate consumer perceptions for the benefit of industrial corporations whose offer is no longer superior.

From the buyer-centric perspective of Right Side Up marketing this approach to branding compounds injury with insult. It turns the byproduct of the original system (improved margins) into *the* purpose of marketing and brand building. The job of the brand is now simply to deliver a brand 'premium': to charge more. And instead of earning this 'premium' by making the system as a whole work better (by delivering 'New! Improved!' products and services at lower cost based on improved economies of scale, for example) it seeks to use artificially added 'emotional values' to persuade consumers that paying the extra money is worthwhile: to get them to pay for the privilege of having 'perceived value rather than absolute value'.

> *'Emotional added value' is a device for consumers to pay twice for marketers' attempts to fleece them.*

Then, as if this wasn't enough the ever-inflating costs of the increasingly elaborate and expensive marketing communications programmes that are needed to invent these emotional values are then added into the price the consumer is expected to pay for the product. The consumer ends up paying twice over for the marketer's cynical attempt to fleece him. And brand building turns into brand hokum: a great soft underbelly in the old system just waiting to be attacked.

TEETERING AT THE EDGE OF THE FUTURE

The net result is deeply frustrating. Recognizing the critical importance of customer knowledge and human emotions represents two enormously important breakthroughs. Both lie at the heart of Right Side Up marketing. But when reverse-engineered into a seller-centric marketing model, far from revitalizing it, they simply exaggerate its faults. They make the old system even more remote. They make its stimulus-response, adversarial character even more obvious. They make its extraction mentality even more pronounced.

Now, think of a future where connectedness begins to take the place of remoteness and where brand management as façade management turns into brand management as interface management. Imagine a world where stimulus-response marketing goes into reverse: into sense and respond. Where an adversarial extraction mentality makes way for mutually beneficial co-operation and co-production. See these transformed relationships enriched and enhanced by emotional (as well as functional) exchange – a sharing of *values* as well as value – and by all the potential of the database and the information age. This is the new high ground offered by agents and Right Side Up marketing.

But seeing it intellectually is not the same as being able to reach it. Marketers have been reaching for this high ground for decades. And each time they have reached for it, it has slipped through their fingers. The 'fault' does not lie with marketers. If they could have made the break before now, they would have done so. But they could not. To understand just how *systemic* the challenge of Right Side Up marketing is, we first of all have to understand why this is the case.

trapped!

> More often than not, we do not perceive the power of the system at play.
> Rather, we just find ourselves feeling compelled to act in certain ways.
>
> Peter Senge[1]

MARKETING MYOPIA REVISITED

Ted Levitt published his classic manifesto for the marketing revolution, *Marketing Myopia*, in 1960. Its aim: to 'underscore the catastrophic results of being product-oriented rather than customer-oriented'.[2]

Central to Levitt's argument was his distinction between selling and marketing. Selling, he said,

focuses on the needs of the seller, marketing on the needs of the buyer. Selling is preoccupied with the seller's need to convert his product into cash, marketing with the idea of satisfying the needs of the customer by means of the product and the whole cluster of things associated with creating, delivering and finally consuming it.[3]

Trouble was, he suggested, what most organizations called marketing was, in fact, selling. Lambasting the US oil industry of the time, Levitt wrote:

> To the extent that the consumer is studied at all (which is not much) the focus is forever on getting information which is designed to help the oil companies improve what they are now doing. They try to discover more convincing advertising themes, more effective sales promotion drives, what the market share of the various companies is, what people like or dislike about service station dealers and oil companies, and so forth ... Basic questions about customers and markets never get asked.[4]

Likewise, he criticized the Detroit car industry. Each year, he noticed, they 'spend millions of dollars on consumer research' yet still display 'unbelievable lags behind consumer wants'. Why? Because:

> Detroit never really researched the customer's wants. *It only researches his preferences between the kinds of things which it had already decided to offer him* [while] ... the areas of greatest unsatisfied needs are ignored, or at best get stepchild attention ... The automobile companies do not seem to listen or take their cues from the anguished consumer. If they do listen, it must be through the filter of their own preoccupation with production. The marketing effort is still viewed as a necessary consequence of the product, not vice-versa [my italics].[5]

As Levitt commented: 'When it comes to the marketing concept today, a solid stone wall often seems to separate word and deed. In spite of the best intentions and energetic efforts of many highly able people, the effective implementation of the marketing concept has generally eluded them.'

Forty years later we still hear the same complaint from people like Peter Drucker, one of the original pioneers of the marketing concept. 'The term "marketing" was coined fifty years ago to emphasize that the purpose and results of a business lie entirely outside of itself,' he wrote in 1998.

> Marketing teaches that organized efforts are needed to bring an understanding of the outside, of society, economy and customer, to the inside of the organization and to make it the foundation for strategy and policy. Yet marketing has rarely performed that grand task. Instead it has become a tool to support selling. It does not start out with 'who is the customer?' but 'what do we want to sell?' It is aimed at getting people to buy the things you want to make.[6]

Misson impossible

The question is, why? Why has this 'solid stone wall' between word and deed remained so solid through all these years? The answer is that Levitt (and Drucker) were asking marketers to do the impossible. Asking the industrial age enterprise to embrace marketing as they described it was asking them to commit commercial suicide. It was like asking a fish to breathe air.

Levitt hinted at this when he noted that 'mass production industries are impelled by a great drive to produce all they can. The prospect of steeply declining unit costs as output rises is more than most companies can usually resist.' This, he observed, 'generates great pressure to "move" the product'.

But this pressure is so great that it's well nigh irresistible. If you are a car company and you have invested $1 billion in a new car plant or platform, if you fail to sell enough cars to cover that investment your firm's future is in doubt. The very investment that creates the benefits you sell also creates the pressure to sell. We cannot have the benefits of mass production without also having production-driven organizations.

Also, no matter how desirable it may be to be customer-oriented, it is the defining fact of the production-driven organization that it is organized around technologies and infrastructure – productive assets. Which means it is *not* organized around customers. Take cars again. Levitt said that marketing was about 'satisfying the needs of the customer by means of the product *and the whole cluster of things associated with creating, delivering and finally consuming it*' (my italics). In his critique of Detroit, for example, he noted that the greatest customer needs – which were (and are still) persistently ignored by the big car companies – arose 'at the point of sale and on the matter of automotive repair and maintenance'.

But to truly satisfy this whole cluster of needs, the car company would not only have to involve itself as a manufacturer making the car, but also as a dealer providing distribution, a garage providing servicing, a roadside assistance organization offering breakdown services, and so on.

Yet then – as now – each of these industries and companies focus very much on their own thing. For very good reason. They require specialist skills and special investments. Making a car, for example, involves putting 10,000 individual pieces together in a way that works perfectly, 100 per cent of the time. And getting this highly complex task right, 100 per cent of the time, at the lowest possible cost, while forging ahead with technical innovation affecting each one of these 10,000 individual pieces, isn't easy. Some of the biggest, most well-resourced, most competent organizations ever known to man put all their scientific, organizational and financial effort into doing this – and they still struggle not to

> *Seller-centric marketing is congenitally unable to fully practice what it preaches.*

make a hash of it. Considering the scale of the challenge in just one area of the cluster, it's not surprising that specialists choose to stick to their knitting.

For these two reasons – the survive-or-die pressure to recoup upfront investments through volume sales, and the need to organize around the requirements of efficient production – industrial age marketers could never implement Levitt's exhortations. This was not because they lacked the necessary vision, understanding, insight, strategic intent, skill, tools, budgets, resources, or anything else. It was because 'what do I make and how can I sell it?' is the internal, *defining* logic of the industrial age organization. This logic is embedded within its DNA. And if it doesn't follow this logic – by selling what it makes – it dies.

So what we have ended up with, instead, is a compromise. Marketing should focus on the needs of the buyer, not the seller, and marketers have applied the precepts of marketing as far as they can – to what they make and sell. In doing so, they have interpreted the core notion of finding out what the customer wants and giving it to him extremely narrowly: 'Given that we make widgets, what sort of widgets would our customers like, so that we can make the widgets that sell?' And (further), 'Given that we have made these widgets, how can we persuade our target customers to buy them?'

Marketing has excelled in this role. But it is not the 'marketing concept' as Levitt intended it to be. In fact, it's quite the opposite. Instead of adopting the marketing concept as an *alternative* to the selling concept, industrial age marketers appropriated it as an *adjunct*, in order to make selling more efficient and more effective. They made marketing *seller-centric*. Sergio Zyman summed it up perfectly when he said, 'The sole purpose of marketing is to sell more to more people, more often, and at higher prices. There is no other reason to do it.'[7]

But Levitt wasn't wrong, he was just before his time. You cannot have consumer-focused marketing without consumer-focused organizations. Unlike production-driven organizations – which are driven by the need to recoup investments made in productive assets such as plant, tools, machinery, technologies and infrastructure – the buyer- or consumer-focused organization's critical asset and investment is the consumer himself. Instead of making its money by organizing *production* and *selling* efficiently and effectively, it organizes *consumers*, demand and *buying* efficiently and effectively. When Levitt was writing, such a beast was a practical impossibility. It isn't any more.

at last! an escape route!

> *The important applications of any significant new technology are usually unthinkable in advance ... people do not solve new problems with an unfamiliar technology. We start by solving familiar problems more efficiently; then we solve those same problems differently; and only when we have reached a threshold of familiarity with the capabilities of the technology do we apply our ingenuity to new areas.*
>
> Stephan Haeckel, Director of Strategic Studies at
> IBM's Advanced Institute of Studies[1]
>
> *Once you've detached information [from the product] everything changes.*
> Jay Walker, founder of Priceline.com[2]

THE INFORMATION AGE OCTOPUS

Wealth creation, organized around consumers buying more efficiently rather than producers producing and selling more efficiently? Organizations organized around consumers and buyers, rather than productive assets? To the industrial age seller-centric mind these are implausible notions. Rightly so. In an industrial age context they are impractical and unworkable. But our economy is changing. We are entering an information age, and it is making new breeds of business beast possible.

To see the potential of these new beasts we need to look closer at the sorts of change triggered by the information age. It does not create one, singular effect. It creates many, different, intertwining effects. Try thinking of it as an octopus where each different tentacle has its own unique economic suction power. These tentacles are latching on to everything they touch, pulling every morsel of every economic activity in a different direction.

As they swirl around it's very easy to get mesmerized by just one or two of them – and to forget that it's not the tentacles that get you, it's the beast as a whole. It's also very easy to fall into the trap described by Stephan Haeckel: to see their potential to latch on to familiar problems – in our case, to help sellers sell more efficiently – while failing to see their ability to grab hold of new opportunities, such as helping buyers buy. So let's look at each of those information age tentacles in turn.

1. Plummeting transaction costs

Driven by Moore's law – where the costs of computing halve every eighteen months or so – the costs of gathering, storing, manipulating, analysing, connecting and distributing bits of information are plummeting. For example, back in 1978, before the PC revolution, it cost around $1 million to process one million instructions per second (called MIPS). By 1998, the equivalent cost was less than one dollar. And there's no sign of that pace slowing.

The implications are profound. A cost trajectory that has lasted for a century is now going into reverse. The balance of costs in every organization – between 'matter processing costs' and 'information processing costs' – is being revolutionized, and re-revolutionized. Between 1970 and 1997, for example, the number of hours it took for the average US employee to earn enough money to buy a car fell by just over 2 per cent. But the number of man hours needed to buy a long distance telephone call fell by over 99 per cent in the same period.[3]

For marketers, falling transaction costs have two critical

effects. First, firms that move furthest, fastest along this new cost trajectory can gain a significant cost (and therefore price) advantage. Cisco Systems, the Internet backbone provider, estimates that every purchase order transacted 'virtually' saves it $46, compared to the costs that would have been incurred processing it by paper, while increasing the productivity of employees involved in purchasing by 78 per cent. Big firms like retailers and car companies undertake hundreds of millions of transactions every year. By opening up cost savings of this sort, the information age is triggering the mother of all cost and price disruptions and doubling and redoubling the importance of price within 'the marketing mix'.

But plummeting transaction costs also have another effect. In the industrial age, the costs of gathering and distributing information remained so high that only those with the deepest pockets had access to information – and therefore to power. But just as the invention of the printing press helped precipitate the collapse of the feudal order, by spreading ideas and knowledge from a tiny ruling elite to the ruled, so the information age is triggering a shift in power from corporations to consumers. Customer agents are a key mechanism in this power shift. They use plummeting interaction and transaction costs to put information power in the hands of the masses.

2. *Ever richer content*

Plummeting information processing costs mean that what was impossibly expensive yesterday becomes a trivial cost today. At the same time, ever more sophisticated information processing capabilities mean we can do more and more with the information we have. Access to ever richer sources of information triggers three massive developments.

a First, it gives a massive boost to the age-old industrial age project of 'New! Improved!' We are living in an era of ever smarter, information rich products and services. Ours is the age of 'chips with everything'.

b Second, it's opening the era of personalization and customization. The industrial age could not cope with complexity. It needed simplicity – standardization – to create economies of scale. The information age points to a completely differ-

ent world of personalized communication and tailored products and services – and therefore ways of going to market
too.

c Third, it puts the database at the centre of virtually every
business – data warehousing, data mining. Every firm lives
– or dies – by its ability to process information: to take in
signals from the marketplace; to use information to create
products in the most efficient manner possible; to communicate the final outcome – its offer – to potential customers.
The information rich database, and the ability to process this
information to get maximum value, now lies at the heart of
competitive success.

Each of these three aspects of information richness opens up
tremendous opportunities for traditional seller-centric marketers. But it also opens up space for agents. Instead of serving
consumers better at the end of a supply chain, agents seize
the potential of personalization and customization to put the
consumer at the beginning of a demand chain: as specifier.
Instead of using the database to gather more and more information *about* the customer, to sell more effectively, agents put
the power of the database in the hands of the consumer to help
them, as buyers, to buy.

3. Digitalization

The third tentacle of the information age octopus is that,
increasingly, anything that can be distributed in digital rather
than physical form will be. The effects are particularly revolutionary for any and all information-intensive industries. Historically, what the consumer has *bought* in these industries is
information, but what he has mostly *paid* for is not the information itself, but the physical costs of delivering that information: for example, bank branches in the case of banks,
newspapers, books and newsagents and physical bookstores in
the case of publishing.

By 'going digital' the music industry will unleash unthinkably
huge amounts of value. It's unstoppable, as is the case for every
digitizable industry – whether it is financial services, travel,
publishing, music or software. And, of course, this distribution
revolution places a time-bomb under every aspect of the industry

concerned: cost structures, power structures, business models, etc.

But the key effect is: to reverse the flow from 'pushing' physical products at buyers, to users pulling or 'sucking' information from databases. This is the natural *modus operandi* of the agent. Digitalization creates room for specialist agents, such as consumer-oriented information agents which seek out, edit and filter the information consumers want to receive.

4. Unbundling

Many activities such as retailing and shopping for non-digitizable items, however, involve a mix of both matter-processing and information-processing activities. The information-intensive side includes searching for, comparing, communicating about, negotiating, deciding, choosing and paying. The matter-intensive side includes storing, handling and transporting physical goods.

The effect of the information age is to increasingly unbundle these processes, to allow the information-processing activities to be done separately from the matter processing. Traditionally, for example, the price of a jar of coffee was printed on the jar, and went with it wherever it went. Once the information about the product is separated from the product itself a whole new array of applications – and business models – becomes possible. Crucially, it unbundles the beast we once called 'the shop' whose foundations lie in an age when products and information about products could not be separated. In doing so it revolutionizes *all* retailing. It fundamentally changes the way buyers and sellers meet: it therefore fundamentally changes the processes of marketing itself.

Agents take this unbundling process one step further. By taking on many of the information-intensive tasks of matching supply to demand and connecting buyers and sellers, agents unbundle marketing itself. They disconnect marketing's generic processes of matching and connecting from selling. They let consumers seize control of marketing itself. That's what buying clubs, infomediaries and solution assemblers do. Just as a private label manufacturer doesn't market the product he makes – letting the retailer do that – agents allow for the negotiation of completely new marketing divisions of labour between buyers and sellers.

5. A tidal wave of downward flows of information

The information age is also an age of communication: of information overload. The cheaper it gets to gather, process and communicate information the more we do it. The most obvious examples of this development are the rise of direct and database marketing, the proliferation of media 'channels' and the fragmentation of audiences.

This opens up tremendous new opportunities and challenges for marketers. The biggest challenge is quite simple. The growing tidal wave of 'downward' flows of information is turning information from a precious resource into a pollutant. And it's turning something marketers once took for granted – consumer attention – into a rare and precious resource.

Earning the consumer's attention, rather than using it, becomes the new marketing imperative. And agents, of course, who work for and on behalf of the consumer, to filter messages, and organize consumer attention and realize its value *for* consumers are perfectly positioned to seize this opportunity.

6. The rise of upward flows of information

The sixth crucially important effect of the information age is the rise of 'upward' flows of information. 'Two way flows of information' and 'interactivity' are not new, of course. The postal service and the telephone have been around for a while. But the information age accelerates and deepens their effect a thousand times over: it's only recently that consumers have started getting used to the idea that they can talk to companies as much and as easily as companies can talk to them.

This changes the way companies do business. Back in 1993, for example, Cisco Systems' call centres were dealing with 4000 telephone calls a month from customers, often relating to highly complex technical issues and taking up to forty-five minutes a time. Five years later it was dealing with 950,000 customer queries a month – via its website.

Marketers have also seized on the possibilities of interactivity and 'dialogue' to develop new approaches to marketing: it's a key theme in relationship, one-to-one and permission marketing.

A move from stimulus-response to sense-and-respond business and marketing systems is made possible by this rise in upward flows of information. A classic example is Dell Computer's 'direct' model – making things to order rather than making things and then trying to sell them.

Upward flows of information make it possible to reverse the flow of traditional marketing, to turn 'the consumer' into a specifier, to place him at the beginning of a demand chain rather than at the end of a supply chain. That's what agents do.

7. The emergence of sideways flows of information

Right Side Up marketing really takes off, however, when upward flows of information are combined with sideways, or horizontal, flows of information: the Internet and Internet-related phenomena such as the e-mail explosion, Internet chat forums, the emergence of on-line communities, of 'electronic word of mouth', and so on. It's still in its earliest stages, but the implications are profound. Cost-effective, mass-scale horizontal or 'sideways' flows of information create the foundations for a whole new set of business models such as auctions, reverse auctions, buying clubs and communities of interest.

Sideways flows of information make it financially and economically viable to aggregate consumer information. Sideways flows of information open up the era of the organized consumer: the Right Side Up era.

8. Automation

The eighth tentacle of our information age octopus is different to all the others: it's about what computers and technology *cannot* do, rather than what they can do. As more things *can* be automated, so, more and more, they will be. And once something is automated, we don't worry about it much.

There is a paradox here. The information age is driven forward by our ever-increasing ability to capture knowledge and skills in the form of software. Yet, no sooner have we done so than we turn that particular process or skill or segment of knowledge into a commodity. That changes the sources of value that lie at the very heart of every business and every brand – especially industrial age brands which were built on the back of efficient, replicated routines. People qualities – such as the innate ability to sense, judge, create, empathize and build relationships with other people – move centre stage.[4] As this happens, the very inner logic of mass marketing begins to dissolve. Because by definition, people are unique.

Marketing, in a world where the unique qualities of individuals begin to matter as much as economies of scale? It sounds like a very odd world. But this is now a massive growth area: using information age capabilities to amplify *people* qualities and concerns – rather than simply reproduce *thing* qualities. We'll also see how a new and highly valued breed of agent – the transformation guide – will fill this gap at the pinnacle of value creation, as far as individual consumers are concerned.

YOU AIN'T SEEN NOTHING YET

Yet, huge as each tentacle's effects seem to be, the information age is still amazingly young. As it matures, it will master a whole new set of 'skills' that will really let its full potential flourish. These include:

- XML languages that make for a far more 'intelligent' and efficient information system
- mass-scale broadband communications
- secure electronic micropayment mechanisms
- systems that reassure citizens about privacy and security
- truly intelligent search agents, which actually help you find what you are looking for rather than just pretending to
- ubiquitous and mobile Internet, e.g. via the TV, mobile phone, car etc.
- peer-to-peer file sharing which really does bring the world of information to your fingertips.

Only a few decades ago computing machines were stuck away in special rooms. Today, a throw-away card that plays Happy Birthday contains more computing power than existed in the entire world before 1950. Soon, today's supercomputers will look nearly as primitive. It wasn't until 1984 – with the launch of the Apple Mac – that the computer took the first faltering steps towards being democratized. The Internet has started gaining mass penetration only very recently. And considering what's already in the pipeline in terms of technological capabilities, it's clear information-age driven changes will continue at lightning speed. As Allan Leighton, former CEO of Asda PLC and of Wal-Mart's European operations, remarks: 'The Internet is an industrial revolution in a microsecond.'[5]

A NEW MARKETING SYSTEM BECKONS

Revolutionized cost structures, completely new types of product, service (and marketing), the root-and-branch disruptions caused by digitalization and unbundling, the transformed power structures and marketplaces created by new flows of information, the new sources of competitive edge thrown up by automation – each and every tentacle does its bit to 'undo' industrial age approaches to marketing.

At the same time, however, they are also helping to generate the win-wins that will drive Right Side Up marketing forward with unstoppable momentum. These include:

- sharing the benefits created by plummeting transaction and interaction costs by interacting in new and different ways
- finding new and more efficient, more mutually beneficial, ways of connecting buyer to seller and seller to buyer
- broadening the exchange between buyer and seller beyond the narrow exchange of money for goods to include new dimensions such as information, insight and expertise, shared values, and more
- reaping the benefits of ever richer, more detailed sources of information: via personalized and customized products and services. Turbo-charged matching of buyers' needs to suppliers' offers is one example
- reaping the benefits of real-time rather than delayed-reaction business systems, e.g moving from make-then-sell stimulus-response modes of operation to make-to-order, sense-and-respond systems which create more valuable customized products and services at lower cost
- new information economies of scale that arise from the aggregation and 'mining' of large amounts of data

▓ new possibilities for information-driven 'mutual process re-engineering', whereby both sides change what they do or how they do it in order to simplify or enrich each other's final outcomes.

Such win-wins are open to every business and every organization. But to really unleash their full potential, information from and about customers needs to be gathered, processed and used. And this creates the space for agents whose prime function is not to organize infrastructure for the purposes of production and distribution, but to organize consumers and the information they generate. These consumer- or buyer-centric organizations break free from the constraints that stopped marketers from applying the insights of marketing luminaries such as Levitt and Drucker. They can follow the logic of 'who is my customer, and how can I serve him?' rather than 'what do I make, and how can I sell it?'. They point not only to new and different ways of 'doing marketing', but to a different sort of marketing system.

PART 2

new dimensions of competition

The agency imperative

Helping buyers to buy, rather than helping sellers to sell, is the wave of the future.

Right Side Up marketing – marketing for and on behalf of the consumer – is emerging to take its rightful place as the centre of marketing gravity.

As it does so, it's transforming the nature of brand and business competition.

How buyers buy, *what* they buy and *who* they buy from are all being thrown into the melting pot.

Every marketer, whether new-style consumer agent or traditional brand, now needs to compete along new dimensions of value.

who is marketing for?

> *You have to have someone who is looking for the product most appropriate to the customer, rather than the customer who is most appropriate for the product.*
>
> Don Peppers[1]

By now the answer should be obvious. Marketing as we know it is *for* sellers. Big corporations, mainly. Marketing is done by them, for them, to help them sell. But what would buyer-centric marketing look like?

Set aside any business or professional objectives for a moment and think about what you, as an individual, would ideally like when venturing out to buy something. Chances are, you wouldn't say no to the following:

- easy, simple access to information about the items that you particularly need or want, including where to source them
- objective, impartial, comprehensive information that helps you make informed comparisons and the best choices
- advice from an expert if the purchase is complex or risky – especially if that expert has a good understanding of your particular needs and circumstances

- ▓ shared experiences from other people who have used the product or service you are thinking of buying
- ▓ the ability to identify the lowest cost source of this product or service
- ▓ assistance in negotiating special discounts or deals, say, via a buying club or reverse auction
- ▓ low-cost, hassle-free transactions. Just compare traipsing around physically from shop to shop with a purchase mechanism like Amazon's One Click
- ▓ perfect fulfilment: delivery when you want it, where you want it

In short, when buyers go to market their dream service comes from someone *who is on their side* helping them to do all these things. This is utterly different to the seller-centric ideal, as described by Sergio Zyman, which is 'to sell more to more people, more often, and at higher prices'.[2]

That doesn't mean the two never meet. Sometimes, seller-centric marketers do things which, to some degree or other, have *the effect of* helping buyers to buy. When a manufacturer advertises a New! Improved! product, he helps make the buyer aware of a new choice and a possible source of better value. When a retailer places competing items on a shelf next to each other, he assists the shopper in the processes of searching and comparing – which is much more than a tied dealer would do.

But these buyer benefits are just small elements within the total seller-centric package. The advertiser advertising his new product isn't doing it to help the buyer source the best value, he's doing it to attract the buyer to his particular offer. And consumers have to work hard to sift through the disparate range of seller-centric marketing activities to pick out the elements that are actually helpful.

A consumer who wants to buy a car, for example, might buy a specialist motoring magazine to find out what the experts think of various competing models, and to discover more about prices. He will pay attention to press and TV advertising from the manufacturers of the models he's interested in. He'll visit dealerships to find out what's on offer. He'll talk to friends and colleagues about their experiences with different cars. And so on. He then has to draw these disparate strands together in order to reach his decision.

Meanwhile, as part of this often complex and time-consuming sifting process, the consumer also has to deal with large volumes of seller-centric marketing activity which do nothing to help him in his buying process. The seller of Brand A, for example, has no interest at all in alerting him to the fact that Brand B might be better, cheaper, or more appropriate to his needs. Indeed, Brand A's marketers may be doing their best to convince him otherwise. After all, seller-centric marketing is not about providing buyers with comprehensive, impartial information but with grabbing their attention and using it to impart biased information: information that puts their offer in the best possible light.

The seller-centric marketer also has a vested interest in avoiding transparency. As marketing researcher Indrajit Sinha points out, buyers have a natural interest in understanding what a seller's real costs are, but 'sellers have a natural interest in keeping their costs opaque to the world outside. They want people to accept the notion that their prices are justified, and they spend a lot on advertising to convey the message that their brands offer unique benefits.'[3]

And if the purchase is complex or risky the seller may well see this as an opportunity, not to help you understand what's going on, but to pull the wool over your eyes. The UK financial services industry, for example, has a glorious track record of doing everything it can to make sure the buyer does *not* have a full understanding of what's going on. How else could it so successfully mis-sell billions of pounds worth of personal pensions and endowment mortgages?

ENTER THE AGENT

It's a commonplace nowadays that the Internet changes the balance of power between consumers and marketers by making more information available to consumers. But there is a difference between a mere availability of information, and a professional service dedicated to sourcing and providing such information. That's what nascent agents are beginning to do. As we saw in Chapter 2, there's now a proliferation of new websites which:

▓ provide consumers with impartial and comprehensive information about product qualities and attributes

* compare prices and features of products available on the Web
* enable consumers to share notes about their experience of products, services and companies, publishing real-time information about bargains and special offers.
* provide bespoke searching services for consumers looking to buy particular items
* intervene in the buying process to tip the scales in favour of the buyer, via reverse auctions or co-buying services, for example.

Now, imagine a meta-website that merged and collated all these functions into one single service that did all these things. Then the buying agent truly comes into his own: doing marketing – those core generic tasks of matching and connecting – for and on behalf of the consumer. In effect, he becomes the consumer's marketing department.

THE CONSUMER'S MARKETING DEPARTMENT

The consumer? With his own marketing department? To the traditionalist, used to definitions of marketing such as 'find out what the customer wants, and give it to him, profitably', the very notion of a consumer having his own marketing department seems absurd. What's he going to do, sell himself?

But thoughtful marketers, like Philip Kotler, have always realized that marketing is not the same as selling, and that both buyers and sellers take part in the core marketing processes of matching and connecting. 'Sellers must search for buyers, identify their needs, design good products and services, set prices for them, promote them, and store and deliver them,' Kotler writes in his classic textbook *Principles of Marketing*. But at the same time, buyers must also search for sellers, identify their offers, compare these offers, make choices, and buy them. 'Although we normally think of marketing as being carried on by sellers,' Kotler noted, 'buyers also carry on marketing activities. Consumers do "marketing" when they search for the goods they need at prices they can afford.'[4]

The assumption that only sellers do marketing is an illusion generated by the industrial age's 'here we are, this is what we have to offer' marketing set up. Under this system, consumers did their form of marketing as dispersed, isolated, amateur individuals. This kept their contribution invisible (individual consumers do not undertake multi-million dollar advertising campaigns) and irrelevant (the individual consumer's buying power is a drop in the ocean compared to the budget of a mighty global corporation).

The difference, then, is not that one side does marketing while the other doesn't. The difference is that one side has done it in an organized, professional way and – so far – the other side has not. As Boston Consulting Group's Philip Evans notes, traditionally:

> sellers have economies of scale in manipulating information that buyers don't. Sellers spend an enormous amount of time and money understanding the competition, the choice, the patterns of behaviour. It's called marketing. Consumers don't do that because they don't have the economies of scale as individual buyers that, say, P&G as an individual seller has. Individual consumers don't have their own marketing department, or rather a purchasing department.[5]

By organizing consumers – and information from and about them – buying agents generate these economies of scale. A service providing rich, impartial information about products or services for an individual consumer would be prohibitively expensive. But investing in the information sources and personalization technologies to do the same for 100,000 or 1 million such buyers brings the unit costs crashing down. Likewise, an agent acting for a single buyer within a marketplace is unlikely to achieve much more, in negotiating terms, than that buyer could by himself. But if the agent can aggregate the buying power of 1,000 or 100,000 such buyers then it's a different story.

BUT WHO PAYS?

Will consumers be prepared to pay for such services? Even the biggest modern corporation finds marketing costs are a heavy burden, so how on earth could consumers afford to employ such marketing departments on their own behalf?

Again, questions like these only illustrate the illusions generated by the old seller-centric marketing system. Consumers' marketing costs only appear negligible because, unlike corporations', they are dispersed across millions of individuals. Add up all the time, money, hassle and attention that consumers generally invest in 'doing the shopping' and it reaches an astronomical sum.

And while the traditional seller monopoly on marketing means that all organized, professional marketing activities are actually conducted by sellers, *they are paid for by buyers* – in the final prices of the products and services they buy.

By tackling both buying and selling costs, agents actually *reduce* the consumer's marketing bill, rather than increasing it.

> *Why should sellers have a monopoly on marketing? Why should consumers subsidize sellers' costs?*

Their first port of call is creating new economies of scale that work for buyers, rather than sellers: economies of scale in the collection and distribution of useful information; the aggregation of buying power.

Their second port of call is to unbundle seller-centric marketing, to strip out those bits that have the effect of helping buyers to buy, and to leave a rump of activities which only add value to one side: the seller. As we saw with the example of the car buyer, currently these buyer-friendly elements of seller-centric marketing come, almost by accident, from a disparate range of players: manufacturers, retailers, different types of media owner. The agent strips these functions out of yesterday's business models and bundles all of these buyer-friendly elements together into a complete integrated buying service, so that the buyer has access to all the product reviews and comparisons, the special offers, the peer comments and the negotiating services in one, single, convenient package.

We started this book talking about win-wins. In the end, the relationship between buyer and seller has to be a win-win relationship. If not, one side will withdraw and both sides will end up losing out. But in the commercial world *equal* win-wins are rare. One side of the relationship usually has the upper hand and calls the shots: setting the terms and claiming a greater proportion of the rewards. It's still win-win, but one side wins more than the other.

Industrial age marketing was a superb win-win machine – in which sellers had the upper hand. Information age Right Side Up marketing is also a win-win system. There are massive benefits to share around. But in this system, the buyer has the upper hand. Marketing is now done primarily *for* the consumer or buyer, rather than for the seller.

Sellers will always have to sell their offers. Of course they will. Sellers will always have to 'do' marketing, just as buyers have always had to 'do' marketing. But the era of organized, professional marketing as a purely seller-centric process is ending. The centre of gravity for *all* marketing – whether carried out by sellers or by buyers – is becoming buyer-centric, just as the centre of gravity for *all* marketing was once seller-centric. To fit this new environment, sellers will increasingly need to recalibrate their marketing strategies. And both consumers' agents and traditional sellers will face a new acid test of successful marketing: is your marketing worth buying?

would your customers buy your marketing?

> Removing waste from the marketing and distribution process and passing value back to the customer is the name of the game. The winners will be the ones who do so most directly, efficiently and explicitly.
>
> Barry Hill, creator of the infomediary experiment Request and now UK Managing Director of Transnational[1]

> Markets are institutions that exist to facilitate exchange, that is, they exist in order to reduce the cost of carrying out exchange transactions.
>
> R. H. Coase[2]

UNBUNDLING MARKETING

Marketing should be worth paying for, not only from the seller's point of view but from the buyer's point of view too. It should be valuable enough for buyers to think it 'worth buying'. Until now, however, the costs of marketing – both the buyer's and the seller's costs – have been bundled into final selling prices, and consumers have had no choice but to pay them. Our information age octopus is changing all that.

Take cars, again. Until very recently, huge car manufacturers with massive brands backed by massive advertising and marketing support budgets controlled everything from product design and production through pricing strategies, distribution, to marketing communications and brand promotion. Dealers were their agents, not the consumer's, jumping to the manufacturer's instructions on promotions, priorities and marketing campaigns. Dealers were extensions of the car brand's presence.

But now a whole range of new Web ventures – pioneered in the US but quickly copied in Europe – are blowing this system of control apart, gathering information about car prices, model attributes, JD Power (or equivalent) assessments, customer reviews, dealer margins and commissions, re-sale values, breakdown propensities and safety records – anything and everything that arms the buyer with better information to negotiate with car sellers.

> *If your marketing was a product in its own right, would consumers be prepared to pay for it?*

Meanwhile, buying clubs and reverse auctions are waiting impatiently for regulatory changes that will allow them to actively intervene in the car buying process on behalf of the car buyer. In this way, the realms of consumer choice are expanding beyond a *choice of models* to a choice of *different types of marketplace*. In crude terms, these marketplaces boil down to three forms:

1. traditional seller-controlled marketplaces
2. neutral marketplaces (such as auctions) set up by third party intermediaries to match buyers to sellers more efficiently and effectively. By reducing buyers' search, comparison and transaction costs, these intermediaries help buyers buy smarter
3. 'buyer controlled' marketplaces (such as buying clubs) set up 'with the aim of shifting power and value in the marketplace to the buyer's side'.

Seller-centric marketers faced with the loss of seller-controlled marketplaces are naturally fighting back. They fear that if they lose control, their brands could be compromised and weakened, their margins reduced, their clout within the marketplace undermined. So they are hastening to shore up their control by a slew of new initiatives: by going 'direct' to the consumer with websites designed to deepen and cement their own relationship with a prospective buyer; by offering ever more 'impartial' information on their own sites, by experimenting with direct, over-the-Internet sales.

But the net effect of this 'channel turmoil' is the same. Different players are competing against one another for the buyer's preference. This time, however, the preference relates not only to the product offering but to how the buyer goes to market, and which avenue to market generates the best value for the buyer. The cars may be exactly the same. But which player's marketing adds the most value – from the buyer's point of view?

Just imagine, for example, the hypothetical case of the Ford Motor Company agreeing to cooperate with the buying clubs and reverse auctions which effectively deliver it its customers 'on a plate' – and using its reduced go-to-market costs to reduce its prices. Meanwhile, arch-rival General Motors stands on its dignity and insists that it will only sell its cars through channels it controls. Only that way can it guarantee acceptable levels of customer service, it claims.

The difference in price between Ford's cars and GM's cars then becomes a key issue. Other things being equal, if the customer does indeed believe GM's customer service is superior and worth paying for, then he will choose to do business with GM. But if GM is merely using its control to persist with seller-centric marketing that adds no value to the buyer, then it loses competitive edge. Ford's prices suddenly begin to seem very attractive.

In one sense, of course, consumers have always had some degree of choice between different channels to market: up-market retailers versus discount chains, for example. But this choice has always been one of degree rather than kind. The new car buying infomediaries, buying clubs, reverse auctions and so on are not just a new form of retailer. They're not selling cars. They compete on a completely different basis. They seek to attract their customers on the basis of who is most efficient, effective and enthusiastic in helping the customer *buy* cars. And as these would-be agents compete for customer preference, the momentum builds. The new focus of competition is whose marketing is most worth buying.

PEELING THE MARKETING ONION

But can this shift really change the way long-established markets work? Buying agents will never get a foothold unless they offer real benefits, including cost and price benefits – so are these potential benefits big enough?

Back in Chapter 4 we discovered the many layers of marketing cost created by the 'here we are, this is what we have to offer' marketing onion: the costs of just-in-case production, distribution and communications, the costs of pushing products and information at resistant buyers, the often futile expense of 'brand wars', and so on. Once we step back to look at these costs, it's staggering to see just how huge they are.

Remember, we are not just talking about trimming a direct marketing or media advertising budget by 10 per cent. We are talking about the operations of a complete marketing system – how our economy matches supply to demand and connects buyers to sellers, or as economist R. H. Coase puts it, 'the cost of carrying out a transaction by means of an exchange on the open market'.[3]

One estimate, by economists John Wallis and Douglass North, suggested that by 1986, 45 per cent of all US economic activity was devoted to 'transacting' – where transacting includes every imaginable cost companies incur in taking their goods or services to market (i.e. not only advertising and distribution but negotiating and signing contracts, assessing and covering risks, etc.). According to Wallis and North's estimates, this figure had doubled over the previous century.[4]

More recent research by McKinsey & Co. suggests that 'interaction costs' – 'the searching, coordinating, and monitoring that people and firms do when they exchange goods, services or ideas' – account for just over a half of all US labour activity. This figure excludes a significant proportion of the remaining half, which is eaten up by non-interactive information processing in the form of individual analysis, data processing, and so on.[5]

The dilemmas these massive 'interaction costs' create for

companies are huge. Currently, around one third of the final price of a car is accounted for by its go-to-market costs. Meanwhile car industry analysts suggest that streamlining interactions between suppliers, car manufacturers and distributors could produce savings equal to 25 per cent of the retail price of a car.[6] Allowing for substantial overlap between these estimates, we are still talking big numbers.

In consumer goods, the challenge – and opportunity – is equally massive. Here's how Unilever Chairman Niall Fitzgerald explained the situation in a recent interview:

> If the man from Mars or the lady who, I guess, comes from Venus, looked at the FMCG [fast moving consumer goods] business as it is today and said describe it to me, and I said: 'Well, I spend 50p in every product finding all the raw materials, manufacturing a product and putting it in a packet and getting it to the factory gate in a form ready for consumption. I then spend another 50p on everything I do thereafter – marketing, selling, advertising, retailers' mark-up – the whole lot to get it from the factory gate into the consumer's home, which might just be across the street by the way, they would say this has to be crackers.
>
> If I put this in the Unilever context, that means we're spending $40 billion getting it to the gate and another $40 billion getting it to the consumer. If you then say to this mythical person, you've got $40 billion to spend on getting the product from here to there, sure as hell he or she wouldn't do it the way we're doing it today.

'Every company has put enormous amounts of resources and energy into improving manufacturing efficiency, into optimizing the supply chain, and generally reengineering their businesses,' Fitzgerald continued. 'Yet what remains and will still be the largest cost in the business is how we communicate with our consumers and persuade them to buy our products. Also how we hear back from our consumers. These areas are still largely untouched.'[7]

THE RIGHT SIDE UP OPPORTUNITY

Some marketers have pooh-poohed Fitzgerald's comments on the grounds that he was simply doing the CEO thing of issuing a wake-up call to his troops – exaggerating to make a point. But such a wake-up call is desperately needed. In fact, Fitzgerald was underestimating the scale of the challenge (and therefore the opportunity) in two crucial ways.

First, he was ignoring the 'kick back' effects of his go-to-market system on that first 50p used in production. As we've seen, marketplace 'noise' created by activities such as 'brand wars' and promotions work their way back up the supply chain, making it extremely difficult for companies to plan and organize production in the most efficient ways possible.

Second, he was only looking at his costs, as the seller. He was ignoring the consumer's marketing costs completely. But these costs are massive. Every day millions upon millions of individual consumers have to search out information about different offers, compare them to their needs and wants, evaluate, make comparisons and make decisions. Helping consumers to reduce these go-to-market costs is becoming one of the most fruitful areas for genuine new product and service development.

Yet most companies continue to ignore these consumer costs of time, money and hassle because they have zero impact on the corporate profit and loss account or balance sheet. Retailers give a nod to the consumer's cost of shopping when they say 'location, location, location' are the first three rules of retailing. But like manufacturers, retailers simply take it for granted that the consumer incurs his own costs of searching, buying, travelling to stores, and so on.

Indeed, as we saw in the previous chapter, in many ways and on many occasions sellers positively benefit from the fact that the consumer's marketing costs are so high. When a buyer decides not to bother with the cost and hassle of poring over the fine print of an insurance policy to weed out the catch clauses or to see if it really is better than a rival offer, the insurance salesman can get away with selling an inferior product. Likewise, when a buyer decides that traipsing from shop to shop to find a cheaper alternative simply isn't worth it, the retailer and/or the manufacturer can get away with charging more for the item. Every day, day in and day out, consumers are in this way choosing to accept inferior deals in order to save on their 'marketing' costs.

The agent's contribution

Now we can see the scale of the agent's potential. In broad terms, think of it as tackling Fitzgerald's 50 per cent go-to-market costs *plus* the effect these go-to-market inefficiencies have on the production systems *plus* the simultaneous reengineering of consumers' go-to-market costs.

Now, of course, the various elements of the information revolution – such as plummeting transaction and interaction costs – mean that *all* marketers both (seller-centric and buyer-centric) have an opportunity to reduce their go-to-market costs. That's a generic. Anybody who doesn't do that will be left behind.

But seller-centric marketers who assume that they can simply deploy these technologies to take these savings for themselves are mistaken. As McKinsey consultants Berryman and Harrington point out, a 'battle between buyers, sellers and intermediaries to capture this value seems inevitable'.[8] This is the precisely the battle that agents join on behalf of their client buyers.

But agents do more than squabble over a share of the growing information productivity cake. That's just the beginning. They open up new opportunities to strip away the many layers of cost created by the old system. At the same time, they pile increasing pressure on traditional seller-centric marketers by offering consumers the extra benefits of 'being on my side', while offering them marketing services that reduce their go-to-market costs too.

Filling the information hole

Marketers have never been able to completely ignore go-to-market costs as a factor in competition. In fact, in recent years they have been rising up the agenda. The lower the total go-to-market cost, the lower the final selling price (or higher the margin). This was a key factor behind the rise of private label products: the fact that they have minimal marketing costs makes them cheaper – and therefore better value. Also, retailing has focused on cutting the costs of its core processes, and increasing value for customers. This has been the secret of outfits like Wal-Mart. It is also one of the reasons why retailers have often come closest to adopting an agency role. Nevertheless, compared to the opportunities now unfolding before us, these attempts to tackle the great incubus have merely scratched the surface.

The first and most fundamental ways that agents tackle the great marketing incubus is by organizing buyers to say, 'Here I am, this is what I want.' As agents construct efficient mechanisms for doing this they start reworking the entire industrial age marketing system, from scratch.

By using mass customization production systems, for example, companies can eliminate the risk and waste involved in the make-then-sell system. By aggregating real-time information about demand from auctions, reverse auctions, buying clubs and infomediaries – rather than by using delayed signals from traditional distribution channels – companies can learn how to make the right number of things at the right times: to bring supply in tune with demand.

> *By enabling consumers to say 'here I am, this is what I want,' agents short circuit seller-push marketing.*

Similarly, by passing on information about interest in offers, agents can help sellers close sales directly with buyers, again avoiding the costs of just-in-case distribution systems. When a reverse auctioneer closes a transaction, for example, the supplier finds out who exactly is purchasing, and can fulfil the order directly.

And by listening to, rather than broadcasting messages at, consumers, they can dramatically reengineer their marketing communications costs. When an infomediary collects and collates information about what his client is interested in, and passes this to suppliers, the suppliers are in a position to target messages directly to people who they know are interested in their offers, now. Compared to just-in-case marketing communications the efficiency gains are mindboggling.

This is a win-win-win. Clients are no longer bombarded with intrusive messages. They may even get paid for receiving messages that they are interested in receiving. The vendor gets a far more efficient marketing communications process. And, of course, the infomediary takes a cut from the whole process.

And who better to 'do' targeting and segmentation than the consumer himself? The cost of searching for the right audience is transformed if this audience organizes itself into a tightly knit, easily identified, easy to reach form such as an online virtual community of interest. If avid collectors of tropical fish gather together in a community of interest, what better forum for sellers of aquariums, fish foods, fish, books about fish, and so on?

A new marketing mix

What is startling about the outline above is how many win-wins there are, once Right Like Up marketing reengineering gets under way. Wins for consumers. Wins for agents. And wins for sellers who, for the first time, are being presented with ways to bypass and short-circuit yesterday's cumbersome marketing processes.

It's one thing, however, for sellers to accept that there are enormous win-win opportunities in embracing agents as co-marketing partners. It's quite another to work out who exactly should do what – to negotiate a new, optimum division of labour between sellers, agents and purchasers.

The task is made more complex by the huge variety of both consumer priorities and types of agent. The optimum division of labour will depend on factors such as what the buyer is trying to achieve and how sophisticated he or she is. For example, music buffs will aggregate around communities of interest rather than buying clubs, which are more suited to less frequently purchased, more expensive items. Meanwhile buyers of financial services will gravitate towards infomediaries, who can add value through extra information and advice, or via reverse auctions which take advantage of the industry's endemic excess capacity.

Also, as far as traditional offer marketers are concerned, giving up some control doesn't mean giving up all control. If a seller manufactures a 'New! Improved!' product, buyers want to know about it. They need the seller to undertake some marketing activity. And car manufacturers will still want to influence buyers' preferences – even if they shift a growing proportion of sales through buying clubs (which, if organized well, could be one of their lowest cost routes to market). So although agents will enable sellers to ease off on some marketing activities, sellers won't want to stop them all. The real trick is to forge a win-win mix that creates the most value for both consumer and supplier.

Conducting the experiments that will lead us to this new optimum division of marketing labour will take time. Nevertheless the underlying message is extremely simple and is summed up by Barry Hill, UK Managing Director of Transnational: 'Removing waste from the marketing and distribution process and passing value back to the customer is the name of the game. The winners will be the ones who do so most directly, efficiently and explicitly.'

CHAPTER 11

do you provide return on attention?

> *The days of high demand and limited supply are over. We are no longer competing to see who can build the factories that will supply the world. It's a new game now. A game in which the limited supply is attention, not factories.* Seth Godin[1]
>
> *Companies that speak in the language of the pitch, the dog-and-pony show, are no longer speaking to anyone . . . We are immune to advertising. If you want us to talk to you, tell us something. Make it something interest-ing for a change.* The Cluetrain Manifesto[2]

In April 1667 the Dutch and English ended a century of conflict over control of the East Indies spice trade with the signing of the Treaty of Breda. Both sides knew its real content: the English had been roundly defeated. The treaty gave the Dutch control of all the East Indies' precious spices: nutmeg, cinnamon and cloves that were worth their weight in gold back in Europe. As a sop to the British, the Dutch conceded sovereignty of a tiny little trading settlement of less than a thousand souls on the inhospitable banks of the Hudson River. They called it New Amsterdam. The British decided to call it New York.

Not long after, the value of spices began to fall. They were starting to become a commodity. Meanwhile New York grew, and grew, and grew. Neither side could see it at the time, but the Dutch victory was all but empty, while the humiliated British had walked away with a prize of inestimable value.

Economic history is full of episodes like this. One day, something has to-die-for value. The next day that value evaporates. Meanwhile other things, long regarded as worthless, suddenly become precious. Not long ago the deserts of Saudi Arabia were seen as a curse, denying all chances of prosperity. Then oil was found underneath them.

Within the world of media and marketing communications, today's spice is 'content'. Content is fast becoming commoditized while the value of audiences' attention – long taken for granted – is rising inexorably. This shift is weakening the once-unbreakable bonds between media and advertising, destabilizing the value trade-offs at the heart of the industry – and opening the doors to buyer-centric marketing communications and the rise of the consumer agent.

The root of this transformation was summed up by Herbert Simon, the Nobel Prize-winning economist, when he said:

> What information consumes is rather obvious. It consumes the attention of its recipients. Hence a wealth of information creates a poverty of attention ... The only factor becoming scarce in a world of abundance is human attention.[3]

Media companies make their money by trading attention in two very different ways. They sell content: news and entertainment that provide audiences with value for attention. And they aggregate and sell these audiences' attention on to third parties: advertisers. The emerging environment of information overload places these two activities within a strategic pincer movement.

On the one hand, content is becoming commoditized. Indeed, excess information is becoming a form of pollutant, clogging up our lives. A few centuries ago, the enlightenment philosopher Condorcet could read every known book in the world. Today, we could spend our entire waking time reading each day's new publications and still not get through them all. If information consumes our attention, an overdose of content threatens to consume our lives. As Simon Gulliford, a marketing adviser to consumer magazine company EMAP, puts it: 'Increasingly consumers are very clearly saying "I want less of" while marketers are saying, "But we can provide you with more!". The consumer reply is, "No! No! Less of . . . *Please!* Time spent staring out of the window is fine. Organize that for me. Now!'

Commoditization of content is at its most extreme on the Internet, where it's beginning to turn traditional media economics upside down. Traditionally, content is expensive to create and distribute but brings consumer attention with it, free. Now, however, transmitting information is tending towards the free (just look at the cost of distributing 100,000 e-mails), while actually winning people's attention gets ever harder and ever more expensive. The emergence of Internet sites which pay users to accept ads, and services like Gratis-Tel which pays telephone users to listen to advertisements, is an explicit recognition that consumer attention is now an asset worth paying for, directly.

A VALUE MISMATCH

The second prong of the pincer movement concerns this rising price of consumer attention. The current media system works by a form of barter – a cashless exchange of value. The media owner hands over content, for free (or at a highly subsidized rate), in return for which the consumer hands over his attention, for free. The consumer saves money by not having to buy news and entertainment. The media owner uses the value of consumers' attention to gain money through the sale of advertising.

Over the years, this system has proved to be a hugely powerful – and flexible – win-win. It's still got a lot of life left in it. But there is a value mismatch at its heart. The one part of the media owner's offer that makes him money – the sale of consumer attention to advertisers – is the one part of his offer that actually offers the source of this value – the consumer – minimal to zero value.

The more valuable the consumer's attention becomes, the more extreme this mismatch becomes. Why should I, the consumer, continue to hand over my attention for free when the economic value of my attention continues to rise while the relative value of the content I'm receiving in return continues to fall? And why should I invest this precious attention in something that gives me little or no return, while handing over massive returns to a third party?

As mere sentiments, these questions are interesting but commercially irrelevant. Agents, however, transform them into a palpable commercial force. In the previous chapter we saw how, by organizing alternative forms of marketplace, agents enable consumers to stop paying the financial costs of marketing activities that fail to provide value to them as buyers. They have a similar effect within the world of media and advertising.

They help consumers insist that commercial communications should provide them with a good return on attention – by providing information that primarily helps them as buyers to buy. Agents do this by making themselves the main source of such buyer-centric information; by competing directly with traditional media owners and advertisers to supply the consumer with superior value for attention in the commercial communications arena.

In addition, they organize consumers to seize back the value of their attention – value they currently hand over to third party media owners, gratis. They do this by organizing consumers to say, 'Here I am, this is what I want,' and helping them to 'sell' this information and attention directly to interested sellers, for maximum return. Net result: just as marketing 'worth buying' becomes a necessity in the emerging buyer-centric world, so does providing value for attention. Sellers who fail to provide buyers with value for attention in their communications risk failing to sell at all.

THE BIASING INDUSTRY

Value for attention means that marketing communications should be a service for the buyer. But most modern marketing communications are nothing of the sort. Seth Godin describes the current approach as 'interruption marketing' – 'the science of creating and placing media that interrupts the consumer and then gets him or her to take some action'.[4] This 'interruption marketing' is a massively expensive lose-lose exercise, he notes:

The cost to the consumer is just too high. Interruption Marketing is the enemy of anyone trying to save time. By constantly interrupting what we are doing at any given moment, the marketer who 4interrupts us not only tends to fail at selling his product, but wastes our most coveted commodity, time.[4]

The win-win alternative is relevance. By definition, a relevant message has value for the recipient. It's also, therefore, far more likely to be acted upon: to be 'effective' from the marketer's point of view too. Segmentation, targeting, database marketing, customer relationship management, one-to-one marketing and permission marketing: these are all ways in which traditional marketers have tried to reach the ideal of the relevant selling message.

> *Power is shifting from the media owner to the attention owner: to the consumer.*

But traditional seller-centric motives and marketing methods invariably scupper the quest for such win-wins. The just-in-case nature of most modern marketing communications means that each individual message is irrelevant to most of the audience. And even if it is relevant – relating to something a particular buyer is interested in buying – it's usually of questionable value. That's because the prime purpose of the seller-centric marketer's communications is to *bias* the audience in favour of my brand: to draw the buyer's attention to my product (even when it is not necessarily the best or most appropriate product); to persuade the buyer to buy my product (even when it is not necessarily the best product); and to encourage the buyer to trade with me on my terms (even when they are not necessarily the best terms). Or, as Godin puts it in the context of so-called permission marketing, to 'over time, leverage the permission to change consumer behaviour towards profits'.[5]

Sellers are therefore forever drawn towards *using* their audiences' attention for their own purposes, rather than providing them with value for attention. Consumer agents, on the other hand, make it their business to gather, analyse and present the information their consumers/clients need to buy more efficiently and effectively:

the impartial expert opinions, the user reviews, the information about comparative prices, data that's useful for negotiating a better deal (such as dealer margins), and information on current special offers and promotions.

COMPETING FOR ATTENTION

Whoever wins the battle for the consumer's attention within the realms of commercial messaging stands to gain access to enormous power and revenues. One way of estimating the current value of consumer attention is to see the vast sums advertisers are currently prepared to spend on advertising. Marketing services conglomerate WPP estimates total global marketing communications spend to be in excess of $1 trillion, just under a half of which is accounted for by traditional media advertising.[6]

Agents are not going to win a significant share of this value easily. As long as traditional media – in the form of mass one-way television, for example – dominates consumers' media consumption, agents will find it difficult to get a foot in the door. They need the interactivity and information efficiencies of digital media to provide their specialist services. They also need to overcome another hurdle. Just like traditional seller-centric marketing as a whole, as the list below shows, there are a number of ways in which traditional seller-centric marketing communications *have the effect* of helping buyers to buy and therefore add value *from the point of view of the buyer* as well as the seller. By trumping this, value agents stand to win the intensifying battle for consumer attention. But as the list also shows agents have the potential to trump this value, every time.

1. Advertising that helps me find the seller I want. The classic example here is classified advertising, which enables me, as a buyer, to find the offers I want – whether they are for jobs, products or services – quickly and efficiently. This advertising is paid for by the seller, but the information it provides helps the buyer buy. It delivers a genuine return on attention.

    Classified advertising's role as a connector of buyers and sellers is simply that of a primitive form of 'virtual' marketplace.

New dedicated websites – or virtual exchanges – can do the same job much more efficiently and effectively. Hence the much-discussed threat posed by online recruitment sites to newspapers' and magazines' classified job adverts, for example. These new online recruitment agencies (which earn their income from transaction and commission fees, rather than by 'advertising' vacancies), threaten to take business away from the traditional media, thereby reducing the subsidies these advertisments provide for editorial content. For both employers and potential employees, online services have the potential to do the job better than traditional advertising. This is true of all buyer-driven searches.

2. The second crucial benefit of advertising, for the buyer, is the role it plays in matching demand to supply. If I, the buyer, think you are selling the thing I want or need, your message is of immediate relevance and value to me: it provides me with the information I need to make decisions and choices. Advertising that is effective from my point of view therefore provides the information I need to work out whether or not this product is 'for me', 'the one I want'. Any advertising (or any other form of marketing communication such as direct mail or public relations) which gives me this information helps me, as a purchaser, to buy. It provides a genuine return on attention.

    However, buyers also know that the information they get from sellers is likely to be untrustworthy – biased, edited and presented for the purpose of helping close a sale. A much better source of information is impartial third party advice. By providing this trusted advice, information agents achieve superior value for attention.

3. A buyer benefit closely related to the 'connecting' function of classified advertising is the role of an ad (or piece of direct mail) as a facilitator of transactions. Direct-response and off-page selling ads are the best example. They create a direct link between the message and the transaction and can be an easy and convenient way for me to buy. This direct linking of message and transaction has enormous potential with the growth of interactive TV and WAP phones.

    A far more 'buyer friendly' form of direct response communication is that offered by infomediaries and reverse auctions. The consumer sends out a signal saying 'I am interested in buying

X', and sellers respond directly with offers which I have expressly asked for. Once again, this gives me superior value for attention.

4. A fourth potential benefit of advertising for the buyer is that it brings things to my attention that I didn't even realize I needed or wanted. This is the core role of all new product or service advertising. A serendipity effect adds another potential layer of value. In nine cases out of ten, the messages I receive are of no value to me, but every now and again something pops up which does interest me – which I wouldn't have known about otherwise.

   Buyers will always be interested in 'New! Improved!' products and services, and to the degree that the seller alerts the buyer to a new benefit, he is providing value to the buyer. This form of marketing communications activity is therefore one of the most robust within the emerging information age environment. However, our earlier caveat about impartial versus biased information still applies. Although it may be of some use for me to know that a new product exists, what I really want is impartial, objective information about it. It's therefore unlikely that I'll trust the seller as my main source of information. While the seller's communication provides me with some value for attention, my agent still provides me with more.

5. Another, less obvious benefit of advertising to the buyer is its future utility. The message you send me today may not be of much interest to me yet, but it may turn out to be useful tomorrow. Today, I don't want or need a purple-fringed flanged carburettor but should I do so tomorrow (if you have managed to make your advertising impinge on my memory), then you will have done me a service. I will know exactly where to look, and you will have saved me time and effort.

   As consumers get used to the capabilities of the Internet – especially the ability to access the information I want when I want it – their attitude towards 'just-in-case' messaging is likely to change. Just-in-time information – the information I want, when I want it – provides far more value for attention than trying to remember a million and one things 'just in case' they might come in useful. Once again, the agent model trumps traditional advertising in the value for attention stakes.

6. A sixth potential benefit for the buyer is that the message is simply valuable in its own right. It's artistic, amusing, entertaining, or says something interesting. It gives me something to talk

about to my friends. I 'consume' the message in its own right – and in the process my awareness and opinion of your product may be positively affected.

If a communication is valuable as a product in its own right then, by definition, it provides value for attention. Some marketers have used this approach very intelligently and very successfully. In the UK, for instance, the soft drinks brand Tango has made marketing communications into a game with its customers – a game that its youthful target audience enjoys playing. This approach has its risks. The biggest risk is that while it provides value for attention to the buyer it fails to provide value for money for the advertiser.

Looking back at Coca-Cola's marketing, for example, Sergio Zyman commented that producing ads that everybody loved allowed the company to be 'misled by the consumer. Everybody loved Coke, but they thought it was OK to love us but they didn't have to buy us. Now we are going back and saying. "No! If you love me, buy me!"[7]

7. Yet another potential buyer benefit of advertising is the message it sends to *other* people about the products that I buy. If an advertiser manages to convince everyone else that wearing Levi's jeans is the sexiest thing in the world, then buying a pair of Levi's is extra-valuable to me. This is the secret of most fashion and luxury advertising: its ability to help me make a public statement about myself. In these circumstances, the marketing communication becomes a critical part of the product itself.

This is another form of marketing communication that will continue to have value in the emerging era. However, by focusing on objective, rational and comparative aspects such as quality and price, agents encourage buyers to take a more rational approach to purchasing and positively favour transparency. Just how far this coldly rational deconstruction of carefully created 'emotional' brand selling points can go remains unanswered.

8. Your message about a product may also reassure me that my decision to buy your product was the correct one. The mere fact that the product is being advertised sends a signal that this is a serious, reputable player prepared to put his reputation on the line, rather than some fly-by-night cowboy. Advertising may also enhance my experience of the product. There are some persuasive theories of advertising effectiveness which suggest

that the real effect of advertising is not to influence consumers' *purchasing* decisions but to influence their *experience* of consumption, by pinpointing the qualities consumers look for when consuming, say, the aroma in a jar of instant coffee.

But in the emerging communications environment, fame and a good reputation rest increasingly not on advertising *per se*, but on word of mouth: in shared consumer experience of actual dealings with a company. In this context, advertising is forever open to the retort, 'They would say that, wouldn't they?' And earning the recommendations of objective advisers may be far more cost effective than trying to buy fame.

THE RISE OF THE TRUSTED, AUTHORIZED MESSENGER

The battle to earn consumers' attention with respect to commercial communications is therefore set to be long and complex. However, as information age technologies kick in, agents gain the advantage: but for one critical twist in the workings of the attention economy.

It's in the nature of all communication that we only know the value of a message *after the event,* once we have consumed it; once we have given it our attention.

This gives good old fashioned interruption advertising an apparently infinite lease of life. Wily advertisers can always find a way of grabbing the buyer's attention and using it for their own purposes. By the time the buyer realizes that the message has little or no value to him, its purpose is met: an impression has been made, a message delivered, and an awareness created. Hence the rise of ambush advertising – advertising designed to catch unsuspecting consumers unawares, when they are least expecting the message: in the sky, on the subway floor, or in a public lavatory.

The ultimate effect of such ever-intensifying attempts to grab consumers' attention, however, is to unleash an attention arms race, with advertisers trying ever harder to cut through the clutter and breach consumers' defences, and consumers trying ever harder to screen out unwanted messages. Result: the marketer becomes 'the enemy'. This is how *Cluetrain Manifesto* co-author David Weinberger puts it:

The fundamental fact of marketing that determines all else is that there is no demand for messages. Marketers talk to people who do not want to hear them . . . As consumers try to tune out the messages, the marketers ramp up the frequency and the obnoxiousness of their programmes to try to break through. The result? How to put this nicely: if you are in marketing, nobody likes you.[8]

But how can consumers screen out unwanted messages if the value of each such message can only be judged after the event? If it's a billboard, the answer (probably) is that they can't. Intrusive advertising, event-based advertising, place-based advertising, covert advertising (e.g. in the form of product placement) are not going to go away.

What the consumer *can* do, however, is pay less and less attention to such messages, and pay more attention to trusted *messengers* instead: messengers who make it their business to provide superior value for attention. As Mike Saylor, CEO of Microstrategy, comments: 'There is a limited appetite for non-permitted messaging, for non-authenticated, non-authorized messaging. In a world where messaging becomes exponentially cheaper, and the generation of messaging becomes exponentially more powerful, and the amount of time it takes to absorb a message remains constant, over time people will stop accepting untrusted or non-authorized messaging.'[9]

Who is best placed to win the role of trusted, authorized messenger of commercial information? Obviously, the agent. Using ever-more sophisticated technologies to achieve their goals, agents seek to act on their consumers'/clients' behalf as information gatekeepers:

▦ by collating and editing useful information from many different sources
▦ by seeking out the information requested by the client
▦ by using new screening and filtering technologies to shield their clients from messages they don't want to receive
▦ by selling clients' attention (assuming they have been given permission to do so)

The inescapable effect of our shift towards an attention economy is that power in the realms of communication begins to shift from sender to receiver; from media owner to attention owner. Agents help the consumer realize the value of his attention. Instead of leveraging the consumer's attention to change the same consumer's behaviour to maximize sellers' profits, as Godin would have marketers do, agents leverage the consumer's permission to change *sellers'* behaviour, to maximize the *consumer's* profit.

THE NEW WIN-WIN

How, then, can sellers respond? One way is to intensify the arm's race with ever more intrusive messaging. Another way is to increase the buyer-centric elements of their own marketing communications; to compete with agents in the provision of impartial, objective and useful information. But there is another way.

> *Agents help consumers realize the value of their attention. This can be a huge opportunity for sellers.*

The rise of buyer-centric marketing communications isn't necessarily a disaster for seller-centric marketers at all. In fact, it represents a massive opportunity to cut costs, improve targeting and effectiveness – to achieve all the things traditional marketers have been trying to do for decades. The opportunity, of course, lies in moving from seller 'push' to consumer 'pull' in communications; in moving towards *consumer managed* marketing communications. When an infomediary 'sells' consumer-generated leads – 'I am interested in buying an X' – to relevant suppliers, he delivers near perfect value for attention to his client (who only receives messages on the subjects he has expressed an interest in). But he also delivers hugely improved returns on communications investment for suppliers by cutting out the excess costs involved in just-in-case, stimulus-response, mind-cuckoo marketing and brand building strategies.

Currently, around 70 per cent of all marketing communications spending attempts to 'preemptively capture the attention of the consumer in advance of the purchase occasion', as McKinsey's John Hagel notes. In emerging reverse markets, where customers increasingly shun this kind of intrusive marketing, 'successful marketers will learn how to list themselves effectively in search environments, how to engage the consumer at the time of purchase, and how to tailor products and services in ways that reduce incentives to switch to other vendors.'[10]

In the emerging environment, agrees US marketing guru Regis McKenna, the ability to 'reach out' to consumers becomes less important than 'being there' when they want to reach out to you. 'Brand and brand management have been taken over by the advertising world,' he says. But 'at the turn of this century branding was really about distribution. And now it is becoming distribution again. But it is not physical distribution, it is distribution of information: brand presence of information – presence of choice rather than awareness of something.'[11]

Such approaches to marketing communications create a genuine win-win that delivers value for attention to buyers while cutting enormous amounts of cost for sellers. For decades, direct marketers have dreamed of perfect targeting. They have dreamed of a time when they have so much information about each individual consumer, and so much technology at their disposal, that they could achieve maximum response for minimum investment in stimuli. This dream could soon come true, but not in the way they ever thought. Perfect targeting will happen. But it will be targeting driven and organized by buyers for buyers.

Targeting, segmentation, relationship marketing, database marketing, one-to-one marketing, permission marketing: sellers have pioneered these technologies and concepts but their natural home lies in agency – in Right Side Up marketing.

CHAPTER 12

how valuable is *your offer?*

> *In the emerging global economy, even the most impressive of positions in the most prestigious of organizations is vulnerable to worldwide competition if it entails replicated routines.*
>
> Robert Reich, former US Secretary for Labour[1]

TOO MUCH CAPITAL

The first half of the year 2000 was not kind to chief executives of 'old' economy companies. In a few short months, the biggest icons of traditional marketing were hammered by the stock markets. A *Business Week* table summed it up. Between March 1999 and May 2000 Coca-Cola's market capitalization fell by $52.3 billion, Procter & Gamble's by £48.6 billion and Ford Motor's by $27.9 billion. Meanwhile, the market valuations of information age infrastructure providers such as Cisco Systems, Oracle and Intel soared by $293 billion, $198 billion and $192 billion respectively. That week, Cisco overtook General Electric to become the world's biggest company, by market capitalization.[2]

Market capitalizations are notoriously volatile, of course. A shakeout soon after quickly rectified some of the grossest anomalies, but pressure on the stars of the old economy hasn't eased. For good reason. When it comes to generating incremental value, they're increasingly stuck between a rock and a hard place.

Take General Motors (GM) – on the surface, it was in rude health. The world's biggest company (in terms of sales, if not market capitalization) had profits of $4 billion in 1999. But once its involvement in car financing, software and businesses such as Hughes Electronics was stripped out, the picture didn't look so good. In its core home market for autos, GM's market share had collapsed, over two decades, from 45 per cent to 28 per cent in 1999. As one cheeky *Fortune* open letter to the board commented, 'The market figures your auto operations are worth little or nothing.' Healthy reported profits don't take account of 'the stupendous sums of capital tied up in GM facilities around the world,' it continued. 'Investors don't believe you'll earn more than that cost of capital anytime soon, maybe ever, and you can't blame them, because you didn't earn it for many, many years.'[3]

As capitalist companies, companies like GM exist to generate returns on the capital they invest. But as *Fortune* pointed out, many aren't doing that any more. With gargantuan legacy assets to feed, crippling overcapacity and cut-throat competition for products which have, in the words of Ford Europe President Nick Scheele, 'relatively little difference in technology and product quality', these icons of the industrial age are finding it ever more difficult to compete.[4]

This is not a passing phenomena, nor is it restricted to capital-intensive heavy industries. It is a product of driving economic forces that lie at the heart of the industrial age economy. As we've seen, in their quest for economies of scale and lower unit costs, for example, companies are driven to invest in ever more productive capacity – only to create the overcapacity that dogs their markets. And by living and breathing what Robert Reich calls 'replicated routines' they are forever undermining their ability to differentiate. By definition, replicated routines are *copies*, and *copyable*. They are rarely a source of differentiation.

This may sound obvious but its implications for modern businesses and brands are profound. Marketing 'worth buying' may transform how companies bring their offers to market. Value for attention may transform how companies communicate messages about the value of these offers. But the Right Side Up revolution is also about the nature of the value firms offer in the first place. Yesterday's market leaders and brand icons cannot simply assume that the things that made them valuable yesterday will keep them as valuable tomorrow. Every brand needs to ask itself: just how valuable *is* our offer?

FROM HARDWARE, TO SOFTWARE, TO WETWARE

The rising importance of 'people value' is triggering a reversal at the heart of modern business.

Industrial age wealth creation is based on replicated routines: mass production of standardized products. Its replicated routines were physical: routines captured by clever bits of machinery, and powered by sources of energy other than human or animal labour. The information age is also based on replicated routines, this time in the processing of information. Computer programs break complex problems down into easily-repeatable routines, thereby automating them. Modern computers can crunch vast quantities of data in nanoseconds, data that would take unaided humans years to analyse. Robot controlled production lines, interactive digital TV, Yahoo!'s customized web pages, Wal-Mart's famous data warehouse, Strategy.com's delivery of personalized information – they are all manifestations of the same thing: a revolution in the automation of information processing. This revolution has only just begun. With developments in computer hardware and software proceeding apace, we are like a ball at the top of a steep hill. We've only just started rolling.

That is the first, massive challenge of information age business: to capitalize on the awesome potential of automated information processing and unleash an explosion of new information-rich products and services.

But there's a twist. Once a problem has been solved and captured by a piece of software, it is effectively solved forever. We needn't worry our little heads about it again. A whole host of problems in production, logistics, accounting, sales and marketing etc. have already succumbed to the onward march of information automation. As we saw in Chapter 8, the faster we forge ahead in these areas – the faster these replicated routines cease to be a source of competitive advantage. Far from liberating us from the differentiation problems created by the industrial age, the information age actually exacerbates them.

But there's another side to this particular coin, and that is that we humans are neither hardware nor software. We are wetware. We are sensuous, biological organisms experiencing life by the way we connect with our environment through our senses. We don't live in a world of calculations. We live in a world of *feelings*. And the faster we automate every possible replicated routine, the faster we hit upon a challenge of a different order. The more important and powerful the computer becomes, the more important the problems computers *cannot* solve become. People problems, in other words.

There are, in fact, vast swathes of life – including business and commercial life – that computers and software simply cannot 'understand'. People instinctively imagine, create, invent, fantasize, innovate and 'see' opportunities. They instinctively feel pride, enthusiasm, ambition, depression or envy. They have moods, opinions and motivations. They make value judgements about what is right and what is wrong. They like reaching out to touch and connect with other people, to empathize, inspire, encourage, crack jokes, have fun. Computers don't do any of these things.

The rising importance of these human attributes is triggering a reversal at the very heart of modern business. For a century, wealth creation has been driven by replicated routines, and made possible by the application of financial and industrial capital to these replicated routines. But as *Wired* founder Kevin Kelly notes, 'Repetition, sequels, copies, and automation all tend toward the free and efficient, while the innovative, original and imaginative – none of which results in efficiency – soar in value.'[5] The bits that are soaring in value, in other words, are the non-replicable bits contributed by people.

The counter-intuitive effect of the information age, then, is to shift the focus of value from financial or industrial wealth to human wealth; to search for competitive edge by unleashing the full potential of people assets rather than *thing* assets such factories and computers.

A NEW ZOO OF BUSINESS MODELS

That doesn't mean we can do away with automation. We would soon squeal if the lights went out or food stopped appearing on the supermarket shelves. Capturing and enhancing the fruits of automation will always be important. What it does mean, however, is that increasingly we are in the privileged position of being able to take the fruits of automation as a given, and to ask, 'What next?'

Looking to the future we can see four core engines of wealth creation – each of them with its own crucially important source of value. The first is the business that specializes in the automation of matter or information processes and provides the infrastructure for everything else. The second is the connector or relationship business, which unleashes the value that comes from connecting people to people in new and different ways. The third is the intellectual property business, powered by people's ability to create, imagine and innovate. The fourth is the passion business: the business of organizing, expressing and enhancing people's feelings, emotions, goals and values.

The infrastructure model

The vast majority of today's major businesses and brands are still firmly entrenched in the first infrastructure model. It comes in a rich variety of forms, including:

- traditional brand manufacturers
- retailers
- financial services companies
- utility operators such as electricity, transport and telecoms
- media owners.

Their common inner logic is driven by the now-familiar question: 'What do I make and how can I sell it?' Traditional manufacturers live or die by their ability to exploit their productive assets.

In retailing, similar considerations apply, except that this time the asset needing to be exploited to maximum effect is property. Most of the firm's investment goes into acquiring and developing this property, and if this investment turns sour the future of the firm itself is in doubt. Its core asset therefore defines its obsessive focus on imperatives such as ensuring maximum footfall and sales per square foot. Meanwhile, in services such as transport and banking, it's the service infrastructure that must be fed: building a bank branch or rail network is an extremely expensive process. The only way that investment can be recouped is by ensuring that as many customers as possible flow through this infrastructure. That way, its enormous costs are shared by as many people as possible.

It may seem inappropriate to include traditional media companies such as newspapers and broadcasters in this category, but in their traditional form they follow the same core industrial age logic. A newspaper may sell information, but the way the business as a whole works – its fundamental economic model – revolves around investment in, and the costs of, printing and distributing matter, in this case paper. The ongoing 'unbundling' of the newspaper industry (for example by outsourcing printing to independent suppliers) is one way these companies are trying to evolve from one model to another.

The huge importance of mass production, economies of scale and unit costs – the inner logic of industrial age wealth creation – made this form of matter processing business dominant in the industrial age. But now, thanks to the information age, other breeds of business are moving centre stage – to take the high ground of value creation.

The connector, or 'relationship', model

Connector businesses come in many forms but, at core, they ride upon new information age potential to bring people together in new and different ways to exchange more, richer value, more efficiently. The generic model is well described by consultants Adrian Slywotzky and David Morrison as revolving around 'switchboard profit':

Some markets are characterized by multiple sellers communicating to multiple buyers. High transaction costs are incurred by both. Often, there is an opportunity to create a high-value intermediary that concentrates these multiple communication pathways through one point, or one channel, by creating a switchboard. The switchboard reduces the costs (of both financial expenditure and personal aggravation) for buyers and sellers, in exchange for a fee to the switchboard operator. The switchboard operator controls the information flow, and even a modest charge per transaction becomes extremely profitable as volume increases.[6]

Switchboard operators are currently gaining great prominence. They include virtual business-to-business exchanges, which have popped up in almost every conceivable industry sector; Internet portals such as AOL.com and Excite.com, which help people reach other people, and information, more efficiently; and auctions such as QXL.com. The various forms of consumer agent, including communities of interest, infomediaries, buying clubs and reverse auctions, also fit this generic model.

The crucial significance of this new type of business is the way it breaks away from 'what do I make and how can I sell it?'. Instead, because it makes its money by connecting one person to another, it follows the logic of 'who are my customers and how can I serve them?'. It's what frees us from the hugely powerful trap of seller-centric marketing.[7]

The intellectual property model

At first sight, the intellectual property model doesn't look very different to the traditional industrial age business. After all, 'New! Improved!' lay at the heart of industrial age marketing, and the knowledge economy (as opposed to an *information* economy) has been gaining pace ever since the days of Isaac Newton.

At root, however, the two are very different. Industrial age brands developed new intellectual property (i.e. new products) to help feed their factories with new orders. Increasingly, in the information age, the emphasis is the other way round: to focus on the development of new intellectual property, and to find factories to exploit its potential when (and if) the occasion arises. The new style intellectual property model is that if I have a good enough idea, I can always get the funding to build a business.

Instead of working to the inner logic of 'what do I make and how can I sell it?', the critical question for the intellectual property brander is 'what ideas do I have, and how can I develop their potential?'. Intellectual property branders realize with increasing clarity that their core asset is not the factory, or even intangible assets such as patents, licences and rights on the balance sheet, but the *people* who create this intellectual property, and the *culture* that unleashes their ability.

At the heart of the intellectual property model, in other words, are the human qualities of creativity – imagination, flair and innovation – rather than replicated routines. And as *Fortune* writer Tom Stewart points out:

> The greater the human capital intensity of a business – that is, the greater its percentage of high-value added work performed by hard-to-replace people – the more it can charge for its services and the less vulnerable it is to competitors, because it will be very difficult for rivals to match those skills.[8]

The operational mindset is also completely different – as Kevin Kelly observes:

> Productivity is exactly the wrong thing to care about in the new economy . . . Machines have taken over the uniform. They love tedious and measurable work. Efficiencies are for robots. Opportunities, on the other hand, are for humans. Opportunities demand flexibility, exploration, guesswork, curiosity, and many other qualities humans excel at.[9]

One key effect of the information age, therefore, is an inexorable tendency for power (including brand power) and riches to shift away from replicated routine producers to the individuals or firms that best act as creators and holders of intellectual property. These include:

- creative artists, including musicians, writers and film makers
- inventors, researchers and developers

▓ knowledge workers, such as lawyers, accountants, doctors, management consultants and advertising executives

▓ problem solvers, talent spotters and opportunity spotters, such as enterprise managers, venture capitalists and entrepreneurs

▓ transformation agents such as management consultants, counsellors and keep fit instructors, who use specialist knowledge and expertise to guide their clients to valued goals.

The passion model

Passion brands are the Cinderella of modern marketing. They've been around for years, but they've always been neglected. With the emergence of the information age and Right Side Up marketing, it's time for them to go to the ball. The best and strongest will emerge as some of the brightest and most influential stars in the information age firmament.

A passion brand is a brand whose core asset is its passion – a pure 'information' brand, in other words. If it sounds odd to describe a passion as an asset, that's only because we are still overly influenced by an accountancy profession that finds it hard to accept that even things it can't touch and weigh can be real. The opposite way of looking it at is this: what more powerful asset can a brand have than a passion which connects directly with the hearts and minds of audiences or 'users', enthusing them, motivating them and engaging them?

Passion brands come in many guises. They include:

▓ charities; which are driven by their concern for the issues and people they exist to raise money for.

▓ crusades and campaigns; such as Friends of the Earth or Greenpeace.

▓ 'callings'; those brands or organizations where the people want to do the job because of its intrinsic value. Public sector health and education are one example. Religious organizations are another.

▓ clubs or communities of enthusiasm; inspired by the excitement, entertainment etc. of the thing that turns them on: football, trainspotting, etc.

▓ creative; where it is people's love of the act of creation – rather than money making – that really motivates them. Musicians, artists, mathematicians and scientific researchers often fall into this category.

Passion brands differ from traditional brands in a number of important ways. The first difference is that a passion brand's exchange with its audience takes place primarily, not at the level of exchanges of money for goods or services, but at the level of meaning: motivations, beliefs and enthusiasms. If you are a fan of Manchester United, an animal rights activist, or a voluntary worker for the Red Cross, the rational selfish economic calculations of the economists' mythical beast *homo economicus* hardly enter the equation. What motivates you is the passion you hold for the game of football and your club, a sense of ethical outrage, or a desire to help people in need.

This is what makes passion brands so potentially powerful. Marketers were amongst the first business people to realize that *homo economicus* didn't exist – that every exchange of money for goods or services is also, to some degree, at some level an emotional exchange too. But the only way marketers could apply this insight was to wrap emotions around cold, instrumental products to make them sell better. An awful lot of modern branding theory still revolves around this interplay between the core functional attributes of the product, and its emotional wrapping.

Passion brands do the opposite. What they 'sell' is the passion – the experience of feeling. Then they wrap products and services – such as affinity credit cards – around this core offering. This chimes perfectly with an ongoing, information age trend within marketing: the staging of experiences which engage people through all their senses – by sight, sound, touch, smell and taste and, if possible, with all their hearts too. Passion branders are pioneering event managers. From global mega-events such as the staging of the Olympic Games through to charity fun runs to the pressure group campaign or political demonstration, passion brands involve their members, fans and supporters by creating and delivering what consultants Joseph Pine and James Gilmore call 'memorable experiences'.[10]

As a result, the relationship between the passion brand and its consumers is very different to the relationship traditional brands have with their consumers. Indeed, the use of the word 'consumer' is particularly inappropriate here. Passion brands don't have 'consumers', they have members, fans, supporters and believers who are active, engaged and involved. This underlines just how remote and distant the traditional brand's relationship with its customers can be. Whereas consumers tend to 'buy' traditional brands in an arm's length transaction, they 'join', enlist or subscribe to a passion brand.

The potential power of this emotional connection with members, fans and supporters can be seen by the way the sponsorship industry has developed. The very fact that a commercial brand sees the need to associate itself with a 'good cause' through a sponsorship or cause related marketing deal is an admission of strategic weakness. The brand cannot generate the warm feelings it craves without outside help.

> *What made brands successful yesterday won't necessarily keep them successful tomorrow.*

Passion brands also deny and reverse the Number One rule of traditional marketing. Instead of trying to find out what their customers want in order to deliver it, they do the exact opposite. Their inner logic is 'what inspires and motivates me, and how can I inspire and motivate other people to join me in this passion?' They are, in other words, very much 'inside out' brands. That doesn't mean that some of them don't use the most sophisticated marketing communications techniques to persuade target audiences to join them, but essentially the process is reversed. What truly matters – the core asset – is the internal passion, not the marketing 'positioning'.

A third difference is that, historically, most passion brands have not been driven by the profit motive. Whereas the traditional brand deploys emotions to sell a product to make a profit, passion brands' approach to money-making tends to work in reverse. They raise money to feed their passion, rather than exploiting a passion to feed their bottom line.

This in turn tends to make them appear to be far more trustworthy and 'real' than traditional brands. While traditional brands are only 'in it for the money', passion brands' driving motives are seen as authentic. They come from the heart, not from clinical financial calculation. And as emotional beings, people warm to them, especially in today's cynical times.

So not only do passion brands have the potential to outgun traditional brands on the emotional 'hard sell', they also have the same potential to outgun traditional brands in the battle for 'share of trust'. This was seen when Greenpeace confronted Shell, over the decommissioning of the Brent Spar oil rig – the public trusted Greenpeace, not the big corporate.

Last but not least, just because passion brands tend to have not-for-profit roots doesn't mean they can't be as ruthless, as clever and as successful as traditional brands when it comes to fund raising. When the Olympic movement or Save the Children embark upon a fund-raising exercise their passion for the cause will lead them to try to be as efficient and effective in raising money (i.e. making a profit) as any commercially-oriented brand.

Passion brands have a range of potential advantages over traditional brands, including a potentially superior share of trust, greater emotional engagement and the ability to market a growing range of affinity products and services to maximize their share of purse. As passion brands intensify their efforts to woo members' and supporters' hearts, minds (and wallets) they effectively raise the emotional bar for all brands, making the seller-centric marketer's 'added emotional value' look thin indeed. For all these reasons, passion brands are emerging from the shadows to claim their status as powerful brands in their own right.

THE RISE OF PEOPLE BRANDS

The creativity that drives the intellectual property business; the emotions that drive the passion brand; the relationship-building qualities that drive the connector brand: the high point of wealth creation is moving away from 'thing reproduction' to 'people amplification': the amplification of people qualities. You can see this in virtually every form of business.

The most explicit people amplification business is where the individual is the brand; where the individual's imagination, creativity, knowledge or judgement is up for sale. This applies to pop stars, comedians, authors, business gurus, barristers and film stars. In these cases what their customers are buying is the individual's specific skills and qualities.

In other instances the customer buys an organization's qualities – qualities which are embedded in, and delivered by, people with specific skills. This is the world of consultancies, law firms and advertising agencies. It is also the world of passion brands: where people's beliefs and enthusiasms are an absolutely crucial magnet. And it's also true of transformation agents: psychotherapists and counsellors, fitness instructors, educators and trainers.

In the third case, contact with people is still a critical part of the brand experience, but not necessarily the prime source of value. Examples include banks, courier, fast food, hotel, leisure and travel companies, where people are 'brand ambassadors' but are nevertheless just one part of a much bigger operational offer.

In the fourth case, the people element has become an important part of what remains basically a product brand. We may buy the products marketed by Disney, Microsoft, 3M and the like, but we know very well that what we are paying for really is the imagination and creativity of the people behind these products.

Finally, there are products where the people element is almost completely invisible, though increasingly vital. This is the world traditionally inhabited by the consumer goods brand. The point here is that in the information age, the age of automation, the only way a business like this keeps on delivering superior value is through the organization's ability to come up with a stream of innovative products – or creative ways of re-engineering processes to minimize costs. As Coca-Cola's former CEO Doug Ivester once commented, 'Everybody falls into the trap of looking at the latest gadget or thinking that creativity has to be in the arts and sciences. But you've got to encourage creativity in staffing, strategy, branding, and business processes too.' As the automation revolution presses onward, in other words, even the infrastructure business is affected, and begins to rely increasingly on human qualities to push it forward.

A brand shake up

In any economic era, brands tend to represent the pinnacles of value creation. In the industrial age, product and service brands representing the fruits of replicated routines ruled the roost. The inner logic of the information age suggests that the high-ground of marketing and branding is set to shift to new forms of value creator. Soap powders may have been the icon brands of the industrial age. They will not be the icon brands of the information age. Consumer agents, on the other hand, are just one of the new forms of value creator and just one of the new breeds of brand. Like yeast in the dough, they are not the biggest or most obvious ingredient. But they are a catalyst, transforming the way the mix as a whole behaves.

Can *you still deliver value?*

AVERAGE LOGIC

The logic of industrial age production is an *averaging* logic. The industrial age was about maximizing economies of scale and minimizing unit costs by producing standardized products and services. Likewise, industrial age marketing produces the same standardized messages, such as mass TV advertisements, for the same standardized unit of consumption: 'the consumer'.

It does this for good reason. It treats people *as if* they are identical because the costs of doing anything else far exceed the benefits. These are primarily information costs. It is too expensive to find out how the costs or opportunities of A differ from B. And even if we find out, it is prohibitively expensive to do anything about it – say, to customize the product or message for both A and B.

The lure of deaveraging is devastatingly simple. It's in the nature of an average that it includes some high values and some low values. If any business can cherry pick the high values, without being dragged down by the low values, then it's clearly on to a good thing.

There's only one problem. The average is a sort of glue that keeps the different elements of industrial age businesses together. The more successfully you deaverage, the more successfully you dissolve the glue. The bits start separating out. The business begins to unbundle. By minimizing the cost of obtaining information about the high values and the low values – and then doing something with this information – the information age makes deaveraging and unbundling possible.

PARETO POWER

The world is a skewed place, and it's astonishing just how skewed it often is. Call it the Pareto Principle or the 80/20 rule or whatever, but the general rule of 'skewedness' applies to virtually anything you care to look at: value of customer grouping, product line, distribution channel etc.

It applies to customers. In the US, for example, 9 per cent of airline travellers account for 44 per cent of airlines' revenues. Just 5 per cent of US households buy 85 per cent of Levi's jeans and just seven million households account for 84 per cent of Diet Coke's annual sales.[2] Likewise in the UK, 16 per cent of UK households account for 73 per cent of fishfinger consumption.

It applies to products. Of 300 Hollywood movies released in one eighteen-month period, just 1.3 per cent earned 87 per cent of the total box office revenues, with the other 296 movies earning the rest.[3]

It also applies to profits. In cars, for example, the Lexus brand accounts for one third of Toyota's total profits but just 2 per cent of its volume. In retail, consultant Brian Woolf tells the story of one US supermarket which estimated that the lifetime value of its top quintile of customers as 976 times higher than that of its bottom quintile.[4] In his book *All Customers Are Not Created Equal*, Garth Hallberg analyses the case of Yoplex yogurt, for whom 16 per cent of its customers account for 110 per cent of its profits, with 20 per cent of the brand's potential profit gobbled up by the costs of marketing to the 53 per cent of customers who never buy the brand.[5]

Segmentation of customers by lifetime customer value, database-driven marketing to ensure better targeting, rationalizing product portfolios to eliminate 'brand tails', 'mass customization' – these are all ways in which marketers are trying to use deaveraging to their advantage. But just how far can this quest go?

ARE YOU TRAPPED BY AVERAGES?

Grafting deaveraging marketing strategies on to businesses that prosper by averaging can be a risky business. Companies start down the road of deaveraging because they see it as a way to make their existing operations more efficient. The further they travel down this road, however, the closer they find themselves to a precipice: the very economic viability of these operations can be threatened. If you don't watch out, you can deaverage yourself out of existence. A good example is insurance.

> *Deaveraging sets off a chain reaction that melts the glue keeping companies together.*

Insurance is by definition an averaging, cross-subsidizing business. Clever marketers have made good money by deaveraging – distinguishing high-risk customers from low-risk; smokers from non-smokers, households by catchment area, drivers by age and sex, and so on. Take it too far, however, and the risk-sharing logic that drives the insurance contract begins to unravel. The better marketers become at targeting the lowest risk customers and attracting them with lower premiums, the higher the high-risk premiums become. Soon, if you happen to be in a very high risk category, the insurance premium begins to rise so high that you no longer see the point of paying it.

As these people stop paying, the insurance company's total income falls. Which means it has to raise its premiums. So the attractiveness to low-risk customers also falls. Besides, if you know you are in a really low-risk category, you might earn a much better return if you simply put your insurance premium into a high interest savings account. The more perfect the information, in other words, the less viable cross-subsidization becomes, because customer A has no reason to subsidize customer B.

A second risk with deaveraging is that it disrupts essential economies of scale. Take an airline like British Airways. It makes most of its money from its frequent flying business class customers. Wouldn't it be nice if it could concentrate all its efforts on serving them? You know the jargon: focus on your most profitable customers, increase their satisfaction, improve their loyalty, boost their lifetime value, and so on. But it can't, because it cannot afford to let seats go unfilled. Every unfilled seat is a cost without any revenue.

So even as BA tries to focus on its most profitable customers, it's forced again and again to discount the seats at the back of the plane, down to bargain basement prices. Result: sometimes those at the front of the plane are paying thirty times more than those at the back – to the increasing disgruntlement of the companies paying these differential fares.

One answer would be to invent a plane that shrinks or stretches according to the number of seats sold. Customized infrastructure, in other words. But the logic of deaveraging actually points to the unbundling of the business itself. One business to focus on high margin frequent flying business people. Another low-cost business to serve holiday makers. And that, effectively, is where BA started heading with the launch of its discount brand Go, and the acquisition of smaller planes to serve business markets – with fewer seats at the back to fill. BA recently sold Go so that it could concenrate on its more lucrative flights, but the problem remains.

And it's not alone. Across virtually every industry, in some way or another deaveraging threatens to set off a chain reaction within companies that unravels the ties that originally bound them together into a single entity in the first place.

CHERRY PICKERS' PARADISE

In most cases, deaveraging favours the cherry picker: the upstart outsider, the new entrant who is not trapped by his installed base.

Take credit cards as an example. Mass market credit card issuers such as the UK's Barclaycard are massive cross-subsidization businesses. According to the Credit Card Research group, on average, 40 per cent of credit card users pay off the entire bill at the end of each month, thereby avoiding interest payments. And the cost of providing them with this interest free credit is born mainly by the 25 per cent of users who are credit card junkies, and are always heavily in debt. For an operator such as Barclaycard, those 40 per cent of credit card users who pay off their entire bill at the end of the month are freeloaders. They take advantage of the service and the infrastructure, but they pay very little towards the cost of maintaining it, never mind towards the card operator's profits. Most of the costs (and profits) are paid for by that relatively small group of heavy card users.

Now imagine an outsider coming in, and finding a way to target this core 25 per cent. Let's assume that their targeting is so sophisticated that they can distinguish between 'good' customers who borrow a lot and remain credit worthy, and 'bad' customers who represent a high risk of bad debt. It's worthwhile offering these 'good' customers a much better deal than they currently get, because they no longer have to subsidize the 40 per cent of freeloaders. It therefore becomes quite easy to offer these key customers a much better deal. And if they can cream off this truly valuable segment, then Barclaycard – the incumbent – is left with two unprofitable rumps of customer segments: the 40 per cent who don't pay their way, and the bad debtors, where the costs of collecting the bad debts often far outweighs the actual sums recovered.

In this way, by slicing off, say, just 10–15 per cent of the right customers, the new entrant could destroy the entire economic viability of his much bigger rival. And that, of course, is precisely what specialist credit card providers such as MBNA and Capital One have been trying to do: inflict deaveraging marketing judo on the market leaders.

Credit cards, however, are just one example of many. Most averaging business models have relatively high operational gearing: the first 90 per cent, say, of revenues is needed simply to cover their operating costs. The next 10 per cent makes all their profit. If a cherry picker manages to steal just 10 per cent, the entire business model goes belly up.

That is exactly what's happening in sectors such as music and books where non-traditional competitors such as superstores and Internet sites are selling high volumes of 'top ten' titles at very low prices. Traditional full-range music and book retailers need these bestseller revenues to help fund the supply and stocking of the other 95 per cent of titles which sell at much a slower rate. Hence the recent warning from Simon Wright, Chief Operating Officer of Virgin Megastores, that high street music retailers need lose only 10 per cent of CD sales to new Internet retailers to be forced out of business.

As the information age unveils the juiciest cherries for all to see, it's sparking an increasingly bitter battle between would-be cherry pickers and scale-driven incumbents. As McKinsey consultant John Hagel points out, 'Traditional corporations may be more vulnerable than they realize. Many traditional business models are economically unstable in the face of the loss of even a small fraction of their best business.'[6]

WHO ARE TODAY'S BUSINESS BUNDLES FOR?

In the last chapter we saw how a new business ecology is emerging – built around infrastructure providers, connectors, intellectual property creators, and organizations that organize and express human passions. Yet, if we look at the modern firm, we can see that it attempts to bundle all of these things together. The firm tries to develop intellectual property, exploit economies of scale and build relationships with customers, all under one roof. And by bundling them together it finds, as McKinsey's John Hagel notes, that it has to 'suboptimize the performance of each'.[7]

Compare, for example, the economic logic of relationship building to efficient production. Building relationships is expensive. It takes time and money to build a long-term, trusting relationship with a customer. It follows that any relationship building business wants to funnel the sale of as many different products and services through that relationship as possible. A business focused on exploiting economies of scale, on the other hand, wants to produce as many of the same unit as it possibly can: because variations and complexity cost it time and money. What it wants, then, is to sell the same unit to as many different customers as possible.

The relationship builder wants to find products for his customers. The manufacturer wants to find customers for his products. Their priorities clash, head on.

The same goes for corporate culture. Innovation tends to flourish in small, loose, informal organizations. But infrastructure businesses seek size, scale and standardization. No wonder they find it hard to innovate. Result: in traditional industrial businesses, where these various processes are routinely bundled together, the needs of one are 'routinely sacrificed' to accommodate the needs of another, suggests Hagel.

But who, in a seller-centric world, bears the cost of this sacrifice? In most cases, it is the buyer. The traditional car dealership is a classic example. It collects and displays cars from factories. It services them. It also acts as a showroom (that is as a source of information for the buyer), offers loans and closes transactions.

> *By unbundling 'marketing' from 'making' agents unbundle seller-centric business models.*

But as Philip Evans of the Boston Consulting Group points out, the car dealership carries out most of these constituent activities rather inefficiently. As a physical distributor it is less efficient than deliveries direct from the factory or from regional distribution centres. As a service provider, it is inferior to specialized repair chains. As a provider of unbiased information to the consumer, 'its value added is negative'. As a provider of finance, it is over-priced. And as a market maker in used cars, 'it exploits the ignorance and anxiety of consumers'.[8]

What has held this rather unedifying bundle together so far has been its stranglehold on something so valuable it overrides all these negatives: 'the consumer's economies of searching: the high cost of acquiring comparative information about price, service, delivery, quality and interest rates.'[9]

Now, as we've already seen, new Internet-based services are transforming these economies of searching. And the value glue which held together the bundle of services we now call a 'car dealership' is beginning to dissolve. Evans calls it 'deconstruction'. 'Deconstruction can occur wherever information economics hold a physical bundle together and wherever the informational activities themselves can evolve into separate businesses,' he suggests. 'Deconstruction will occur when deaveraging releases economic value – when activities cross-subsidize one another, or when the economics of one activity are compromised for the sake of another.'

If Evans is right, deconstruction will affect all the traditional business bundles that have dominated the marketing scene for decades; manufacturers, retailers, and media included. Most manufacturers are both makers and sellers. But as we've seen, consumer agents can unbundle the making from the selling to do the core matching and connecting tasks better and cheaper.

The same is also true of traditional retailers. Their business models are constructed around the economics of handling goods: gathering them together in warehouses, distributing them to shops and displaying them in shops. But one key benefit of the shop to the consumer is that it helps the shopper search, compare, choose and pay. And this can be achieved far more efficiently on the Internet.

Likewise with the media. The modern media is a bundle of editorial subsidized by advertising. But as we saw in Chapter 11 the Internet is creating new, and more efficient ways for both buyers and sellers to connect, thereby threatening the advertising subsidy to editorial. How many magazines and local newspapers could survive, for example, if classified ads migrated *en masse* to new forms of virtual exchange?

Manufacturers, retailers and media owners as we know them in their current form are hardly going to disappear overnight. Their existing momentum is far too great for that. But as deaveraging kicks in they will need to discover new forms in order to flourish. As we move towards a Right Side Up world, in other words, not only is *how* companies go to market being transformed along with the *sorts* of value they offer within these markets – so are the very entitites that create this value.

And once again, we find the consumer agent at work, this time in the guise of one the most virulent forms of unbundler. By focusing specifically on the information-intensive tasks of matching supply to demand and connecting buyers to sellers, agents are riding with the current of information-driven deaveraging. They also expose the seller-centric nature of many existing business bundles – such as the traditional car dealer.

That doesn't mean the end of all business bundles, however. If all the different strands of service currently bundled into a car dealership were separated out into different businesses, buyers would have to invest an enormous amount of time and energy scrabbling around to put a complete solution together. Bundles can and do add value. But in future, if the bundle is to flourish, it must add value to buyers as much as it adds value to sellers.

do you offer 'value for time'?

> Time is the ultimate non-renewable resource. *Anon*

THE VALUE FOR TIME REVOLUTION

Money is the currency of commerce. Time is the currency of life. In the end, what people buy is value for time, and that's where the focus of competition under Right Side Up marketing moves to.

The value-for-time revolution has profound implications, though they are deceptive. It splits once integrated markets down the middle, shifts the focus of value creation from products and services *per se* to the quality of the customer's life, and transforms the key questions marketers have to address. And once again, it exposes the producer-centric nature of industrial age marketing.

Industrial age marketing revolves around value for money – a neat phrase that sums up the two core dimensions of competition: price and quality. But, price and quality are actually vendor-centric notions. They are about the price of *my* product, the quality of *my* product. Value for money focuses on the value of *my* product.

Value for time, on the other hand, is essentially consumer-centric. It's about the value of each minute and each hour to that human, the price he has to pay – not only in money, but in time – to achieve the things he wants to achieve. It is about the quality of *his* life.

Marketers who define value in terms of products, rather than in terms of the ways people spend their time tend to see price solely in terms of the financial returns they can levy. They remain oblivious to the often time-consuming processes that surround the transaction itself: searching for solutions, arranging transactions, assembling these solutions and ensuring delivery. This is precisely the entry point for many of the new breeds of information age brand: the infomediaries and buying clubs, the outsourcers and the integrated solution providers.

These consumer agents locate their specific forms of value creation in their customers' life rather than in factories or infrastructure. Before we look at these trends in detail, however, let's quickly deal with two issues. First, the whole 'time famine' issue is a puzzle. Objectively speaking, it seems we have more free time than ever. So why do we feel under such time pressure? Second, if you look at the history of marketing through value-for-time eyes it's astonishing how powerful value for time has *always* been: it's *always* been there, we just haven't looked for it before.

Time famine?

Perhaps one reason why we feel under time pressure is a shift in the focus of our lives. For example, one hundred years ago, survival was still the main item on most people's agenda.[1] Now, however, we have enough time to lift our eyes from the daily battle for survival to wonder what else we could do with our lives. And, thanks to the information age, we are also realizing than even if we lived to be 100 years old, we would still not have enough time to do all the things that we would ideally like to do.

Certainly, even ninety years ago ordinary people had less time to play with. In 1910 the average worker worked 3000 hours a year:

that is nine and a half hours a day, six days a week, week in week out, with no holidays, paid or unpaid. Working hours in advanced industrial economies have almost halved since then, to around 1600 in Germany and 1850 in the US. Even the over-worked Japanese have it easy compared to ninety years ago: their average working year is 2000 hours.

At the same time, however, the industrial age has been obsessed with time compression. At work, the clock rules. The pressure of deadlines is never far away. Productivity means producing more in less time – with fewer man hours. This has been compounded recently with business's endless attempts to squeeze more activity into less time through concepts such as speed to market, just in time and inventory turns per year.

The post-war workforce genderquake – the rise of the working woman – means that families as a whole have less time for domestic chores. And because traditional divisions of labour between men and women have been only partially renegotiated, working women in particular are under constant pressure to juggle: work, home, childcare, etc.

But the most important drivers of the 'time famine' phenomenon are probably more subtle. Compared to ninety years ago, when we were working like dogs, we live in an age of relative plenty: 77 per cent of UK consumers now say they have everything they need – there are no material comforts missing from their lives – which means that we have the luxury to worry about things other than survival and sustenance.[2]

At the same time, the information age is both expanding our horizons and choices and making it ever more difficult to cope with them. Developments such as electrification, central heating and the TV mean we no longer have to while away long, cold dark winter evenings. Instead, if we choose to we can sit in warm, light homes bombarded by the media which reminds us of all the amazing things we could do with our lives: places to see and experiences to enjoy, skills to master and things to learn, foods to sample, music to listen to – things a typical agricultural worker in an isolated village of 100 years ago would have never known or thought about.

Confronted with this ever expanding choice, possibility, potential, the chances of our ever having the time to do a tiny fraction of the things we want to begins to seem ever more remote. The higher and broader our horizons get, the more frustrating our inability to 'have, or do, it all'. As we've just seen, one central effect of an age of information overload is attention poverty: a poverty that stems from the fact that we all still have only twenty-four hours in our day.

The time economy

Not everybody suffers from time famine, of course. We still have a tiny minority of time rich, money rich people, and large numbers of time rich, money poor, such as the unemployed and large sections of the retired population. But the fastest growing sections of the population seem to be among the time poor, money rich and the time poor, money poor. And if we step back a bit, we can see that throughout human history even the time rich have hankered after better value for time. In fact, you could argue that value for time has always been a key driving force in human economic activity.

Virtually every breakthrough product or service has won its popularity because it offered better value for time. Humans are incorrigible 'betterists'. We don't just adapt to our environment, making do with what we have got, we strive to change it for the better. Since the year dot, we have tried to make our time on this earth better, easier, simpler and more enjoyable. We have sought ever more comfortable shelter, fuel to cook with and to warm our homes, clothes to make ourselves more comfortable or to gain self-esteem and status, tools to do more things with less effort in less time. Inventions like the plough and the wheel could be seen as the first 'convenience' products: labour saving devices that enable us to do more, in less time, with less effort and hassle.

Likewise, trade is just another way of maximizing value for time. In early agrarian societies, most people spent a lot of time making things for their own use. But trade flourished whenever people realized that other people could make the same or better things in less time than they could (for whatever reasons, such as proximity to a valuable resource or superior skill). To this degree, money (and therefore value for money) was only invented to oil the wheels of trade – trade in time, in value for time.

The industrial age merely accelerated this process. Basic products such as cloth and clothing, processed flour or a loaf of bread offered consumers better value for time. A factory can turn out far more pieces of clothing or loaves of bread per hour than anyone could hope to do by weaving and sewing, kneading and baking at home. One of the things a consumer buys when he buys a manufactured article of clothing or a loaf of bread, therefore, is a time saving.

Just imagine life without the elements of infrastructure such as running water or electricity, or the enabling technologies such as cars and fridges for which they provide a platform: having to fetch water in buckets from a well, not being able to use any electrical product, not being able to speak to someone instantly over a distance (but having to wait for a message to reach them physically), not being able to travel quickly from A to B, having to scrub your clothes by hand, having to shop every day because the food you buy goes off so quickly.

The second half of this list includes some of the products that exploited the potential of this infrastructure and its enabling technologies. They were among the biggest and most successful packaged goods brands – brands which helped to shape and define what we now think of as marketing. Again, what they all have in common is their convienience (improved value for time). Tea bags eliminate the hassle of dealing with messy tea leaves, and offer a quick, simple cup of tea. Canned baked beans are the early version of fast food. Disposable nappies save the time (and unpleasantness) of washing, drying and ironing terry towelling. And so on. Each one moved the ongoing value-for-time revolution one step further.

The retail revolution is no different. Superstores dominated not only because they offered lower prices, but because they offered superior value for time: the convenience of a car park; of a huge range of goods (which reduces time spent shopping around); of an ever expanding range of services (such as financial services, or the ability to buy petrol, which follow the same time-saving logic); of extended opening hours, and so on. In fact, it is difficult to think of any successful product, service or brand which has not jumped to a new level in the endless race to deliver improved value for time.

THE GREAT VALUE FOR TIME CHISM

Even so, most companies are still only scratching the surface of the great value-for-time revolution. There are two sides of the value-for-time coin. Their importance cannot be overestimated. They are:

- **minimizing low 'value-for-time' time:** there are many things in my life that I don't like doing. If I possibly can, I would like to spend less time doing them. Any product or service which helps minimize these low value-for-time activities is valuable to me. This is what the UK's Henley Centre calls 'streamlining'.
- **maximizing high 'value-for-time' time:** there are things in my life that I enjoy doing, that enrich my life. If I possibly can, I would like to spend more time doing them. Or, if my time is limited, I would like to enrich this time by stuffing as many positive, fulfilling, rewarding experiences into it as possible. So any product or service which helps me enrich the time I do have is also valuable to me. The Henley Centre calls this 'elaboration'.

The quest for better value for time is creating deep fissures in virtually every single consumer market. Once-integrated markets are dividing into two as consumers make value-for-time driven choices.

This great division between streamlining and elaboration raises issues which straightforward value-for-money considerations simply do not address.

The food industry, for example, is dividing into 'streamlining' convenience and fast food, and elaboration – the night out with friends at a restaurant or gourmet cooking as a home hobby. In mature western economies traditional grocers continue to lose 'market share' to the food service industry: fast food outlets, restaurants, canteens, home delivery pizza outfits etc. which feed this just in time mentality. In the US, the grocery industry's share of stomach is now hovering at a mere 50 per cent. In the UK, the food service share of stomach is close to 35 per cent and rising rapidly.

Similarly retailing is dividing into replenishment/chore shopping and shopping as a leisure activity. This split is also seen in travel. Brands that are failing either to reduce low value-for-time aspects of their offer, or enhance high value-for-time aspects risk being stranded in a very uncomfortable commercial no man's land.

Tackling the great value-for-time division isn't necessarily easy, however. Seen from a value-for-time perspective, exactly the same product can represent two totally different sets of meanings, depending on the value-for-time mindset of the user. For a DIY-phobe who hates spending time and money doing DIY, a power drill is probably a distress purchase, full of resentment and anxiety. For the DIY enthusiast, on the other hand, it is a thing of joy and pleasure. These are not *product* attributes. They have nothing to do with the product at all. They are *customer* attributes reflecting the different value-for-time priorities of different people.

> *Value for money relates to the product. Value for time relates to the person.*

As the information age unfolds, competition between firms and brands will increasingly revolve around addressing these two sides of the value-for-time coin – saving time, and doing more enjoyable things with the time we have got. But the split has another crucially important effect. It opens up a vast swathe of new forms of wealth creation.

Time enrichment

Robert Blatchford, the nineteenth-century English socialist, said it all. 'Man's bodily wants are few,' he declared in his bestselling pamphlet *Merrie England*. They include food, clothing, shelter and fuel. And all are best used temperately. Man's mental needs, however, 'are infinite'.

Blatchford divided man's mental needs into three: Knowledge, Pleasure and Intercourse. 'Of Knowledge, there are almost numberless branches, and all of them fascinating,' he enthused.

Then there are Pleasures and their name is legion. There are such pleasures as walking, rowing, swimming, football and cricket. There are the arts and the drama. There are the beauties of nature. There are travel and adventure. Mere words cannot convey an idea of the intensity of these pleasures . . . Then as to Intercourse. I mean by that all the exaltation and all the happiness that we can get from friendship, from love, from comradeship, and from family ties. These are amongst the best and the sweetest things that life can give.

Blatchford wrote his pamphlet in 1893. Over a hundred years later modern consumers are coming round to the wisdom of his words. Compared to our physical, bodily needs our mental needs are infinite. We are entering what US consultants Joseph Pine and James Gilmore call the 'experience economy', where the goods and services that provide our relatively limited bodily wants become the stage and props for experiences which enrich and enhance the little time we have on this earth:

In the full-fledged 'experience economy', instead of relying purely on our own wherewithal to experience the new and wondrous – as has been done for ages – we will increasingly pay companies to stage experiences for us, just as we now pay companies for services we once delivered ourselves, goods we once made ourselves, and com-modities we once extracted ourselves.[3]

Along with the notion of 'agency' (of being 'on the customer's side'), this deceptively simple distinction between two forms of value for time emerges as one of the key drivers of the Right Side Up marketing era. The two go hand in hand. So far, we have discussed only one species of consumer agent – the buying agent. But as we'll see, other forms of agent that act for their client to provide better value for time in different ways will have just as big an impact in the long term.

The rise of 'just in time'

Just in time has been a hugely important theme in business-to-business markets for decades. But only now is this mentality – together with its huge operational challenges – migrating to consumer markets.

Just in time represents the beginnings of a completely new consumption mindset, as long standing drivers of human behaviour begin to lose their grip. Drip by drip we are beginning to accept the miracle of industrial age plenty and to take it for granted. This is fundamentally changing our attitudes towards use of time. Take food. Shopping is a planned activity, done with one eye to the future. Deep down inside, it is driven by a 'just in case' mentality: 'I had better buy these provisions, just in case we need them at some time in the future.' But nowadays the supermarket shelves always seem to be full. So why spend so much time 'hunting and gathering' and searching for food just in case we might want it at some time in the future?

In an age of material scarcity, a 'just in case' mentality is crucial. But in an age of relative material plenty that begins to change. We no longer have to plan our lives around making sure the larder is full for next week. And as this sinks in, slowly a new mentality is taking hold. If I no longer have to worry about whether I will have enough food tonight, I will worry about it when it matters to me: when I'm hungry. Nowadays 70 per cent of Americans (asked at four in the afternoon) have no idea what they'll eat that night.

Coca-Cola began to understand the significance of the shift from just in case to just in time (and value for time) decades before other marketers began to see it. Rather than expecting consumers to go out searching (hunting and gathering) for a place to buy Coke, the company decided to be within arm's reach of desire, making sure its drinks were available wherever consumers happen to be; to be there when we decide we want it; just in time. Coke's recognition of value for time goes a long way to explaining its phenomenal success as a brand.

This growing 'not only do I want it, but I want it *now*' mentality doesn't stop with food and drink. It also applies to information-based products. As US marketing consultant Regis McKenna points out, we expect ever more products and services – such as access to cash, the ability to communicate, the ability to listen to music or access sports news etc. – to be there, where we are, within arm's reach of desire, just in time.

This, in turn, points to another shift. A just-in-time product or service is convenient for me: it fits into my life as I happen to be living it. It does not demand that I stop what I am doing to go out hunting and gathering the products and services I need. It adds value 'in my life'. Instead of my having to plan and organize my time around the convenience of the supplier, the supplier has to plan and organize his time and operations around my convenience. Instead of Mohammed always having to go to the mountain, the industrial age marketing mountain is coming to Mohammed. Instead of consumers 'going shopping', shopping and marketing are coming to where consumers physically want to spend their time, whether at work, at home, 'online' or at events and venues: wherever and whenever it gives good value for time.

THE BATTLE FOR 'SHARE OF TIME'

Competing for 'share of time' is a very different matter to competing for 'share of market'. Take a stunningly simple example. What exactly happens when a consumer decides to buy a home delivery pizza rather than go shopping for food? A typical conversation might go like this:

> 'What shall we do tonight?'
> 'Let's get that video Sally recommended.'
> 'Good idea! But what shall we do about food?'
> 'Oh. Let's order a pizza.'
> 'That would be a nice.'

Value for time lies at the heart of it. Not only have the couple in question decided to 'outsource' the hassle of shopping and cooking to a third party (one value-for-time decision), this decision itself was prompted by another, higher-order value-for-time decision: how to spend their time that evening. The decision about what 'product' to buy was a byproduct of a previous and 'more important' decision about use of time.

This value-for-time decision has untold knock-on effects for the traditional product-focused marketer. Back in the supermarket, he is still engaged in traditional 'brand wars'. Brand A of flour (or anything else) is slugging it out with Brand B and Brand C (the own label version). All of them are investing (as heavily as they can afford) in advertising and in-store promotions, in order to gain 'share of mind', win brand preference, close the sale and achieve 'brand loyalty'.

Similarly, each individual supermarket is slugging it out with its rivals to win these consumers' footfall, share of purse and loyalty. Yet, as far as our video watchers are concerned, all these brand wars are a complete irrelevance; a waste of time and money. If marketers are to compete for share of customer time, rather than maximize share of market as defined by product or service category, they are competing potentially with any other offer which might offer that consumer better value for time. This is a key strategic problem facing toy maker Lego, for example. Lego has a very high share of the traditional toy market. But kids are spending more time on things like video games. The money has followed the time, and Lego risks being boxed into having a big share of a shrinking cake.

RETHINKING PRODUCTS, MARKETS AND INDUSTRIES

Value for money focuses attention on the product. Value for time focuses attention on the person. In doing so, it sweeps aside industrial age notions of product category, 'market share' and 'industry'. Products, markets and industries are all defined by the attributes of the producer. Value for time – value 'in my life' – does not respect or recognize these category and industry boundaries, or the assets they rest upon.

The soap powder market is defined by what soap powder manufacturers are trying to sell. If we focus on the person and what he wants to achieve with his time, we do not discover a soap powder market. We discover a market for fresh clean clothes, ironed and ready to wear. And we become aware of all the time, money and effort that consumers invest in achieving this result. A business that delivers fresh clean clothes, ironed and ready to wear is very different to a business that makes and sells soap powders.

Marketers tend to think they are addressing the challenge of value for time by recognizing the importance of 'convenience'. But when product-centric marketers think about convenience, they naturally think about it in ways that can help them sell their product and keep their core asset – their factories – busy. So they try to embed convenience into their product, as another selling attribute. They might, for example, offer a ready prepared pizza base, or even a ready prepared frozen pizza, rather than a packet of flour. Likewise, retailers – who are fixated on feeding their particular core asset, their store base – seek to embed convenience into their store offer: better parking, easier choice in the fixture, shorter queues, and so on.

But the home delivery pizza sweeps these forms of infrastructure – along with the traditional divisions of labour between manufacturer and retailer – aside. The home delivery pizza is not made in a factory. It's made locally, around the corner. It's not sold in a superstore. It's delivered to the consumer's door.

This sums up the value-for-time dilemma for the seller-centric marketer. Attempts to embed 'convenience' or value for time in traditional offers can only go so far before they come up against the driving logic of 'what do I make and how can I sell it?'. Car makers, for example, are currently bending over backwards to stuff ever more value-for-time gadgetry into their cars. They are turning the modern vehicle into a mobile entertainment and music centre, a mobile office, a mobile communications centre (including satellite navigation systems), and a mobile eating and drinking environment. But in the end the real value-for-time issues involved in owning and running a car – the traffic jams, the parking irritations, all the hassle involved in acquiring, maintaining, repairing, running, insuring and disposing of the car – cannot ultimately be addressed by producing 'New! Improved!' cars. To genuinely address value for time, marketers need to look beyond traditional seller-centric market and industry boundaries.

New brand alliances

Winning share of customer time is something few traditional marketers can achieve by themselves. The ever-present need is to work with other organizations to 'round out' the total experience.

To tackle the hassles of car acquisition and maintenance, for example, car makers need to work with car sellers, car insurers, roadside assistance organizations and mechanics. Enhancing the value for time mundane product or service may involve linking it with completely different sorts of value. In Germany, for example, Milka, the Kraft Jacobs Suchard chocolate brand, has drawn on its Alpine heritage to work with ski manufacturers, ski resorts, retailers and event organizers – such as the FIS – to tap into high value-for-time Alpine health, travel and entertainment activities.

> *Winning share of customer time is something few traditional marketers can achieve by themselves.*

Management consultants Roland Berger & Partners call this 'co-revolution' – where several non-competing partners work together at all levels within and across the value chain to leap to a new level of value as far as the consumer is concerned. As Roland Berger & Partners point out, invariably, this involves reengineering assets and capabilities – 'co-revolution is not based on existing infrastructure' – and going beyond existing industry boundaries.[4]

But sometimes the challenge of value for time is even more fundamental. To truly tackle the nightmares of the traffic jam and the hassles of parking, for example, car makers would need to enter the killing fields of public policy and planning. They might even have to accept that fewer cars on the roads would create value-for-time benefits for customers. This is difficult, when every sinew of your organization shouts the imperative: 'Sell more!' We'll see later how new breeds of brand – brands which are not driven by the need to sell more – are preparing to muscle in on such territory.

As we've explored the Right Side Up revolution, we've seen how it transforms not only how companies go to market and the ways they communicate, but the sorts of value they offer, and the nature of the entities that create this value. Now, with value for time, we can see how this transformation reaches back even further, to the very way we think about – and organize – industries and markets; into the very processes of wealth creation itself.

At the same time it opens up new opportunities in the arenas of time enrichment, by bringing value creation into the heart of the consumer's life, by actually helping to change consumers' lives for the better. But to be 'allowed in' is a challenge in its own right: you don't invite every stranger through your front door. You have to trust them.

why should *people trust you?*

> *It is not instrumentally rational to trust instrumentally rational people.*
> Martin Hollis[1]

If there is one sure-fire candidate for the prize of 'marketing disaster of the 1990s' it must be Monsanto's attempt to introduce genetically modified (GM) foods into Europe. GM foods – or Frankenstein foods, as they came to be known – may be wonderful. They may be safe. They may be the perfect expression of 'New! Improved!' But they were still a marketing disaster. Because consumers trusted neither the product nor the company. As *Financial Times* columnist Philip Stevens noted at the time, the real Frankenstein in these foods lay not in the food itself, but in people. It was called mistrust.[2]

THE CHANGING NATURE OF TRUST

Brands originally flourished because they kept their promises. People could trust them. In the early days, when markets were flooded with shoddy and adulterated products backed by outrageous and dishonest claims, a good wholesome product that delivered what it promised really did add value.

It added value for the consumer, who was no longer being ripped off. And it added value for the producer, whose brand attracted repeat custom – the launching point for improving economies of scale. The focus of trust was therefore fairly and squarely on the offer and has been ever since. And why not? This space is potentially infinite. Competition revolves around marketers finding something extra to promise, and organizations having to stretch their capabilities ever further in an attempt to keep these extra promises.

With the information age and marketing Right Side Up, however, new dimensions of trust are opening up. They relate more to the building and maintenance of *relationships between people* than to the making of offers and the closing of sales. This is the beginning of a whole new ball game.

In an era when connections and relationships begin to be as valuable as the individual exchanges that take place within them, the issue of *motives* begins to raise its confusing, ugly head.

A child trusts his mother because he knows she loves him. A consumer trusts a brand because she knows it's in the (enlightened) self-interest of the seller to keep his promises. The two are entirely different. And until now, they've been kept neatly in different compartments. The first is for human relationships. The second is for commercial relationships. Now, slowly but surely, the distinction is being blurred. The question of motive is joining the issue of performance to transform the nature of the trust battleground. Its implications run extremely deep.

When Monsanto faced the pressure groups over GM foods, it wasn't an ordinary marketing battle. It wasn't two producers arguing over whose offer was best. It was between an offer-marketer and a passion brand. When the general public was asked to choose between them, they chose the one whose motives they trusted. Seller-centric trust revolves around performance. Passion brands add trust in motives to the equation.

Monsanto didn't fail, therefore, to clear any old trust hurdle. There's little doubt, for example, that the general public 'trusts' Monsanto to be excellent within certain narrow boundaries of scientific expertise. Monsanto failed to clear the two trust hurdles that lie right at the centre of Right Side Up marketing: 'Are they the sort of people who would . . . ?' and 'Can I trust you to be on my side?' Agents triumph by clearing both 'performance trust' and these new hurdles to beat all comers in the trust stakes.

NO TRUST, NO WIN-WIN

Before we examine these shifts, however, let's remind ourselves why trust is so important. You can't see it or weigh it, but trust is a hugely powerful economic force. As writer Matt Ridley argues, 'It is as vital a form of social capital as money is a form of actual capital.'[3] It's the heart of win-win.

If two sides to any transaction do not trust each other, then the costs of that transaction are likely to balloon out of control. So much so that one or both sides may decide that the transaction is not worth the candle in the first place.

Traditional economic theories assumed perfect markets where the costs of exchange were zero. They simply ignored inconvenient facts such as the costs of mistrust. Path-breaking economic thinkers like R. H. Coase and Douglass North, however, have shown just how expensive mistrust is, both directly and indirectly.

As North points out, a lack of trust – 'the uncertainty that the other party will find it in his or her interest to live up to an agreement' – creates all sorts of new and extra transaction costs. Observes North, this 'transaction cost will reflect the uncertainty by including a risk premium, the magnitude of which will turn on the likelihood of defection by the other party and the consequent cost to the first party'.

On a grand scale, cold wars and arms races – which can be unthinkably costly – are examples of this risk premium. Contracts, laws and law enforcement agencies are all attempts to minimize these transaction costs. But they are also a cost in their own right. So are many business processes which – with a fresh eye – can be seen as forms of institutionalized mistrust. Like checking a delivery against an invoice, for example. Add all this up and we come to

North's key conclusion: 'Throughout history the size of this [risk] premium has largely foreclosed complex exchange and therefore limited the possibilities of economic growth.'[4]

Brands, businesses and societies which manage to build trusting relationships therefore free themselves from an enormous cost burden. As US thinker Francis Fukuyama notes: 'Widespread distrust in a society imposes a kind of tax on all forms of economic activity, a tax that high-trust societies do not have to pay.'[5] The same, of course, can be said of firms in their relationships with key constituencies, including customers.

But the costs of mistrust are only one side of the issue. The benefits of trust are equally huge. Commenting on relationships between manufacturers and retailers, for example, Nirmalya Kumar, professor of marketing and retailing at the International Institute for Management Development at Lausanne, notes that 'by developing trust, manufacturers and retailers can exploit their complementary skills to reduce transaction costs, adapt quickly to marketplace changes, and develop more creative solutions.'[6] As we'll see, the point is just as well made about

> *The new acid test for trust is no longer trust in the product, but in the people behind the product.*

the relationship between consumer and supplier or agent. When you trust the other party, you are prepared to share all sorts of things – such as confidential or sensitive information – that helps both sides get far more value out their relationship.

Trust, then, is not merely nice to have. It is a potential economic superpower. Those who have most of it, across most dimensions, have a huge competitive advantage.

THE INFORMATION AGE GOLDFISH BOWL

But why are trust hurdles rising? Traditionally the focus of trust was on a promise or 'unique selling point' and, whether it was delivered or not. Then, brand management was a relatively simple affair. Brand managers could define and control the agenda. They controlled the flows of information and they could turn the spotlight on the things they wanted to highlight. As long as they got the promise right in terms of relevance and value, and delivered it, everything was hunky-dory.

But brand managers no longer control the flows of information as they once did. The shift started a long time ago, with the rising importance of the media. Nowadays, thanks to an all-pervasive media, brands swim in a goldfish bowl of information that enables and encourages consumers to peer behind brand managers' carefully constructed brand façades to look at the 'reality', not just the sales glitz. This warts-and-all view of the brand has been encouraged by things such as the media exposé. Exposing corporate malpractice is an excellent source of news, and a good way of attracting audiences too. Companies have learned the hard way that a TV programme or newspaper story about corporate malpractice can empty the organization's trust bank, overnight.

Closely related to the media spotlight is the rise of the pressure group. Pressure groups hardly existed when most brands were born. But they have become expert at finding ways to grab the media's attention, and using it to compel corporations to change the things they do. Pressure groups' campaigning tactics revolve around trust: they are designed to cast doubt on the integrity and trustworthiness of their corporate opponents.

Both pressure groups and the media link in to a third factor: rising consumer sophistication. The generation that's reaching retirement age now is the first generation to have lived their adult lives in a full-blown brand marketing, media-intensive environment. Consumers are now 'marketing literate'; they have seen it all before. They are no longer dazzled by smoke-and-mirrors marketing razzmatazz.

They know brands are façades – invented to help close sales. And once you know something is a carefully constructed façade, designed to sell you something, it becomes harder to trust it. Hence *Cluetrain Manifesto* co-author David Weinberger's prediction that 'Within the next five years the point will be reached where delivering a marketing message will make your company look arrogant and manipulative. And it will look like you are hiding behind your message, afraid to engage in the real market conversation with real customers.'[7]

Through sometimes bitter experience consumers are also increasingly aware that every brand is the product of a complete supply chain. The environmental lobby and numerous health and food scares have combined to make consumers extremely aware that there is no such thing as a 'pure' product which simply – miraculously – appears on the shelf. On the contrary, every product is created by a supply chain. And at every step along that supply chain decisions are made which affect the integrity and quality of the product, how it is made, how people, animals or the environment are treated in the process, and so on.

What's more, with rising affluence, people can more easily afford to express their opinions on these matters. When you are no longer worried about where your next meal is coming from, you can afford to worry about other things, such as whether the tuna in your sandwich was caught using dolphin friendly fishing techniques.

The list could continue, but it makes the point: the focus of trust is shifting. And this shift is not going to stop.

ARE THEY THE SORT OF PEOPLE WHO WOULD . . . ?

Consumers already expect to be able to peer behind the brand façade to a degree almost unthinkable a few decades ago. Back then, for example, what went into a product was not something manufacturers made a fuss about. They wanted to focus buyers' attention on the benefits, not the ingredients. Today, consumers expect to be able to inspect many different types of information: about which ingredients are used or not used, about research and production processes (such as animal testing), environmental impact, social impact, and so on. Companies like Monsanto, or Shell, that fail to ride these waves of scrutiny and criticism get punished.

It's true, of course, that some consumers care much more passionately about issues like these than others. Some pundits predicted that consumers as a whole would be prepared to pay a premium for so-called 'green products', for example. It never happened. But 'green' didn't disappear, either. Instead, environmentally friendly policies have been increasingly accepted into mainstream business. And the net effect was the same. The sphere of trust has expanded beyond the product's immediate benefits to the organization's behaviour in society.

The same is happening with broader issues of social responsibility and 'ethics in business'. Seeing these issues in terms of a market segment, or a particular target audience, misses their deeper significance. If you are always aware that every product or service is governed by decisions which may affect you, your children, the environment etc., you also become aware that by buying that product you are 'voting' for, or endorsing, these decisions in some way or another.

Events over the last twenty years or so – driven by the rise of the information age – mean we have crossed a rubicon and cannot go back. Buying a product is no longer 'value free' any more. To some degree, no matter how small, it is about *values* as well as value. This is even true of those consumers who decide they do not care whether a product uses CFCs or child labour. The genie of awareness is out and cannot be put back. Deciding to ignore it is a positive decision.

This element of values, as well as value, is set to rise for a very simple but important reason. The genie of awareness underlines the fact that every brand, every offer, is not just a soulless, valueless, 'objective' transaction. It is brought to market by *people*: people with certain behaviours, attitudes and motives. And therefore we should scrutinize these people, not just their products. The focus of trust shifts inexorably to 'are they the sort of people who would . . . ?'[8]

This question has some terrifying implications. It is, for example, completely open-ended. We could finish the sentence in an infinite number of ways. It could be 'Are they the sort of people who would destroy the environment', or 'exploit children in the third world', or 'side with oppressive regimes', or 'hide important information', or 'mis-sell me a personal pension'. It could be anything.

Perhaps even more terrifying to the traditional brand manager is that 'are they the sort of people who would . . .' acts like a lightning conductor to the heart of trust. Take child labour as an example. If those organizations are proved to be 'the sort of people who would exploit children in the third world in the quest for a quick buck', then the chances are they would also be 'the sort of people who would exploit *my* children in the quest for a quick buck'. If they are the sort of people who have been economical with the truth about one issue (an issue which doesn't affect me directly), then they are also likely to be the sort of people who would be economical with the truth about *another* issue (which *does* affect me directly). If they are *those* sort of people, how can I trust them?

The rising tide of concern about social responsibility, ethics and environmental performance among consumers therefore does not represent pure altruism. On the contrary, it is a highly sophisticated form of selfishness. No matter what the specific issue is, it boils down to trust. Proving that 'in this organization we are the sort of people who have integrity' is completely different to proving that 'we are offering a product that does what it says on the tin'.

For the traditional brand manager, this is a seismic shift. Brand managers in the past have been consummate puppeteers. They have stayed behind the scenes, pulling the strings of their brand puppets to engage their audience, while remaining hidden, unknown and anonymous. The shift towards 'are they the sort of people who would . . . ?' – like everything else in the information age – reverses the flow of information. Brand management as mask management is dead. Branding is no longer just about how we would like to present, or 'position' ourselves. It is also about 'who we are'.

> *Trust in product performance is not enough any more. The question is are you on my side?*

Trust angels and trust cannibals

A world of informed, sophisticated, sceptical – even cynical – consumers: this is the environment in which information age brand wars will take place; an environment where trust in the people behind the brand increasingly takes centre stage.

In this environment, brands find themselves competing as hard for 'share of trust' as they do for share of market. And strange new forms of brand warfare begin to appear. Nowadays many brand campaigns are designed to cast doubt on the integrity of the people behind the enemy brand; to become a trust iconoclast or cannibal – a brand that survives by 'eating' other brands' trust.

Pressure groups pioneered Trust Cannibalism. But the tactics are now being picked up for 'mainstream' brand warfare. Richard Branson's Virgin group is an expert Trust Cannibal. Whenever it enters a market its message is essentially the same: 'The incumbents are not on the customer's side. They are anti-customer: ripping customers off, confusing them, failing to deliver genuine value. They are only in it for themselves.'

In the UK, supermarkets like Asda and Tesco have also started honing their skills as Trust Cannibals. When they discount over-the-counter medicines, books, perfumes, jeans and trainers they are not simply indulging in good old-fashioned price promotions or price warfare. They are attacking the manufacturers' motives. 'These people cannot be trusted, because they are trying to rip you off' is their message. Thus, when Tesco started selling grey market-sourced designer clothes at discount prices, it said its ability to do this 'shows the enormous margins brand manufacturers expect to milk from the market place. It's a scandal for ordinary shoppers that we are working hard to resolve.' For which read: Tesco is on the customer's side. These other brands are not.

Trust Cannibals operate by engendering controversy which undermines the public's trust in their victims. Controversy, however, creates its own dynamics. The first and natural response to hearing an allegation against a company or a brand is to want to hear 'the facts', to get more information. Yet, invariably, the more information we have access to, the more we 'know', the more we realize how *little* we know.

Take the GM foods saga. Consumers were worried about what *could* happen as a result of the introduction of GM foods. However, they quickly realized that the issues involved – the science, the research and the details – were far too complicated for them to fully understand. So they turned to 'experts' for help and advice. But these 'experts' disagreed. And there were doubts as to their motives. Some were funded by 'the industry'. Some were backed by pressure groups. Everyone seemed to have a vested interest. There was no one to trust. So most consumers opted for the safest course possible.

Such dynamics are not unique to GM foods. They are a characteristic of information age debate: the more we are flooded with information about a subject, the less certain things become, the less we seem to *know* for sure. And even if we had the time or inclination to really get to the bottom of one issue – say, Nike and its use of third world labour – we would never have the time or inclination to get to the bottom of every such issue. In an age of information overload, we cannot be experts in everything.

So one of the strongest emotions generated by such debates is not to want to know more, but to want to *worry* less. What we would really like to do is *outsource* our worries to somebody who we can trust to make the best possible decisions – 'to do the best by me' – given the known facts. The opposite of the Trust Cannibal, then, is a new type of superbrand, the Trust Angel, who worries about and addresses these issues for me so that I don't have to. Trust Angels win the battle for trust at a completely new level: the level of *agency*.

CAN I TRUST YOU TO BE ON MY SIDE?

Honesty, integrity, a strong moral code or set of principles – these are the sorts of human quality that engender trust. But we also know that most people are not saints. And most companies are not organizations of saints. For a Trust Angel to win our trust we need something else. We need to know why it's on our side.

Getting a sudden attack of moral qualms is not good enough. In fact, it can be downright suspicious. That was another of Monsanto's problems. When European consumers asked the question, 'Are you the sort of people who would do the best by me?' of Monsanto, they gave it the thumbs down. They decided that Monsanto weren't the sort of people who would put preserving the environment ahead of pushing their products. And once they decided that, all the scientific facts in the world counted for little.

Monsanto lost the trust argument, in other words, not because people didn't trust its science or its products, but because they didn't trust its *motives*. *Financial Times* writer Philip Stephens summed up the mood like this:

These giant multinationals now speak as if their mission is to save humanity, to put food in the mouths of the starving and medicine within reach of the sick. Baloney. Monsanto, a company that has spent many, many millions promoting its image as a guardian of the planet has one ambition: to create value for its shareholders.

There is nothing wrong with that . . . But these corporations should not expect the rest of us to be conned by their synthetic altruism.[9]

Such comments go right to the heart of the issue of trust in a Right Side Up marketing environment. Let's put the issue as starkly as possible. Imagine you have a choice of doing a transaction with one of two parties. You know Party A is entering this transaction to make as much money out of you as possible. You know this because he's told you many times. His job – he never stops saying it – is to maximize shareholder value. In other words, he has openly declared that he is being paid to further the interests of someone else, not you.

On the other hand, you have employed Party B to act as your agent. He gets rewarded to the degree and extent that he is effective in acting on your behalf; getting you the best deal; being on your side; looking out for your interests. Given this knowledge of the two parties' various allegiances, which are you predisposed to give your business to?

The answer is obvious. The very knowledge that seller-centric marketers are acting in the interests of sellers, rather than buyers, tends to eat away at the very trust that is so crucial to the success of their brands.

Faced with this terrible dilemma, seller-centric marketing has come up with a good answer. It goes something like this: 'While maximizing shareholder value may be the purpose of the organization, the only successful means to this end must be to satisfy and delight customers by providing them with the best possible value. Our brands must consistently provide our customers with superior value, and they have to earn the customer's trust in this respect.' What's more, the answer continues, 'We have a vested interest in maintaining this value and this trust, because that is how we maintain our market share and our income.'

It may be a brilliant answer. But it's not watertight. It succeeds only by evading the issue – by substituting rational, instrumental calculations of benefit for trust. But as philosopher Martin Hollis points out, this is not a strong basis for trusting anyone at all. It's a bit like putting our trust in man who says honesty is the best policy. Such a man is not actually honest. His real commitment is not to honesty itself but to the best policy – the calculation of gain. And one day it may no longer be the best policy to be honest.

That's how agents trump seller-centric brands in their trust heartlands. First, it's more instrumentally rational for us to trust someone who we pay to be on our side than someone who we know is paid to prioritize the interests of a third party such as shareholders. Second, as the focus of trust shifts beyond promises being kept to include people's motives. What we want to know is whether these people are actally *trustworthy*. And as we'll see in Part IV, that opens up a whole new ball game: the game of *values* as well as value.

Does this mean that traditional brands cannot survive in this new environment? No. To the extent that old offer-based win-wins still apply, nothing changes: transactions will still be closed. It's unlikely, for example, that an impulse purchase such as an ice-cream will need to fight too hard on the 'be on my side' trust front. But this sort of trust is a very limited, arm's length sort of trust. It's not the sort of trust upon which real relationships between people are built.

We started this chapter noting the huge economical potential of trust. As long as exchange was one dimensional – money for goods – offer- or performance-based trust worked just fine. But if companies want to leap to new levels of value creation based on new dimensions of exchange, such as the sharing of information, or being 'invited into my life' to help me enrich my value for time, they also need to leap to new dimensions of trust. Climbing up the information age value curve (and not being left behind) also involves climbing the trust curve. This, in turn, changes what it takes to build a brand.

who are brands for?

> *Today's brands are product or vendor centric brands – they are state-ments about the quality or attributes of the product or vendor. On the Internet, the most powerful brands will be customer-centric brands.*
>
> John Hagel[1]

MARKETING'S PERSONALITY DISORDER

Psychologists talk about a narcissistic personality disorder as characterized by a grandiose sense of self-importance, fantasies of unlimited success, power and brilliance, a belief that one is superior, special and unique, a constant seeking for attention and admiration, and a preoccupation with how well I am doing and how favourably I am regarded by others.

Modern marketing has its own narcissistic personality disorder. It's called branding. The brand as we know it is a vehicle of organized corporate narcissism. Despite everything marketers like to say about knowing, understanding, getting close to and focusing on the customer, building and managing brands as we know them is the ultimate exercise in egocentricity.

The brand is a carefully constructed package of information designed by me about me – about the special attributes of *my* product or *my* service. My market research is preoccupied with what you think about me, and what I can do to make you think I'm even better. My marketing communications are designed to grab your attention so that you pay your attention to what I want to say to you. These communications are designed by me, to flatter me, so that you see how wonderful I am. I say that I want to understand you when I develop these communications, but that's only so that I can achieve these goals most effectively. The ultimate purpose of my brand communications is not for me to understand you, but for you to understand and admire me.

When I do things to 'build' my brand I do them because I want you to become *my* customer and be loyal to *me*. And I do all these things to further my own purposes, not yours. I invest in my brand because I want it to maximize the returns it generates for me. My marketing is designed to influence your behaviour to my benefit, by buying more of me or paying more for me. In my dreams, I would like you to become my brand ambassador, spreading the good word about me.

When I measure 'brand value' I measure the value of my brand to me, not to you. When I talk about marketing or advertising effectiveness, my concern is how well it achieves my objectives cost effectively, not yours.

When we view him in this light we can see why the modern seller-centric marketer has a problem. In a very deep sense, modern brands have very little concern for the consumers they profess to have so much interest in. Brands as we know them are not *for* the consumer. On the contrary, as former P&G brand manager turned consultant Michael Lanning comments, most companies (and their brands) are 'thoroughly self-absorbed egotists [who] can only understand relationships in terms of themselves . . . The egotist fails in many relationships and can't understand why.'[2]

We've seen why this happened. When wealth creation revolved around entities driven by 'what do I make, and how can I sell it?' and 'here we are, and this is what we have to offer' brand narcissism was perfectly natural and understandable. It was the only option. Its downsides were also tempered by the saving grace of consumer choice. But as we stumble into a new world where the consumer says, 'Here I am and this is what I want,' and where new forms of buyer-centric business start operating according to the logic of 'who are my customers and how can I serve them?', this seller-centric narcissism begins to look very odd indeed.

THE BRAND MELTING POT

Now it's time to draw some strands together. Everything we have discussed throws another piece of fuel onto a fire that's heating the once-rock-solid seller-centric model of branding to melting point: the disintegration of the win-wins that traditional brands were built upon and the rise of new information age win-wins that require a buyer-centric approach to marketing; the ascendance of new buyer-centric concerns such as 'is your marketing worth buying?', value for attention and value for time; economic shifts that are changing both what forms of value are most prized and the entities that are best placed to create them; the leap to new dimensions of trust such as 'are they the sort of people who would . . . ?' and 'can I trust you to be on my side?'

Together these transformations add up to the new imperative of the agency: brands must be *for* buyers and consumers if they are to flourish. This new buyer-centricity does not demand a single, uniform approach or business model, however. Buyer-centricity affects brands representing both organized consumers and traditionally organized producers. It's a generalized phenomenon, bubbling up all over the place in different forms and having its effect at many different levels. We are, for example, moving towards a new brand ecology populated by:

- brands which represent buyer or consumer attributes rather than seller attributes – such as communities of interest and passion brands.
- brands – such as buying clubs and reverse auctions – which act for buyers in the marketplace to 'extract value from vendors, rather than the other way round', as McKinsey's John Hagel puts it.[3]
- brands whose core purposes include using information to help buyers to buy – such as infomediaries.

▓ seller brands which, in response to those pressures created by all the above, find it necessary to ramp up the elements of their marketing which *have the effect of* helping buyers to buy, rather than simply helping the seller to sell.

The list doesn't end here. There are also other forms of buyer-centric brands such as solution agents, which deal with supplier brands on behalf of their clients to assemble the solutions they want, and transformation agents, who work with the clients to help them achieve their personal goals.

So does this mean that sellers, seller brands and seller marketing are doomed? It's true – as John Hagel remarks – that 'what gives brands power today will not be sustainable in the future. New forms of brand will emerge that will be even more powerful than existing brands.'[4] But as we've seen, the emerging business ecology has room for – it positively needs – infrastructure and intellectual property creators as well as relationship or 'connector' businesses and passion brands. And these forms of business have to sell to survive. The big change is not that sellers and selling are disappearing. It's that narcissistic seller-centric *marketing* has reached its sell-by date.

BRAND MANAGEMENT IN FLUX

For buyer-centric and seller-centric brands alike, therefore, the combination of new information age technologies and the rise of buyer-centricity mean a root-and-branch shake-up of what it takes to build and 'manage a brand'.

Brands are not dying. As concentrated packages of information, brands are a perfect information age communications vehicle. All the techniques of branding – the logos, slogans, colour cues, design, brand names, jingles and so on – are designed to communicate large quantities of information in nanoseconds of attention time. Precisely because these techniques are so powerful they are spreading, to become ubiquitous. Far from hastening 'the death of the brand', the information age ensures its triumph – and metamorphosis. But the more ubiquitous the process of 'branding' becomes, the more branding *per se* is being separated from 'selling'.

Instead, branding is becoming a generic communications device.

That's why, today, everything and everybody is becoming 'a brand': people such as pop stars, athletes, film stars and politicians; places such as tourist destinations and business centres; events such as the Olympic Games; causes and crusades such as Greenpeace. Like fish, fowl, mammals and bacteria, each one of these beasts has a different place in the brandscape, and there is no one rulebook that can encompass them all.

The rise of new flows of information – upwards from buyers to sellers, and sideways from buyer to buyer – does, however, mean that many characteristics of traditional brand management are fading. The traditional brand was built around a selling proposition: it was (at worst) the lipstick on the gorilla designed to make the offer look as attractive as possible and close the sale. It was complete: a prepackaged bundle of attributes which gave the consumer a binary choice – he could either take it, or leave it. And this prepackaged bundle was 'managed' by a control freak brand manager who wanted to control everything about his brand: product attributes, design, packaging, brand personality, communication idea and execution, media strategy, distribution strategy, pricing strategy and so forth.

> *Seller-centric brands are narcissistic through and through. Now branding needs to be reinvented.*

Don't expect any of these attributes to survive the Right Side Up revolution intact. Brand management as façade management is increasingly untenable, for example. As *Cluetrain Manifesto* co-author David Weinberger points out, there is a fundamental difference between marketing 'messages' which corporations manage in order to persuade consumers to buy their offerings, and conversations that take place naturally between people. 'The Web is creating networked markets that defy the old broadcast model of marketing. These new markets are choc-full of conversations,' he says. 'How are you going to manage these conversations? You're not. As soon as you try, you destroy them.' These emerging networked markets 'are unwilling to be branded', continues Weinberger. 'They will not sit still for one-way marketing communications.' Instead, 'markets are now branding companies'.[5]

The onset of marketing 'worth buying' and the imperative of providing consumers with value for attention means that traditional just-in-case, mind-cuckoo approaches to building brands now look increasingly counter-productive. In the emerging 'here I am, this is what I want' era, earning word-of-mouth recommendation and being there when and where I want you (or information about you) rise up the agenda.

The notion of a brand as a carefully constructed bundle of emotional and functional attributes also looks increasingly tenuous. The bundle as used in branding was never real in the first place. It was invented and artificial, designed to influence – or manipulate – consumers into closing more profitable sales. But now, ever stronger passion brands are helping so-called 'consumers' to amplify and express the real emotions in their lives. And as we'll see, the rise of 'brand experience' and new dimensions of exchange between organizations and clients are reinforcing the need for genuine, rather than ersatz, emotional engagement (when and if it's appropriate).

In an era where buyers' experiences of brands is more important than the messages marketers send about them, the things that brands *do* also become more important than the things brand managers so painstakingly try to *say*. As Dave Allen, Chief Executive of Enterprise IG remarks, 'behaviour = brand = reputation'. [6] And what marketers say inside the organization becomes as important a part of 'building the brand' as what they say outside.

In fact, changing information flows means that increasingly, rather than acting as masks behind which corporations can hide, brands are turning into windows, through which the public chooses to peer into the heart of the corporation. Chief executives are now realizing that the brand is not just an offer, but 'an organizing principle' – critical to decisions as to what sorts of value they wish to create, and how.

The rise of 'interactivity' and 'dialogue' meanwhile challenges long-held assumptions about brands as offers and the role of 'choice'. Making offers as take-it-or-leave-it choices doesn't fit with anyone wanting to build a genuine relationship. As one-to-one marketing pioneer Don Peppers notes, traditional brand messages have been *broadcast* messages: the same to everyone who receives them. Marketers like to talk about their brand communications creating 'a relationship' with customers, but this relationship is on a par with the customer's relationship with a film star like Robert De Niro. 'You know who he is, you have an opinion about him, and you may even love his movies (the product), but it's doubtful that he knows you.'

This essential remoteness means that in the industrial age context, 'a brand's primary role isn't to maintain a relationship with a customer but to serve as a *substitute* for such a relationship'. Peppers adds, 'You can't have a relationship with an audience, only an individual.' [7] His point, of course, is that real relationships have to be two-way, where 'the product maker is actually willing to change how he or she treats an individual based on the customer's input.'

Once the marketer is changing what he offers in response to the individual customer's input the consumer has a voice: he doesn't have to choose 'exit' if he doesn't like what's on offer. Instead, he can say : 'I would prefer it like that, please.' In other words, he can ask the brand to go beyond choice to become a service. This changes what it means to manage a brand, as Bob Tyrrell, chairman of RISC Futures in Paris, points out:

> Where branding is public, the ethos of service is personal and intimate. Where brands are based on values with universal reference, the values of service are unique and particular. Where brands do the talking, service is about listening. Where brands know best and are confident, service is deferential and assumes the customer knows best. Where brands wait for the consumer to come to them, service goes to the consumer. [8]

One way of looking at this shift, suggests Tyrrell, is to think in terms of facility providers and users rather than suppliers and customers. In a user/facility model, Tyrrell notes, the watchword is not 'choice' but 'specification': it is the user who specifies what he or she wants, how and when. That way, the brand becomes more like a menu in a restaurant than a Buy Me! message. And the marketer's resources become 'my tool' for achieving my ends.

This helps to turn the supplier's brand into 'my brand'. My Yahoo! is a classic example. My Yahoo! lets the user stamp his own personality and preferences on the Yahoo offering. Procter & Gamble's reflect.com experiment is an attempt to apply the same thinking to traditional packaged goods. Reflect.com is a venture selling cosmetics and toiletries online in a way that lets consumers configure their own products to suit their own skin type, hair colour, style preferences. P&G – the quintessential traditional brand manager – is now letting its consumers specify the attributes of 'their' brand rather than push *its* brand at them. The name reflect.com expresses the shift perfectly. When consumers look into it or its products they see themselves reflected back.

Reinventing brands

In fact, the attitudes expressed by this icon of marketing apply equally well to traditional seller-centric marketers and to would-be up-and-coming buyer-centric superbrands. 'We don't have the answers. We just know that the 1950s, 1960s mass push big bang model [of marketing] is not as effective as it used to be, and it certainly isn't as efficient,' says P&G CEO A. G. Lafley. 'In the past, it was mass marketing and it was push, basically. Push packaged product, push the advertising on to the telly: turn it on as loud as you can, keep it on as long as you can, sample as broadly as you can for as long as you can. That's the way we did it it.'[9]

But now, says Lafley, 'we have to reinvent branding. We have to reinvent marketing, and we have to reinvent marketing with the customer [i.e. retailer] . . . What we are trying to do now is find different business models, different launch models, different branding and marketing models.'

Lafley has pinpointed the challenge now facing both buyer-brands and seller-brands. And as they begin this quest they face a series of common, critical issues. Bearing in mind the eight critical questions of buyer-centric marketing we've just discussed in this part of the book, we're now in a position to investigate what happens when old and new clash, mingle and mix.

PART 3

create value 'in my life'

While the old model of wealth creation revolves around maximizing the potential of the producer's assets, the new Right Side Up model revolves around maximizing the individual consumer's assets: the production of personal wealth, the outcomes I want in my life.

Whereas the old model was focused on realizing value in the form of money within a marketplace, the new Right Side Up model has a much broader perspective: realizing value for time in the form of the richest, most rewarding life possible.

In Part 3 we focus on the operational side of creating value 'in my life'; how it spawns new forms of consumer agent and the competitive imperatives it generates for agents and traditional sellers alike.

create total solutions

> *Reach the profit zone by ... finding ways – beyond merely selling the products – to help customers in the difficult, expensive or time-consuming areas of their process.* Adrian Slywotzky and David Morrison[2]

'THE CONSUMER' PLC

Think of 'the consumer' as a business. In generic terms, businesses do three things. They acquire raw materials or inputs. They process these inputs, working them up into a product or service. And they sell them to realize a profit.

As consumers, we do exactly the same with our lives. We acquire inputs – the products and services we buy. We work them up into the outcomes we want: say, processing and assembling the ingredients of a pizza into the final pizza. And we realize the profit – we eat it and, hopefully, enjoy it: an experiential rather than a monetary bottom line.

Along the way, we do all the things the typical firm does – except without professional help. We do purchasing, we invest in capital equipment (such as homes and cars), we have to do accounting, distribution, logistics, manufacturing and operations (making that pizza), personnel ('recruiting' people like plumbers), and generally managing the whole caboodle: planning, forecasting, organizing, administering, coordinating, searching for useful information, comparing, weighing and judging, discussing and deciding, transporting, processing, assembling, maintaining, repairing, and so on.

For working women especially, 'juggling' is now an essential skill. Juggling is a high stress, high risk, time and attention consuming activity. At any second, things could start crashing around your ears. That's why, as UK retail consultancy The Store points out, there is a huge and yawning gap in the market for 'life managers' and 'decision agents' which help sort this mess out for us.[2]

> *What sellers sell – the end product of their value chains – is just the raw material of the outcomes we seek in life.*

Buying agents, which assist us in sourcing the key raw materials of our life, don't really address these issues at all. They are just the first wave of Right Side Up marketing. Later, we'll discuss the emotional side of creating value in my life and the rise of transformation agents, which help their clients reach their personal goals. But for now our focus is solution agents, which help their clients in these tasks of general life management.

THE SOLUTION PERSPECTIVE

We've already come across the essence of the solution perspective. Why bother spending all that time searching for and buying and processing and combining all those ingredients for a pizza (and washing the cooking utensils afterwards) if you can source a delicious piping hot, ready-made pizza to appear in your life, as if by magic? But why stop at pizzas? The same philosophy could be applied to complete swathes of 'my life'.

Take my financial affairs, for example. Wouldn't it be nice to find someone who could ease the burden of administering my financial affairs and maximize the value of my financial assets and money flows? This would involve taking an integrated view of the complete range of currently separate products and services – bank accounts, loans and savings, mortgages, pensions and insurance policies – and putting them together in such a way that they work best for me in two ways: making me as rich as possible; and using up as little of my time and attention as possible.

Or what about home maintenance? Things always go wrong. Roofs leak. Washing machines break down. Walls get dirty and need painting. Floors need cleaning, and so on. Wouldn't it be nice if there was just one person I could go to who made sure that these things got sorted for me? Even better, someone who kept an eye on these things so that they got fixed before they went wrong?

Then there's home replenishment. A buying agent may find me the right items at the best possible price, but wouldn't it be nice if I could go a stage further in the area of routine replenishment (re-stocking potatoes, washing up liquid and toilet paper, for example) and have someone take responsibility for making sure that these items are always to hand, and that I never run out of them, so that I don't ever have to worry about them again?

Another potential area for change is personal mobility. Cars are one of the greatest convenience products ever. But owning and running one is often a complete hassle. Organizing insurance, arranging maintenance, keeping it clean and repairing it after accidents. These things always seem to impinge on my life just when I need them the least. Wouldn't it be nice if . . . ?

THE PERSONAL PRODUCTIVITY REVOLUTION

In fact, come to think of it, when it comes to the production of our own lives, there are a million and one such 'wouldn't it be nice ifs', from assistance in arranging the diary ('remember, it's Aunt Agatha's birthday next week, should I send her some flowers?'), to keeping the garden looking respectable. But they have never really been tackled by organized service providers. The industrial age only ever really tackled the first phases of what we could call the personal productivity or personal profitability revolution.

Phase one began with the industrial revolution, when we started outsourcing the production of specific items to people who used factories to make them better and cheaper than we could individually. Phase two came after the Second World War when we started automating our own homes with labour saving devices, such as washing machines which saved us from back-breaking clothes scrubbing. Since then, these two revolutions have continued to unfold with a proliferation of convenience products, from the disposable nappy to the chilled ready-meal.

But now we are on the verge of the third stage where, like many modern businesses, we seek to outsource complete non-core processes – where 'non-core' includes anything that doesn't directly boost our personal bottom line. This third revolution involves a fundamental shift in the location of value creation. In the first two, companies created value somewhere else – in their operations – and brought it to market so that we could buy it. Phase three is about creating value in *my* life, in *my* operations. As Regis McKenna remarks, it 'amounts to a reversal of the pattern of the past, in which consumers or users of things had to arrange their lives according to the product or service desired.'[3]

Sometimes marketers give a superficial nod to this third personal productivity revolution with vague references to the rise of the so-called service economy. But 'the service economy' is a weasel phrase: it obscures and confuses more than it clarifies.

In chapter 14 we saw how the word 'convenience' helps to mask the true importance of value for time. Seller-centric marketers tend to see convenience as just one of many attributes of their offers, when often it's the other way round.

'Service' is another word created by the industrial age marketer: it's simply a catch-all to cover everything that is not a product, just as colour is a catch-all word to describe everything that is not black or white. When somebody says something is a service, that's all they are telling us: that it's *not* a traditional product. They are not telling us what it is. It's rather like somebody telling us that something has a colour but refusing to tell us whether it is magenta red, cadmium yellow, lime green or prussian blue. It leaves us none the wiser.

Does the service we are talking about take the form of expert advice from a lawyer or accountant? Is it a service created by an infrastructure dependent system such as a flight to New York? Or is it a service as in the personal service of a waiter in an Italian restaurant? These 'services' are as different as chalk is to cheese. To lump them all into one category and say we are moving into 'a service economy' is vacuous.

Indeed, if we look a little deeper, we can see that in a very important sense products are services too. As Kevin Kelly notes, it's not what you sell to the consumer that matters, it's what you do for him.[4] A packet of soap powder helps you do the washing. A loaf of bread does the kneading and the cooking for you, so that you don't have to. Every product does something for you: every product is a service too. The issue, then, is not whether you sell products or services, but the degree to which you help lead the third phase of the personal productivity revolution.

Failing between stools

Industrial age firms have shied away from this revolution for many reasons. Traditionally, these arenas offered up little scope to realize economies of scale. Where these needs do enter the commercial arena, they still tend to do so in a pre-industrial form: domestic help and craft labour such as the plumber, for example.

Often, firms have had no incentive to tackle these tasks anyway. Why bother taking on tasks which consumers are undertaking for free? As we will see in our discussion of total purchasing cost, the last thing a retailer wants to do, for example, is take on the costs a shopper incurs travelling to and carrying goods from his shop. Tackling these issues often disrupts industrial age divisions of labour. A car maker helping me run my car would be stepping on the toes of the dealer, for example. And besides, providing complete solutions is actually a different business to selling ingredients to those solutions.

Solution economics

So why should any new-fangled solution agent be able to venture into territories even the best industrial age marketers have not dared to enter? The answer, of course, is that the information age is the catalyst of change, making new bundles of value creation viable where they were not before. Agents add value in a mixture of five key areas.

First, they use information age technologies to address the information-processing side of solutions: the planning, organizing, coordinating, information gathering and transacting side of things. Money is simply a particular form of information, for example, and at root my personal financial agent is simply a supremely efficient information processor. He searches the market for the combination of products and services that, when assembled together, make the most of both my money and my time. Tools like the Internet mean that these tasks can be done far more efficiently than ever before. They are making a service that was once the preserve of the very rich – a personal banker and investment adviser – accessible to everyone.

Please note: this is not the same as 'cross-selling'. As we'll see later, in many ways it is the complete opposite. My personal financial agent may not provide *any* of these products or services himself. In fact it may be a positive plus that he doesn't. That way, I know he's not making recommendations because of a vested interest. His task is merely to use information technologies to seek out the best mix of products and services for me (the lowest interest rate debt, the highest interest rate savings, etc.) to assemble them so that they create a complete integrated solution, and to administer them efficiently.

The second economic ingredient of solution agency is people simply paying for work that they would rather not have to do themselves. There is nothing new here, except for one thing: if new bundles of value are created – which really create value for time (which is what this is all about), people will be prepared to pay for them.

The third key economic ingredient is the creation of new economies of scale. If a personal financial manager is simply doing it for me, it's likely to remain pretty expensive. But if he's doing it for thousands of people, he can invest in software and infrastructure which sends his (and therefore my) costs plummeting. Likewise, my personal mobility provider might achieve crucially important local economies of scale. Imagine, for example, if he signs up 50 per cent of the households on a particular street. There are now fifty cars, say, within walking distance of my home, all being managed by the same operator. What opportunities are there for car sharing, car pooling and car hiring there? So and so at number 123 has a pick-up which I could really use to get that stuff for the garden. Would he let me hire it for half a day? The personal mobility provider would be in a position to set up necessary insurances, make the connections and facilitate the transaction – and take a small fee for his pains.

What we 'buy' when we buy a car is not really the car itself, but the mobility. As Peter Drucker points out: 'The customer never buys what the supplier sells. Value to the customer is always something fundamentally different from what is value or quality to the supplier.'[5] Our real personal mobility needs take many forms. We want a nifty town runabout for inner city chores. We may want a fast, powerful car that speaks 'status' to speed us to an important business meeting 200 miles away. We may

> *Sellers create value in their operations. Agents create value in their clients' operations: their lives.*

want a cavernous vehicle to take the family on a camping holiday. We may want a small truck to move large or heavy items. But we cannot afford to buy four or five cars, so we make do with one: a compromise.

But what would happen if, as part of an annual mobility contract, our personal mobility provider gave us extremely convenient access to these different forms of mobility? We might end up not *buying* any cars at all. Instead, we would spend the money with a personal mobility contractor who would provide us with the sorts of cars we wanted, when we wanted them (and who took on all the chores of ownership for himself). Some car hire firms, such as Sixt, are already edging towards these sorts of solutions.

Another side to these economies of scale is the benefits of specialization. By focusing on just one specialism – say, personal mobility – the agent can afford to invest in infrastructure, knowledge and skills that the consumer would never bother investing in. This specialist knowledge is an important source of added value in its own right.

The fourth driver of solution agency is to combine permutations and combinations of the above three with other information age business models: the virtual exchange, the buying club and the infomediary. The personal financial agent, for example, who acts for 100,000 clients suddenly has tremendous buying power in the market, say, for mortgages. The personal mobility provider who's providing fifty cars in 1000 locations across the country suddenly has enormous buying power with car companies, insurance companies, roadside assistance organizations, spare parts suppliers, etc. He can use this buying power to help bring these services within reach of individuals.

Likewise, a home replenishment agent is in a good position to begin acting as infomediary. Information about clients' buying habits and preferences (on an individual and aggregated basis) would be highly valued by suppliers, for example, who would be prepared to pay for it. They may sign up the replenishment agent to help them beta-test new products; or as channels for sampling campaigns and so on (assuming the clients' permission, of course). What retailers currently do in their stores, in other words, would now be carried out by a replenishment agent in people's homes – 'in my life'.

Alternatively a utility company selling gas, electricity or water may adopt a HomePro.com model and act as an honest broker or agent, providing access to pre-vetted and trusted craftsmen, such as plumbers and electricians – and doing all the things HomePro.com does to add value and earn money. Even the most intractable 'solution space', the domestic chore, might be tackled by a HomeHelp agent.

The fifth element of added value is 'mutual process reengineering' whereby both parties to a relationship change the things they do in order to jointly tackle and reduce the total costs of the process in question – to mutual benefit. Internet banking, for example, dramatically reduces the costs to both the banker and the customer. Wherever such opportunities for win-win mutual process reengineering arise, they invariably transform the industry concerned.

The power of solutions

When two or more of these different value-adding ingredients combine, the effects can be explosive.

The solution revolution has already begun in one huge area: 'food solutions'. Whether it's eating out at restaurants, leisure and shopping destinations, eating 'on the hoof' from fast food outlets, or ordering home delivery meals, the consumer 'demand' is clear: 'I no longer want to organize my life around your food ingredient production and distribution processes. I want you to organize food solutions around my living processes.'

Another growth industry which has already demonstrated the power of these ingredients – when combined in the right way – is the packaged holiday. The first ingredient in this breakthrough was rising affluence. People had more money to spend. They could afford a foreign holiday. Ingredient number two was the burgeoning growth – and falling cost – of commercial air transport: a new technology. Air travel was breaking out of its previous preserve for the elite to become a mass market.

Ingredient number three was a realization that for most consumers the real 'cost' of the holiday was not the flights and hotels, but the hassle, stress, doubt and angst of arranging and coordinating the holiday as a whole: finding the right flight and hotel, making sure that flight times meshed with hotel bookings, arranging the flight and the transfer from the airport and connecting to the right hotel in a foreign land, and so on. Typical solution assembly costs.

Ingredient number four was demand aggregation. By offering the same basic solution to many hundreds of holiday makers, packaged holiday suppliers assembled massive buying power in relation to suppliers of flights, hotels, transport etc. They then used this buying power to reduce prices to way below what individual holiday makers could negotiate for themselves. Finally, ingredient number five was their ability to combine all these ingredients together to create a valued experience – value for time – that was excellent value compared to what else was available at the time.

The packaged holiday companies did not run hotels, airport transfer operations, or airlines. They acted as meta-brands – adding value by combining their separate ingredients together. (If they subsequently moved into operating airlines this was a case of classic vertical integration, and does not subtract from their key source of original value.)

Today, these same ingredients – rising affluence, a burgeoning new technology (in our case information and communication technologies) that's rapidly penetrating mass markets, high purchasing and solution assembly costs (in terms of time and stress as well as money), the potential for demand aggregation and improved value for time – are all present in the areas we have discussed. Entire consumer arenas accounting for an extremely high proportion of total consumer spend – such as personal finance, personal mobility, health, home maintenance and the sourcing of household provisions – are set to be revolutionized by the arrival of solution agents.

Improving customers' system economics

The solution revolution is already well under way in business-to-business marketing. In business-to-business sales outsourcing is now a major force, for example. Lubricant makers no longer merely sell specialist oils, they work for large manufacturers keeping tabs on excessive wear and tear, identifying its causes and tackling it with their expertise and products. Instead of selling oil, they take responsibility for a part of their customers' lives: keeping the machines going at an optimal level.

Retailers and other distributors outsource the complicated, expensive business of logistics to specialist third party providers. And, under the slogan of 'just in time', car manufacturers outsource responsibility for replenishment to suppliers: it is up to the supplier to make sure that his client always has the right amount of stock to hand, rather than the client having to keep tabs on stock levels and keep on making new orders.

In fact, if we look back to our list of 'wouldn't it be nice ifs' we can see that the solution agents simply apply the principles such as outsourcing, just in time and vendor managed inventory to the consumer's life. But to do so, they will also need to embrace the mindset shift which is already sweeping many parts of the business-to-business world: the realization that the best way to prosper yourself is not by charging your customers as much as possible for as little as possible, but by helping your clients prosper. As *Discipline of Market Leaders* author Fred Wiersema comments, 'It requires taking responsibility for customers' results ... customer-intimate suppliers know that customer performance is the name of the game.'[6] It's the agency mindset, in other words.

The job of the solution agent is, in the words of consultants Adrian Slywotzky and David Morrison, to improve customers' 'system economics'.

> Companies that implement a customer development model invest heavily to understand their customers' economics and *find ways to make them more favourable*. They reach the profit zone by first probing how their customers buy and use their products and then finding ways – *beyond merely selling the products* – to help customers in the difficult, expensive or time-consuming areas of their process [my italics].[7]

In the PC market, for example, companies have long realized that the cost of computer hardware often totals only 15–20 per cent of the total cost of owning a PC. That's why companies like Dell increasingly sell their goods on the basis of 'lowest life cycle cost', including the cost of getting the PC to the desk, keeping it there in working order, removing it from that desk, and finally disposing of it.[8]

One of GE CEO Jack Welch's great insights, is that:

> senior executives valued the specific product much less than a new approach to an old process that would dramatically reduce the total cost of the process and would improve their company's profitability ... This system economics perspective required Welch to move GE beyond the traditional product/sell relationship to a true business partnership where value is created for both parties by creating solutions that increase the profitability of both the customer and supplier.[9]

Solution agents simply apply the same mindset to the consumer arena. As in close business-to-business partnerships this means new levels of trust are vital. Old fashioned product trust is not enough. And as in close business-to-business partnerships they take responsibility for the customer's performance in a particular area with this proviso: increasing the consumer's 'profitability' is not just about money profitability; it is also about time profitability – maximizing the customer's personal value for time and productivity by cutting money, time and hassle costs 'in my life'.

The solution agent's challenge

Buying agents challenge traditional seller-centric marketers by shifting the focus of competition from the quality and price of the offer *per se* to the quality and price of its marketing, from the point of view of the buyer. Solution agents represent a very different but equally fundamental challenge. By shifting the focus of competition from the quality and price of the *ingredient* to the quality and price of the *solution*, they deliver a triple whammy:

> *By working on a different dimension of value, agents render old divisions of labour irrelevant.*

- they deliver superior value
- in a way which reduces total marketing cost
- while rendering the ingredient – and its marketing, and its branding – invisible and irrelevant.

If I buy a ready made sandwich I am unlikely to care about the brand of butter or mayonnaise inside it. There's an important point here. By taking marketing to a higher level – that of the solution rather than the ingredient – solution agents push further down the road of reengineering marketing processes and costs begun by the buying agent. Take an analogy. The average car nowadays has around 10,000 separate parts. How many cars would be on the road today if, instead of offering them all assembled and ready to go, consumers were expected to purchase each part separately, and to put them all together under their own steam? Answer: very few. By combining the car into one single solution manufacturers deliver value at a new level for which consumers are prepared to pay large amounts of money.

Now, just imagine the marketing cacophony – and the massive

extra cost – if the competing suppliers of each one of these 10,000 parts were all frantically scrabbling to attract the attention of would be buyers through high profile marketing and brand campaigns. The notion is so absurd it hardly bears thinking about. Not only would the consumer have to incur the cost of assembling these ingredients together, he would also have to invest the time and attention necessary to understand the competing claims of all these ingredients *and* to cover their marketing costs in the final price he pays.

Yet, in the average superstore there are 20,000–30,000 separate stock keeping units and brands all screaming for our attention, and all demanding that we invest time and attention understanding their relative merits, comparing, choosing and purchasing, and then assembling them into the solutions we want. Each one of these ingredients expects the consumer to subsidize its marketing costs to the tune of 100 per cent. Value-wise, it doesn't add up.

'Ingredientization' is therefore one of the first threats posed by the solution agent to the ingredient marketer. The second threat is to his core business model: creating value 'in my life'. This involves a completely different set of skills, infrastructure, cost structures, operating processes etc. to creating value in a factory and then bringing it to market. We don't have to go far to see just how different the two business models are. We can see it right in front of our noses. The pizza parlour provides a perfect illustration.

What makes a home delivery pizza different?

- ▓ it focuses on desired outcomes (a piping hot, delicious, ready to eat pizza) rather than making and selling ingredients (flour, tomatoes and cheese)
- ▓ it obviates the need to shop for, transport and process these ingredients
- ▓ it obviates the need to assemble and combine these ingredients into a desired outcome
- ▓ in doing so, it captures a relatively large share of customer purse (in comparison to the separate ingredient suppliers and retailers)
- ▓ it fundamentally alters traditional divisions of labour between buyer/seller and consumer/supplier
- ▓ it eliminates the need for a grocery retailer
- ▓ it renders the brands of both the ingredient suppliers and the

retailer either irrelevant or invisible. (If the pizza parlour uses a branded ingredient, its customers don't realize it)

▓ in doing so it transcends traditional industrial divisions of labour between manufacturers and retailers. The pizza parlour is a manufacturer, retailer and logistics service provider all rolled into one

▓ it subsumes these many separate ingredient brands into a new, single, bigger, broader, brand offer

▓ it deploys a completely different operational infrastructure (i.e. many small relatively cheap local outlets, compared to a few, highly expensive centralized facilities)

▓ it renders traditional sources of competitive advantage – e.g. manufacturer and retailer marketing and brands, and economies of scale – irrelevant

▓ it turns the *outputs* of industrial age marketing into the *inputs* of solution marketing: it uses an already existing industrial age infrastructure (e.g. a supply of ingredients) as the raw material, or foundations, of a new type of offer

▓ it is driven by completely different operational and financial drivers

▓ it operates on a 'sense and respond' basis rather than a 'make to order' or 'buy then sell' basis

▓ it offers customized rather than standardized products

▓ it is available when and where the customer wants it

▓ it is literally and metaphorically 'closer' to its customer than traditional manufacturers and retailers (e.g. in terms of physical distance and proximity to the customer's desired outcome).

A point worth stressing: not only does the solution provider 'ingredientize' typical seller-centric offers while sidestepping the infrastructure strengths they once saw as giving them competitive advantage, he also transcends the divisions of labour between them. The pizza parlour renders the division of labour between ingredient manufacturer and ingredient retailer irrelevant. The personal mobility solution provider renders the division of labour between car manufacturer and dealer irrelevant. He occupies a different commercial 'space' completely. And while every product or service assumes a division of labour between producer and consumer, every division of labour assumes its own operational infrastructure. You cannot change one without changing the other.

Solution agency is to seller-centric marketing, in other words, as chalk is to cheese. Sandra Vandermerwe, professor of international marketing and services at Imperial College, London, sums up the challenge – and the opportunity – like this. The 'old capitalism' could 'seldom, if ever, achieve . . . totally integrated experiences. It pushed more and more discrete products or services through the system and could never produce the required linking benefits . . . Consequently, there were interruptions at critical points in the customer activity life cycle and huge value gaps were created.'[10] These huge value gaps – or market spaces – are the stomping ground of the solution agent.

A new breed of superbrand

We can now see why total solution agents are key contenders for the role of tomorrow's superbrand. First, they own or control a much greater share of their customer's total spend, both horizontally and vertically. Horizontally, because they bundle a whole series of offerings together into one package. Vertically, because their solutions will usually encompass all or most of the customer's activity cycle from searching for the right products and services, through to purchase to fulfilment. If British Airways succeeded in its stated aim of creating a branded experience 'from contemplation to reflection', for example, it would be dealing with its customer from his first enquiries about travel times, routes and prices through to purchasing tickets to getting the customer to and from the airport, arranging hotel bookings and car hire, as well as managing the customer's experience of the airport and aeroplane.

Second, solution agents gain a much larger share of their customer's 'life' – and trust. Commenting on Unilever's My Home initiative, for example, Maureen Johnson of The Store points out that trusting someone to clean your home entails much higher levels of trust than buying a packet of stuff from them. It's taking trust 'out of the back of the kitchen cupboard'. Indeed as we've seen, for services such as home maintenance or personal finance trust in 'the people behind the service' is crucial.

This is the logical future of relationship marketing. Consumers will have information-sharing, high-trust relationships with only a tiny handful of especially important brands – brands which are deeply embedded in their lives, and where the time and effort invested in building that relationship is deemed worthwhile.

The third factor driving the rise of these superbrands stems from the first two. Total solution providers are, effectively, a new form of meta-brand, or brand of brands. They are literally *super*brands, rising up above and encompassing the many separate and partial offers currently made by most traditional brands.

Boston Consulting Group consultants Philip Evans and Thomas Wurster point out in their book *Blown to Bits* that any business strategy which relies on one-stop shopping, cross-selling or cross-subsidies, all anchored on a putative 'relationship' with the customer, is vulnerable, as information age deaveragors sniff out the core nuggets of value, separate them from the other bits, which offer no added value to the customer, and provide a much better specialized offering.[11]

> *Solution agents skim the world of sellers' offers and use them as the raw material of total solutions.*

But this sort of deconstruction creates a problem for consumers. It massively increases their search, purchasing and solution assembly costs. It creates the conditions for new types of *re*construction. Solution agents effectively *dismantle* yesterday's business models (such as retailing), take out the parts they want and put them together with other parts to create completely new and different business bundles. As McKinsey's John Hagel points out, with limited time and unlimited choice, customers will likely focus their attention on providers that best understand their needs and can, as a result, maximize their return on attention by delivering highly tailored bundles of products and services.[12]

One of the core features of these new business is that, like yesterday's retailers, they funnel a wide range of product and service ingredients through to the consumer in bundles. That makes them a new breed of meta-operator – a service coagulator or coordinator, a retailer of retailers, a brand of brands.

A further complication is that there are no clear boundaries between solutions. Is managing financial transactions a separate solution, or a part of *every* solution? How far up the solution ladder should you venture? While the car is a 'complete solution' in one sense – 10,000 parts all assembled together and ready to go – it's just one ingredient of the personal mobility agent's service. Or take health. Currently, the health care industry is focused on 'disease management' (i.e diagnosis and cure). Slowly, however, it is moving towards disease prediction and prevention. But in future, Vandermerwe suggests, it will move even further towards 'total wellbeing' and 'life extension management'. Here, the focus shifts towards preserving and prolonging the *positive* health of the patient (or to be more exact, the 'unpatient'), rather than waiting only to treat the sick.

This completely changes the nature of the market. Or, perhaps, it creates an entirely new market. Whereas patients are people who are sick and require a cure, 'unpatients are those people who are not ill and who will pay for products and services that prolong that fact,' notes Vandermerwe.[13] This is a very different market space to the one we know now. And it requires a very different mix of technologies, skills and expertise, including, perhaps, pharmaceuticals, biogenetics, food, information technology, healthcare, fitness, cosmetics and nutrition.

So near, yet so far

Many a retailer, utility provider, car hire firm and financial services company can see huge potential in solution agency. But moving from one to the other isn't easy. It's not simply a matter of cross-selling, or brand extending as many seller-centric marketers instinctively see it. Creating new connections between products, services and industries, and integrating their offers into new solutions is different to actually creating these offers in the first place. Being in the business of offering a seamless experience of a journey from contemplation to reflection is a completely different business to the business of filling planes and propelling them through skies.

By transforming traditional divisions of labour between industry sectors, manufacturers, retailers, service providers and consumers, solution agents take traditional players way beyond their existing 'core competencies'. And no matter how much they would like to migrate from one model to another, established incumbents are often trapped by their legacy assets. British Airways may want to influence and manage the customer's experience 'from contemplation to reflection', but when the customer first contemplates his trip, considering times, dates, prices, connections, offers and so on, can he really trust BA to give him impartial advice as to which airline to fly with? How can BA possibly recommend that the customer flies Delta or United when it has a spare seat waiting to be filled on its flights? To beat off the rise of online travel brokers, airlines have had to face this conundrum, swallow their pride (and immediate competitive instincts) to create joint websites that give impartial information, rather than 'selling' information. They have had to move from a seller-centric to a buyer-centric approach.

The same goes for each step of the process: to be a truly impartial solution organizer, the agent must rise above the incentives of each of the ingredient providers. The seller-centric temptation is to embrace the superficial phraseology of 'total solutions' as a cover for the age-old dream of cross-selling. Selling more and more separate ingredients is not the same as providing an integrated solution.

Ford is currently busy extending its business into all manner of car-related consumer services, in line with Chief Executive Officer Jacques Nasser's vision of Ford as 'the world's leading consumer company that provides automotive products and services through world class brands.' These initiatives include buying Internet sites (it owns a stake in Microsoft MSN's Car Buyer service), the acquisition of the European roadside tyre and exhaust service Kwik Fit, and buying stakes in car dealers (which were formerly kept rigidly separate). This is in addition to its decades-old move into car-related financial services.

The question, however, is whether the acquisition of more and more solution ingredients necessarily leads towards the creation of a more integrated solution. Buying up or developing a range of separate brands representing different elements of the solution, for example in the car industry with the car itself, the loan to pay for the car and the roadside service, can end up as another form of conglomerate: a finger in many different pies which create no particular synergy for the consumer.

Strategists' hopes that a company like Ford will come to 'own' the customer relationship, which will make it more able to cross-sell from one part of the business to another, are also classic examples of yesterday's seller-centric thinking. Unless there is a genuine mutual re-engineering of transaction and other solution costs, or a genuine move towards a meta-branding customer agent role, there is no real benefit of this aggregation of separate ingredients to the consumer. It is not a win-win strategy. It's simply an old-fashioned growth/ diversification strategy. Despite their superficial similarity, the two are in fact exact opposites.

Making and selling ingredients will never go away. It is an essential activity. Nevertheless, emerging breeds of meta- or super-brands are subsuming these ingredient brands into fuller, broader, more valuable solutions. As Maureen Johnson comments: 'Ultimately this will lead to major brand rationalizations. The battle will be between suppliers, retailers and new brokers to identify the new solutions and portals which will be valued by consumers in the future.'

Solution agents are different from traditional ingredient sellers both operationally and philosophically. Instead of making and then selling, they 'skim' the world of sellers' offers using them as the raw material for their solutions. They attempt to maximize their profits by improving the customer's 'system economics'; by creating value 'in my life'. One way they do this is by minimizing their clients' purchasing and transaction costs.

minimize total purchasing costs

> An empowered customer becomes a loyal customer by virtue of being offered products and services finely calibrated to his or her needs. That amounts to a reversal of the pattern of the past, in which consumers or users of things had to arrange their lives according to the product or service desired.[1]
>
> Make it easy for your customers to do business with you.
>
> Patricia Seybold[2]

WHY 'PRICE' IS A RED HERRING

Price is a seller-centric notion. It relates solely to what the seller can charge for his offer, and not at all to the real costs the buyer incurs in his dealings with that offer. The price of a box of eggs, for example, bears little relation to the total costs involved in searching for, buying, transporting and assembling those eggs into an omelette. A crucial element of total solution thinking is to address *all* these time, money and hassle costs: to address total purchasing cost rather than mere price.

The gap between formal monetary price and actual purchasing costs can be huge. Adding value by closing this gap is fast becoming a critical battleground in the contest between competing agents, and between agents and traditional sellers.

Consider a big ticket item like a computer. If I want to buy a computer, I am likely to:

- ▦ spend money on specialist magazines which give me up to date information about what's on offer, from who.
- ▦ spend time reading and digesting this information.
- ▦ spend money and time travelling to various computer shops to look at what they have to offer, and to see what's available.
- ▦ spend money and time making the purchase.
- ▦ spend money and time carrying the computer back to my home.
- ▦ spend time in the nightmare process of unpacking, installing software and generally setting up.
- ▦ spend time learning how to use the equipment and the software. And so on.

All these are costs are incurred by me in addition to the monetary price I pay in the shop. They are incurred simply in order to realize the value offered by the computer manufacturer. And they add up. Say, for instance, the computer buyer spends a total of ten hours researching, shopping around, travelling to and from shops and so on: if he earns, say, £20 an hour, as far as he is concerned, the purchase costs him £200 more than the in-shop price. And that's not counting the monetary costs of research (magazine purchases, for example) and travelling. Or the stress and hassle.

Yet because these costs have no impact on either the manufacturer's or the retailer's bottom lines they are all but ignored under the old system. These customer go-to-market costs are the customer's problem. They fall between the stools of industrial age divisions in marketing labour – divisions of labour which are built around sellers' production, rather than consumers' purchasing, processes.

A NEW DIMENSION OF COMPETITION

Now, imagine if, instead of having to go through this rigmarole, I had an expert friend whom I could trust to immediately recommend the best buy for my particular needs. And imagine that being the thoroughly useful chap that he is, he also knows where I could get a discount, and orders and arranges delivery for me. That is what agents set out to do. And that is why, under Right Side Up marketing, any seller wanting to compete effectively must address not only the quality and price of his offer, but the quality and price of the buyer's purchasing process as well.

For agent and seller alike, this battle is already well under way as companies rush to seize the opportunities opened up by plummeting information processing and transaction costs. The most direct way of doing this is to use lower transaction costs to reduce the customer's direct purchasing costs or to cut prices. UK electrical components supplier RS Components estimates that by using its website for purchases, customers can cut the costs they incur in raising an order from around £60 to £10. Likewise, banks want customers to bank online, airlines want travellers to buy tickets online (and so on) because the costs of conducting these transactions are so much lower than through traditional methods. Once these costs structures are transformed, the benefits can be passed back to the buyer in the form of lower prices.

A second way to reduce total purchasing cost is to streamline the purchasing process itself. For example, RS Components also tries to save customers time and hassle by allowing them to check stock availability online, review their order history, or repeat orders by simply pressing a button. Another example is online banking, which saves the customer the time, money and hassle of travelling to bank branches, queuing and so on.

One of the ways Dell Computer Corporation has kept ahead of competition has been by creating customized websites for major corporate customers that enable them to get a complete overview of their business with Dell and allow individual purchasers within the corporation to make purchases within pre-agreed price deals, track orders and delivery, and so on. It is turning its internal operational data into a value-adding service for the buyer, helping the buyer through all his buying processes. In the consumer arena, Amazon.com has set a new gold standard for convenience with its one-click book buying system which remembers the customer's personal details and does all the work for him.

Such services fulfil the first four points of e-commerce guru Patricia Seybold's five basics of success:

▓ don't waste my time
▓ remember who I am
▓ customize your products and services to me
▓ make it easy for me to order and procure service.

thereby going a long way towards achieving the fifth basic: 'make sure the service "delights" me'. The winning strategy for e-commerce can be summed up by a simple maxim, she comments. It is 'make it easy for your customers to do business with you.'[3]

Please note: quality and price are taken as a given here. Making it easy for your customers to do business with you – seeing the whole purchasing process, rather than just the attributes of the offer, from the customer's point of view – is now critical. Just how critical can be seen by the meteoric rise of Charles Schwab, whose entire business strategy has been driven by its determination to be among the first to use new technologies to reduce the costs its customers incur in making transactions.

In 1989 Schwab was among the first financial services firms to use touch tone phones to make trades. It quickly went on to create special trading information software for customers to use on their home computers. It led the market in 1995 in offering much lower cost electronic trades with the launch of its website e-Schwab.com.

At each stage, Schwab seized the opportunity not only to cut transaction costs, but to use reduced transaction costs to change the nature of the offer and to redefine the rules of competition. In its first incarnation, for example, Schwab cracked open the traditional broker's bundle of advice and trading, allowing individual investors to choose a stripped down – and therefore a much lower priced – pure trading service instead.

In its second incarnation, Schwab recognized the continuing

demand for financial advice, and noted that much of this advice was provided by sole traders or small partnerships which incurred significant administrative costs and hassle in running their business. So Schwab offered to cut their transaction costs too, by using its systems to let them do their invoices, orders and monthly statements at a much lower cost. This was a stroke of genius. Previously, Schwab had been seen as an enemy by these brokers. Now, with its offer of lower transaction costs, it recruited them as allies – and in return they channelled a growing proportion of their business through its systems.

Schwab's next move tackled customer transaction costs yet again. Increasingly sophisticated investors were buying into a range of mutual funds, and swapping assets among them. But each swap was a time consuming and costly task – involving many different phone calls and letters to the fund they were moving funds from, and the fund they were moving funds to. So Schwab created OneSource, which allowed its customers access to any fund through one phone call – to Schwab. And Schwab assembled all the information about all the customers' investments into one statement.

Just as Schwab's move into broker services turned the old market upside down, turning enemies into friends, so OneSource did the same with the mutual fund market. Mutual funds had been incurring substantial marketing costs to reach potential investors through traditional marketing methods. Now they could access key customers with one single, simple route. This substantially cut their own transaction costs – so much so that they were willing to waive the transaction fees they traditionally charged their customers. Schwab thereby managed to transfer the cost of acquiring mutual funds from the customer to the fund, thereby reducing its own customers' transaction costs even further. In other words, Schwab used its focus on customer transaction costs to turn the industry upside down.

Why most e-tailers will fail

If Charles Schwab is an example of how to succeed in tackling customer purchasing costs, e-tailing is usually an example of how not to. Most e-tailers are doomed to fail because they fall between two different sets of stools: the trade-off between information processing efficiencies and matter processing efficiencies; and the difference between being a retailer (i.e. a seller) and acting as a buying agent.

Traditional retail economics revolve around the costs and complexities of matter handling: moving physical bits of stock through the supply chain and displaying them in hugely expensive prime-site retailing locations. Shoppers also incur significant matter processing costs: the costs of carrying themselves to the shop, and carrying themselves and the stuff they've purchased back home again.

The promise of e-tailing is that it can dispense with large tranches of these costs. By displaying inventory on a website, the e-tailer doesn't need to invest in prime-site retail outlets, and the consumer doesn't have to travel to the store to inspect the produce. The retailer – for whom ranging decisions were once tightly limited by available shelf space – can now expand the range of products he offers. Likewise the shopper's search and comparison costs also plummet. Clicking one's way through a website – or between websites – is far less time consuming than traipsing from physical store to physical store.

> *As long as the Internet is simply used to do old things – like retailing – better, its real potential will be stifled.*

It should be a win-win, in other words. But there's still the little matter of getting the goods from the supplier to the customer. In the grocery industry, for example, consumers traditionally took on the cost of picking items off shelves, assembling them into shopping baskets and carrying them to their front doors. The Internet grocer who brings such pre-assembled shopping baskets to the door takes on all these costs for himself. And the extra costs and complexity he incurs in doing this can easily gobble up any money he saves from displaying inventory on the Net. Unlike e-banking, where total transaction costs are reduced, most e-tailing simply ends up squeezing the economic balloon: shifting the same basic set of costs from one party to another.

Of course, this trade-off between information processing savings and extra fulfilment costs depends on a whole range of factors such as order value, order frequency, perishability, size (as well as touchy-feely factors such as trying on a pair of shoes). But there's another factor holding e-tailers back, and that's their failure to seize the potential of the Net to go beyond selling and become the consumer's agent.

Unlike a buying agent, an e-tailer is not in business to help the buyer search for the best possible product at the lowest possible price. The consumer still has to incur such costs. And by replicating the fundamentals of shopping on the Web, rather than rethinking the whole process of shopping, the e-tailer passes by the opportunity of really reengineering the way customers and suppliers connect.

Here's just one example. If I buy a jar of coffee in a shop, I have to repeat the process (say) once every three weeks. Every time I run out of coffee I have to go shopping for some more: do a new search, compare competing offers, make a choice, make a payment, and so on. Coffee powder sellers, knowing that I will be back in the market in three weeks' time, need to organize their selling activities as a non-stop attempt to get me to switch brand preference.

How much time and money could be saved on both sides if I negotiated an annual supply contract instead? How much would the supplier be prepared to pay me for the privilege of pushing his brand rivals out of the picture for the next twelve months, and for the consequent chance to cut back on promotional, advertising and other marketing activities? How much more efficient would this be, if an agent conducted these negotiations on behalf of, say, 5000 customers – or 5 million? How much more efficient could the process become if the agent did the same for a whole range of frequently purchased, routine replenishment items? How much more could he improve the deal if he structured the negotiations along the lines of a reverse auction, whereby each major supplier bids for the contract? And how much more efficient would the fulfilment side be if it could be organized around the planned, regular replenishment of these routine items?

Like Charles Schwab, an agent pursuing these opportunities would be seizing on the real potential to cut transaction costs and revolutionize an industry along the way. An e-tailer, on the other hand, is just a shopless shop. That's the trouble with e-tailing. It's a halfway house revolution. Like jumping halfway across a river it often ends up being worse than not having tried at all.

The difference between a shopless shop and a true buying agent is rather like the difference between a horseless carriage and a motor car. When the internal combustion engine was first invented, the first car makers saw themselves as making horseless carriages. They concerned themselves with replacing the horse with an engine, and kept everything else pretty much intact. As long as they did this, the motor car remained firmly stuck on the margins of transport. A plaything of the rich, a novelty. The reason was simple. The horse and carriage industry was a craft industry: you could never achieve economies of scale by trying to mass produce horses. But the only way to really unleash the potential of the internal combustion engine was by mass producing it.

As long as the engine was seen simply as a substitute for a horse, the horseless carriage went nowhere. As soon as it was seen as the prototype of a new business model – mass production – then its cost began to plummet and its value began to soar.

The same goes for the Internet. As long as it is simply used to do old things – like retailing – more efficiently, its true potential will be stifled. Only when it is used to create entirely new business models – which generate new economies of scale in the aggregation of information from and about consumers to revolutionize transaction costs for buyer and seller alike, will its full potential be unleashed. Tackling customer purchasing costs is just the first step. The real opportunities only become obvious when the burdensome costs of a 'push' stimulus-response marketing system are lifted.

reverse the flow

> In unpredictable markets, customers themselves become unreliable predictors of their future needs. Premiums now flow to those who sense early and accurately what their customers currently want and who respond in real time.
>
> Stephen Haeckel[1]
>
> Let the customer pull the product from you, as needed, rather than pushing products, often unwanted, onto the customer.
>
> James Womack and Dan Jones[2]
>
> Your customer will speak, and you will listen. Your customer will ask, and you will both make, together.
>
> Don Peppers and Martha Rogers[3]

FROM PUSH TO PULL

In many ways Right Side Up marketing is the mirror image of the seller-centric marketing we were used to:

- Under the old model 'the consumer' acted as the last point of the supply chain. Under the emerging model he is the first link in a demand chain.
- Under the old model he was a passive target of marketing activity. Under the new model he is an active specifier.
- Under the old model marketing was all about developing the right stimuli to provoke the right responses in terms of changed behaviour. Under the new model, sense-and-respond takes the place of stimulus-response: elicit the right stimuli from the client in order to give the right response.
- Under the old model the consumer was merely a unit of demand, a source of cash in exchange for goods or services. Under the new model, it is information – stimuli – gleaned direct from the consumer that drives the whole system.

The benefits of reversing the flow in this way can be massive. Dell has already become the classic example of the benefits of moving from push to pull marketing systems.

For Dell, the benefits include:

- Minimizing (even eliminating) inventory (of components in factories and of stock with dealers and distributors). Capital tied up in such inventory eats up cash and reduces return on assets.
- Access to customer information: the transaction is 'owned' by the manufacturer not the distributor.
- Speed and market awareness: the company is alerted to changes in market conditions and customer requirements much sooner than traditional 'push' operators where these signals are muffled by weeks, or even months, of inventory in the distribution pipeline.
- Lower distribution costs: particularly those arising from dealer commission and dealer support.
- Lower marketing costs: a higher degree of the organization's marketing is conducted through existing relationships, rather than having to 'reacquire' each customer after each transaction.
- Improved customer relationships, as the salesman takes on an advisory, rather than 'selling' role, guiding the customer to the best way to meet his specification within his price range.
- Increased customer loyalty, as these advantages are translated into lower prices for more appropriate, tailored products.

By acting on the instruction of the customer, rather than trying to sell something it has already made, Dell has been able to trump its competitors on two counts. First, it has a better offer. It is able to match what it makes to what its customers want, in ways that other suppliers cannot. Second, it also has a cheaper offer, because of the costs it is able to strip out of the system.

As CEO Michael Dell remarks:

> By developing and building to order only the systems that our customers wanted when they wanted them, we were able to virtually eliminate the excess cost tied into buying too many components, having to store them, and then selling the surplus at a loss. This enabled us to speed up the process of configuring and delivering our products, saving us time and allowing us to pass on the savings to our customers.[4]

The win for Dell, of course, is that it can still generate healthy margins and rapidly grow within this system.

The reverse in flow is now being applied to some degree, in some aspect of operations, in virtually every industry. Fashion retailers such as Hennes & Mauritz, Gap, Benetton and Zara, for example, have forged ahead of their rivals by building effective sense-and-respond manufacturing and replenishment systems: systems that let them track changes in fashion as close to real-time as possible, and which allow new items to be designed and shipped in weeks. Result: a far greater ability to ride high on new fashions when they arise, and far fewer write downs on stock which is still unsold at the end of the season: the perennial danger of relying on forecasts.

In the car industry players like Ford now hope to have mass-scale built-to-order systems operational within a few years. The potential savings are almost unthinkably huge. In the US, at any one time, around $60 billion of finished vehicle inventory is stuck waiting in parking lots somewhere within the system: about sixty-four days' worth of supply. Moving to pull mode could see these lead times plummet to ten days or less, freeing up billions of dollars worth of cash. And that's not counting the customer satisfaction benefits of being able to order and buy the car you want, and the marketing cost savings of not having to push cars that people don't want to buy.[5]

Meanwhile in financial services, banks like First Direct broke the mould by making its services available to customers when they wanted it (twenty-four hours a day), where they wanted it (at the end of a phone line), rather than expecting them to bank when and where the banks found convenient. Now, with the boom of Internet banking and other financial services, such 'reverse the flow' approaches, which put the customer in charge, look like becoming the norm. And, as information processing costs fall, the potential of 'reverse the flow' approaches reach further and further into areas once strictly reserved for standard, mass produced items such as pizzas or P&G's Reflect.com experiment.

But there is a snag with this 'direct' explicit model for reversing the flow. It assumes that the buyer and seller have a close, direct relationship where information can quickly, easily and readily flow between the two sides, and where the customer is prepared to invest the time and effort in making this relationship work. For a high ticket item like a computer or a car this may be the case. But what about other sectors, where there are simply too many suppliers of low ticket items, and where investing time and effort in a direct relationship is unlikely to reap worthwhile rewards?

Or where the incremental benefit in customizing the product or service doesn't justify the extra costs? It's not realistic, for example, for Coca-Cola to start customizing what goes into each can depending on the whim of each individual consumer.

FROM STIMULUS-RESPONSE TO SENSE-AND-RESPOND

Seeing the consumer as the specifier – at the beginning of a demand chain rather than a passive 'consumer' at the end of a supply chain – can make it all seem like hard work. It takes a lot of time and attention to keep saying, 'This is how I want it,' and often people may simply not be bothered: inertia is one of the most powerful forces in marketing.

But not all sense-and-respond systems rely on hyperactive consumers. One of the most powerful forms of agent is the one consumers delegate detailed decision making to. For example, the consumer might say to his agent, 'Please make sure that my savings earn the highest possible interest rate within these risk limits. As long as you do that for me (say, by reinvesting them every night in the highest yielding overnight fund) I don't want to know anything except how much money you have made for me over the last six months.' Or he might say, 'Please keep me supplied with household goods in these categories. As long as they are good quality, and are replenished regularly, I don't really care what brand you choose.'

In this way, the consumer can actually reduce his input, while still acting as the beginning of a demand chain. Also, some sophisticated sense-and-respond marketers may work by responding to implied, rather than explicit, demand signals. For example, instead of eliciting an order from the customer and then acting upon it, retailers increasingly use scanning data to sense what consumers are 'saying' they want from their purchases, and responding to these shifts in demand as quickly as possible. As Stephan Haeckel, Director of Strategic Studies at IBM's Advanced Business Institute, explains, a sense-and-respond mode of operation is where it is the organization's behaviour that is driven by customers' stimuli: 'by current customer requests – tacit as well as articulated – rather than by firm-forward plans to make and sell offerings'.[6]

> *One of the most powerful forms of agent is the one consumers delegate detailed decisions to.*

Retail systems of a decade or two ago were based upon manufacturers pushing stock at retailers, and encouraging them to take more through devices such as volume discounts. Increasingly retailers are sending orders to suppliers based upon what was sold in the stores over, say, the past twenty-four hours. Wal-Mart was the pioneer here. It has invented an implicit pull mechanism based upon highly sophisticated information systems and fast and flexible logistics systems. Instead of buying products from manufacturers and then trying to sell them – a classic push approach – it is moving towards a situation where it only sources what sells. Wal-Mart estimates that in 1987 only 26 per cent of in-store replenishment decisions were driven by customers, as expressed by their behaviour at the checkout. The vast majority were driven either by traditional producer promotional activity or by internal department manager decisions. Already by 1996, 90 per cent of replenishment decisions were driven directly by consumers.

But what started out as a cost-cutting, efficient replenishment exercise has led to some profound changes in marketing theory and practice. Policies such as everyday low pricing, for example, are designed to minimize the 'noise' (and incremental supply chain costs) created by traditional stimulus-response marketing activities such as promotions. And retailers' attitudes towards learning and market research has begun to change. As one director of a major UK retail chain admitted: 'We have given up trying to understand our customers. And that's helping us cut a lot of complexity from our business.' The board member was not saying that understanding customers is a waste of time and money. He was saying that it is sometimes better to understand customers by sensing what they do and responding to these actions, rather than spending an awful lot of time and money constructing elaborate theories about customer motivations, so that equally complex marketing strategies can be developed to change these motivations in the hope of altering customers' behaviour.

Manufacturers increasingly realize that intensive stimulus-response marketing activities such as promotions no longer work. The opportunity, however, is to also embrace a sense-and-respond mode of operation and reconfigure production systems, to synchronize production runs as closely as possible to demand, rather than retaining old-style batch-and-queue systems along with high levels of buffer stock, lying around wasting money in warehouses. Synchronized production is one of the key 'improvement concepts' within the grocery industry's efficient consumer response initiative.[7]

FROM JUST IN CASE TO JUST IN TIME

Many of these ideas were first pioneered a long time ago in a completely different environment: in the business-to-business relationships between Japanese car component suppliers and car assemblers such as Toyota. But their application to the consumer-facing industries becomes more apparent every day. Again and again, we find the same outcome: consumer pull is not only better than 'push', it's also cheaper.

But it can also require massive operational and infrastructure changes – even bigger, perhaps, than those which revolutionized the car industry's supply chains and business relationships.

Take a simple example: the food industry. We've already seen the potential difference between old and new infrastructure with our discussion of traditional mass food production and retailing versus the home delivery pizza parlour. The characteristics of these two types of business couldn't be more different. The first, producer-push model is remote in terms of both time and distance. The factory could be hundreds of miles away, the store a car journey away. The product spends an awful lot of time passing through the supply chain as inventory: from factory to warehouse, from warehouse to store, from store to kitchen.

The model is also remote from the consumer perspective. Going shopping is a planned activity. There is a gap in time between the decision to have a pizza and actually eating one. The producers' marketing mirrors this gap between desire and fulfilment. Marketing communications focus on creating a place for the brand in the consumer's mind – a memory and set of associations which lie dormant until the consumer is in the shop, making a purchase decision, at which point they (hopefully) get triggered into life to influence that decision.

This old model is also highly centralized and highly dependent upon capital investment, in factories, in logistics systems, in stores. Because of this high up-front investment, both the manufacturer and the retailer are driven by the need to realize economies of scale. The one saving grace: all these costs create high barriers to entry.

The pizza parlour, on the other hand, is extremely close in both time and distance. The gap between desire and fulfilment is probably less than half an hour and half a mile. The model is also highly decentralized: one 'factory-cum-shop' combined, on virtually every city street corner. Speed and flexibility replace economies of scale as key drivers: it is the ability to respond to customers with what they want, when they want it, that's the key to success. And barriers to entry are very low. In place of traditional stimulus-response driven systems, we are moving towards what Martin Christopher,

Professor of Marketing and Logistics at Cranfield School of Management, calls 'marketing logistics'. Here, the aim is to create 'the responsive organization [where] the critical interface [is] between the market place and the organization seeking to satisfy customer requirements'.[8]

Increasingly, the responsive organization is an organization that responds to its environment in real-time. Take Internet banking. It is, says McKenna 'real-time experience . . . created from self-service and self-satisfaction by customers. It is instant response. Real-time occurs when time and distance vanish, when action and response are simultaneous . . .[it] is characterized by the shortest possible lapse between idea and action; between initiation and result.'[9]

FROM RIGID TO FLEXIBLE

The challenge to the traditional marketing mindset – and processes and tools – can be profound. The old model has built-in time lags between clearly differentiated functions and processes conducted by different sets of people. First, there is market research and analysis. Then there is product development, using the insights gleaned from that market research. Then there is the product launch: communication of the product's benefits through the media. Then there is the product purchase, in the shop.

The emergence of two-way flows of information begin to blur all those boundaries, of time, function and process. For a business whose main interaction with customers is from the call centre or Internet, market research can be conducted in real time. This necessitates a real-time response. Marketing ceases to be about using marketing communications to get customers to do the things you want them to do; it is about sensing what the customer wants now, and responding to that expressed need, now.

As McKenna points out, 'this flips the whole model'. The emerging model is about access and presence, where 'I get a lot of information so I can respond to what it is you are demanding of me: trying to figure out what you want, where you want it, and when you want it . . . Instead of trying to fruitlessly predict the future course of a competitive or market trend, customer behaviour or demand, managers should be trying to find and deploy the tools that will enable them, in some sense, to be ever-present, vigilant, and fully prepared in the brave new marketplace where information and knowledge are ceaselessly exchanged.'[10]

The classic metaphor of the industrial age is the production line: amazingly efficient at producing things, but a completely senseless, inflexible machine. The organization that this production line is a part of is a command and control organization: working to carefully laid plans, which are made long in advance. Its brand managers are inveterate control freaks, wanting dictatorial powers over every aspect of their brand's existence: its performance attributes, its packaging (down to the slightest change in colour), its positioning, its personality, the tone and voice and content of its advertising, and so on.

Reversing the flow to work in real time involves bringing the old industrial age machine 'alive'; developing a nervous system for it made up of real-time information flows between various parts of the organization and, crucially, between it and its customers. Filling the information hole at the heart of the old system is rather akin to giving it senses. Just as we humans take in information from our environment in the form of senses like sight, hearing, touch and smell, the successful marketing organization of tomorrow needs to build its own real-time senses.

For some organizations, like Dell, the main sensory mechanism is the website, which customers interact with, sucking information from, placing orders on, channelling queries by, and so on. For others, like Wal-Mart, it may be scanning-based information on transactions. But both need to be highly sensitive, and able to work as close as possible to real time. As *Wired* founder Kevin Kelly notes, 'With few exceptions, nature reacts in real time. With few exceptions, business must increasingly react in real time.'[11]

The organization also needs to be able to respond to changes in that environment in real time – and to reconstruct that machine to give it reflex-style flexibility; the ability to act on the messages sent by those sensory systems. As Jan Andreae, President of Dutch grocery retailer Albert Heijn, told the first European Efficient Consumer Response grocery industry conference in Geneva in 1995, moving from push to pull means accepting that 'consumers' desires should not just influence our business decisions – they should direct our business operations . . . That is a frightening concept, because it means giving the consumer real control, a real impact on stocking, delivery, supply, category management – every aspect of our business.'[12]

BEYOND ARISTOTELIAN MARKETING

What is noticeable about these shifts is that they emanate from disciplines such as IT, supply chain management and logistics rather than advertising or brand management.

In fact, the traditional strongholds of marketing are now proving to be the most backward: the areas most resistant to new ideas and to change. That's not only because change is operationally difficult. It's because it represents a deep philosophical shift too.

By its very nature, the old system bred a 'push' mentality. It bred Aristotelian marketers. Aristotle believed that the natural state of a body is to be at rest. So to explain the ceaseless motion he saw around him, he had to invent a prime mover who ceaselessly moved things around. At root, that's how marketers see themselves: as the prime movers of markets, having to work ceaselessly to stimulate the market into motion, for fear that otherwise it would wind down to a state of inertia.

Stimulus-response marketing adds more cost and complexity than value for customers.

When Newton came along, however, he said the opposite. The natural state of affairs is for things to be in motion. And they are only slowed down or stopped by an opposing force, such as friction. The pull marketer is an instinctive Newtonian, believing that real markets naturally generate demand. If demand has to be continually stimulated, it is not a real market.

The real marketing challenge is not so much to 'create' demand, in other words, but to respond to it. Aristotelian marketers, on the other hand, tend to regard their Newtonian peers with horror. For them, the Newtonian prescription for the way forward looks grey, dull and lifeless. As ceaselessly active prime movers, Aristotelian marketers are never satisfied with their marketing budgets: their natural instinct is 'the bigger the stimulus, the bigger the response' (tempered, of course, by scrupulous scientific investigation into which stimuli are effective, and which are not). Yet as we've seen, as often as not, the stimulus rarely actually adds value for the customer. It simply adds cost and complexity.

SENSE-AND-RESPOND MARKETING COMMUNICATIONS

We've already discussed the gut-wrenching implications of 'Newtonian' marketing: it ends with the question: 'would your customers buy your marketing?' Either your marketing adds value as a service to the customer in its own right, or it's an unnecessary added cost and burden, just waiting to be stripped away. And one way of making sure this happens is by letting the customer take the driving seat. As Regis McKenna comments: 'The new marketing model reflects a shift from monologue to dialogue in dealings with customers. The result is a reversal of traditional consumer and producer roles, with the consumer dictating exactly how he or she would like to be served.'[13]

Let the consumer dictate exactly how he or she would like to be served in terms of marketing communication? Until very recently such a notion would have seemed absurd. The way information was gathered and distributed, via TV programmes and newspapers, for example, simply did not allow for such a possibility. But now, thanks to new technologies, that's changing.

Take Strategy.com. It promises to recast the way we think about media. Launched by US software firm MicroStrategy in July 1999, it seizes on the opportunities created by digitalization to create an entirely different media offering. It uses digital distribution channels only – such as the Internet, telephone or wireless device – to offer subscribers only the information they want, when they want it, how they want it. It allows users to specify, for example, that they want news about shares relating to Marks & Spencer, but not Tesco. And they can specify even further: to receive a message if the M&S share price falls below price X or rises above price Y.

Starting with such investment-related services for the financial community, Strategy.com is quickly spreading its information – providing wings from finance to sport, news, traffic and the weather – and eventually on to around thirty specialist channels. For example, its traffic services allow users to specify that it contact them, by phone, every day at 7 a.m. to alert them of any traffic jams on particular roads; or to download to their PC information about the weather in Madras, India – the destination for their business trip or holiday tomorrow.

The contrast with traditional media is absolute. Traditional media operates on a producer-push model: the media owner and its agents decide what content to distribute, and when to distribute it. Strategy.com lets the user decide not only what information he wants but also when and how he will receive it.

And there is no reason why this should not apply as much to advertising as it does to news. Using a communications infrastructure such as that being created by Strategy.com, consumers will be able to specify which advertising messages they want to receive, instead of being broadcast advertising messages whether they like them or not. For example, if a consumer wants to buy a car, he can announce that he would like to receive advertising messages about, say, saloon cars in this particular price bracket. The fact that he has made this announcement makes him extremely valuable to advertisers, who now have the chance to communicate only to those individuals with an explicit, declared interest in their product. For the consumer, this turns advertising from a nuisance into a service.

We have already discussed this principle of consumer-specified marketing communications in the context of the infomediary. Players such as Strategy.com are creating the infrastructure to make this principle a reality: to reverse the flow of marketing communications along with that of production and distribution.

THINGS FALL INTO PLACE

With technologies such as this all the pieces of the jigsaw begin to fall into place. Just as the industrial age system could not work without mass production *and* mass distribution *and* mass advertising – they all reinforced each other – so Right Side Up marketing only begins to gel when the 'push to pull' can be applied to marketing *and* distribution *and* production.

And once again, the agent emerges as the linchpin, because it is through agents that the fuel of the whole process – information from consumers in both individual and aggregated form – is gathered, stored, analysed and passed on in useful, efficient ways. As long as there is no institution capable of taking on this information-aggregating role, then the move from push to pull will always be limited to exceptions such as Dell. But with the emergence of a new breed of businesses capable of taking on this role (some new, some evolved from industrial age business forms such as retailers) Right Side Up marketing can begin, at last, to work as a system: complete, integrated, with critical mass.

Sense-and-respond business models are not a universal panacea, however. Every sector will need to negotiate a new division of marketing labour between buyer, seller and agent; a new 'marketing mix'. Few, if any, sectors are naturally all 'push' or all 'pull'. Most will display a complex mix of both. In groceries, for example, a significant driving force behind the growth of online ordering is a consumer desire to automate routine replenishment chores. Yet, at the same time, consumers want to be stimulated with new ideas for meals: new recipes, new ingredients, and so on. A degree of marketing 'push' in these areas is therefore positively welcomed.

Likewise for some kinds of business, a sense-and-respond approach may be wholly inappropriate. In a whole range of intellectual property-driven businesses, from pharmaceuticals to movies, for example, what consumers and customers are looking for from providers is creativity, imagination and innovation: things they didn't know they wanted; that they hadn't conceived of before. Sense-response mechanisms are not suited to the selling of imagination.

Likewise, passion brands are almost by definition not sense-and-respond brands. They are inside-out brands, driven by what ignites members' and supporters' enthusiasm to promote that enthusiasm. To that degree, they are inherent 'push' marketers. In other sectors, such as fashion and luxury goods, stimulus-response marketing communications are part of the product: a good deal of what the consumer 'buys' is what the advertising says about himself.

But these caveats do not alter the fundamental message. Just as sellers will continue to 'do' marketing within a buyer-centric marketing system, so stimulus-response activities will remain within a system whose core defining characteristic is no longer the push of top-down information from seller to buyer, but the pull of information from buyer to seller.

Reversing the flow helps both buyers and sellers to cut waste, costs and complexity, to streamline processes and improve their relationships. It enables customers to access better products and services at lower cost. And it helps supplying organizations to improve responses and speed, and their ability to learn, while boosting (or at least preserving) their margins. But the way we have discussed the shift so far makes it sound like a technical matter. That's often how the principles of reversing the flow first start being applied – as a cost-cutting technicality in certain business-to-business contexts (such as streamlining stock control and order processing in the car industry). This is not how it ends up.

These technicalities end up as a critical ingredient of the Right Side Up marketing revolution – as enabling technologies. But no matter how right the technologies are, if they are applied within the wrong relationships very little will happen. And while many of the initial win-wins unleashed by this shift arise simply from the benefits of dismantling and superseding the costly inefficiencies and rigidities of the old system, in the long-term, that's not enough to sustain the new system; to propel it forwards. It needs its own virtuous circles. The nature of these new virtuous circles has been hinted at in our discussion of the examples of Dell and Wal-Mart. The secret lies in waking the sleeping giant of wealth creation: 'the consumer'. And as we shall see, the only way to do this is to move beyond industrial age 'Buy Me' approaches to marketing, to embrace 'Join Me!'

think 'join me!'

> *The largest productivity gains of the next decade will come from companies that demolish the demarcation line between consumption and production.*
>
> Charles Leadbeater[1]

> *'Buyer' and 'seller' just aren't descriptive enough of what's really going on. What we need to talk about instead is mutual exchange ... a web of economic, information and emotional exchange.*
>
> Stan Davis and Christopher Meyer[2]

> *1:1 marketing is collaborative, rather than adversarial. Collaborative marketing occurs when you listen as the customer speaks, and when you invite the customer to participate in actually making the product, before asking the customer to take it.*
>
> Don Pepper and Martha Rogers[3]

THE SLEEPING GIANT OF WEALTH CREATION

Industrial age marketing invented the notion of the consumer as a unit of demand for sellers' offerings – as a source of money for sellers. But people are not only a source of money for sellers. They invest all manner of things – time, attention, energy, information, communications and emotional commitment – in their efforts to produce the outcomes they want in their lives. If we view wealth in this broader sense – of what people invest, create and value in their lives – we can see that 'the consumer' is a massively important (and almost completely ignored) engine of wealth creation.

If we recognize the consumer's ability to invest resources other than money – such as time, information and emotional energy – it becomes clear that industrial age marketers are singularly unable to tap these resources. Their obsessive focus on exchanging money for goods and services – on 'the market' – excludes all other forms of exchange: all the other ways or dimensions in which value might be traded.

One of the many clichés mouthed by executives of seller-centric firms is that 'the customer is our greatest asset'. What they really mean is that the customer's *money* is their greatest asset, if they can get their hands on it. Once we look at value from a buyer-centric point of view, however, we can easily see that money is just one of many assets consumers invest in their lives.

Solution agents recognize the importance of these resources by focusing on the creation of value 'in my life', rather than merely bringing the ingredients of this value to market. By doing this, they pave the way for many new dimensions of exchange: of information, time and emotional commitment. The bottom line is that any organization – whether seller or agent – that fails to trade with the consumer along these new dimensions fails to tap additional resources that are fast becoming the key to competitive edge.

There is only one problem. Unlike the typical natural resources of the industrial age which could be mined, felled, reaped or sucked out of the ground at will, the new natural resources, consumers, have minds of their own. Consumers are alive. Conscious. Intelligent. So, this resource, unlike the others, cannot be extracted. It has to be *volunteered*. When prospectors come sniffing around looking for a way to tap this resource, the consumer wants to know 'what's in it for me?'. And the prospector has to have a very good answer: an answer good enough to persuade the consumer to 'Join Me!'.

The new cornucopia

Actually, the section heading above is wrong. It's a cornucopia all right. But it's not really new. It is as old as the hills. But previously the consumer's contribution to value creation has been dispersed, unaccounted for, taken for granted, overlooked and condescended to. Every day, millions of consumers spend time, money and effort searching for information about the goods and services they want, trying to find them, make decisions about them, pay for them, carry them to where they want them, work on them, assemble them into the solutions they want, planning and organizing when and how they are going to do all these things, and so on.

In modern firms, where these tasks are organized on a mass scale, we have special terms to describe these functions: such as purchasing or buying, manufacturing or operations, marketing communications, accounting, logistics and general management. Every activity and cost is pored over in great detail. Academics and management consultants study every example of best practice. People follow careers in professional 'functional specialisms' which focus on just one discipline.

We've seen how, by tackling these tasks in an organized and professional manner for consumers, solution agents open up new vistas of possible value creation. Much of this value is unleashed by crafting more productive divisions of labour between supplier and consumer. These divisions of labour are so deeply entrenched in the old system they they have become almost invisible. Consumers and marketers alike simply take them for granted.

This is how Priceline.com founder Jay Walker describes them:

> An absorbed cost is when I drive to the store and use my own gas, labour and car depreciation. I absorb that cost. When UPS, on the other hand, has to drive in the other direction to my house, it's an explicit cost – gas, Teamsters, and depreciation. Guess what? None of those things scale. Not only that, they now have to be, explicitly stated in the transaction, shipping and handling costs.[4]

What would retailing look like, if consumers charged retailers for their absorbed costs? What would advertising and marketing communications look like if consumers charged for their time and attention costs? Alternatively, how much are consumers prepared to pay for somebody to do this work for them – as in the home delivery example? Creating value 'in my life' is all about renegotiating these divisions of labour, thereby opening up rich new dimensions of exchange. Let's look a little closer at the resources the consumer can, and does, bring to the party.

Information

Information from and about consumers is filling the information hole at the heart of industrial age marketing, and driving its top-to-toe reengineering. But there's more. Consumers and customers can volunteer a wide range of information, including personal data, observations and comments, suggestions, complaints and insights, all of which are potentially invaluable to companies, especially if their competitors are denied access to this information. It's not only about the slug trail.

> *Traditional marketing all but ignores the time, effort and emotional energy consumers invest in their lives.*

Sandra Vandermerwe underlines the potential value of information from an 'installed customer base' by listing the ways they can contribute. These include: asking for advice (not necessarily related to your product or service), sharing confidential information, inviting you to be involved in important meetings, asking you to solve problems, accepting your ideas and advice, giving positive (and negative) feedback, giving information on competitive offerings, discussing future plans, discussing options rather than discounts, relying on expert contacts referred to you, involving you early in decision making, and even allowing you to take decisions for them. Above all, she says, 'they want you to succeed', which is perhaps the biggest prize of all.[5]

This input of information becomes even more important in fast moving markets, as Stephan Haeckel points out:

Increasing information intensity breeds smarter customers and competitors, whose behaviour becomes less predictable as they interact with one another more rapidly and frequently ... As a result the fundamental transaction of the information age becomes an exchange of information about value (from the customer) for delivery of value (from the firm). The customer becomes the indispensable source of information about value as well as the final arbiter of whether or not it has been delivered.[6]

Money
The money consumers typically pay for items in a shop is typically a lot less than the full financial costs they incur. For example, a consumer may spend additional money on information about 'best buys' or travelling to and from a shop.

Work
Consumers and customers routinely work hard to realize the value of the products and services they purchase. Ikea customers take on the task of assembling their furniture. Internet banking customers do the transaction processing for their bank, for free. When customers input transactions on an online banking service they do work that was once done by paid staff.

Expertise
Consumers have to invest in their own expertise before they can get the full value out of most offers. Car companies could not survive if consumers did not invest large amounts of time and money in learning how to drive. Software companies depend upon users learning how to use their software. Expert customers (while often the most challenging) tend to be the most valuable. A wine connoisseur who has invested many years in developing his or her knowledge of wines will expect more of a wine merchant than a novice but – if satisfied – will also buy a lot more, at higher prices.

Emotion
Consumers invest enormous amounts of emotional energy – stress, angst, enthusiasm and joy – in searching for, acquiring and using the products and services they buy. The degree of this investment separates mega-brands from also-rans.

Communication

Consumers have always talked about products and services to each other. 'Word of mouth' has always existed as a factor in communication. But now, with the Internet acting as a megaphone of customer-to-customer communication, with agents such as epinions.com actively organizing this channel, and with people trusting independent third party information more than they trust selling information, the willingness (or not) of the consumer to act as a mouthpiece or ambassador for a brand can be crucial.

Attention

When the scarcest resource is attention, when consumers pay attention to a piece of marketing communication they are investing a valuable asset. When a customer makes a complaint or suggestion he is investing time, attention and information into his relationship with the organization. A customer opting for 'exit' rather than 'voice' is choosing not to make such an investment.

Time

All the above activities take up precious time which – along with attention – is one of the most valuable resources in the information age.

Resource and infrastructure

Consumers often invest in resources which sellers take for granted. Consumers use their own cars to carry shopping, their own PCs to surf the Internet, their own cookers to cook food brands, their own washing machines to use washing powder brands. They use their own electricity and phone bills to run their computers and TVs, and so on. The importance of these investments to marketers often only becomes apparent when a market is in its early stages: take the way that the early growth of the Internet was hampered by the fact that few consumers owned PC's, or the way the development of consumer goods markets in many countries is prevented because consumers do not have access to utilities and home appliances.

Consumers don't only consume, therefore. They invest every resource that companies invest to create value and go to market. They help produce value from products and services. And when all these potential contributions are taken into account, 'the consumer' should be acknowledged as the sleeping giant of modern wealth creation.

CREATING WEALTH TOGETHER

Companies that win access to this hugely powerful resource stand to gain an almost unbeatable competitive edge. The race is now on – among both new agents and traditional seller-centric brands – to win access to as much of this resource as possible. 'Join Me!' marketers, for example, are going out of their way to recruit their customers as information and insight partners: to 'turn our customers into teachers', as Michael Dell puts it. 'Our best customers aren't necessarily the ones that are the largest, the ones that buy the most from us, or the ones that require little help or service,' he says. 'Our best customers are those we learn the most from.'[7]

'The best way we've found to stay in tune with our customers and keep them happy is to engage them in a cooperative mutually beneficial dialogue,' he adds. 'The key is the dialogue – not just talking at, or talking to, your customers but talking with them – and really listening to what they have to say.' The benefits of these *voluntary* inputs of information can be massive: Dell built a multimillion dollar business around pre-installing customers' proprietary software in its factories, for example. The suggestion came from just one customer (BP) which was fed up with the cost and hassle of installing the software after the computers were delivered.[8]

Sophisticated companies have long sought to involve customers in beta-testing their new products. Kevin Kelly tells the story of Microsoft, which sent out 350,000 beta-tests of Windows 98. He estimates that, at a total cost of around $3000 per test, the net customer contribution to the development of Windows 98 was in the region of $1 billion – probably more than Microsoft itself invested.

When Amazon.com recommends books to a customer on the basis of previous purchases, a subtle process of information exchange is taking place. Call it 'co-training', if you want. The customer realizes he is training Amazon.com as to his tastes and preferences, while Amazon trains the customer to get most value from its services and infrastructure. Loyalty schemes and clubs are another common way companies are soliciting information from customers. Meanwhile, encouraging comments, suggestions and complaints either directly, or via infomediaries such as Planetfeedback.com, is rising up the corporate agenda. So are user groups, 'consumer boards' and customer forums, which are all becoming increasingly common. As Regis McKenna remarks:

> Enlightened companies invite customers to sit on advisory boards, work as partners in the refinement of specifications and testing, share benchmark data, and fine-tune the balance of supply and demand. Customers have an equal say in such areas as design and inventory management. Customers – like vendors – are treated like partners.[9]

Marketers are trying hard to use the information gleaned from each consumer's slug trail as the building blocks of relationships: targeting more relevant and timely messages and offers, anticipating customer needs, reacting faster to changes in the customer's circumstance, and so on. It's all potentially valuable stuff. But at a certain point, if you want to access really useful, proprietary information you have to ask for it. 'Join Me', rather than 'Buy Me' becomes a necessity.

Co-production

It is now a commonplace that consumers are an essential part of many brands' production, or value delivery, process. 'Customer self-service' is now a priority among corporations seeking to reduce their administration and transaction costs.

But this stretches far, in many directions. The whole burgeoning sector of customized products and services depends on the input of information from the customer. Says Kevin Kelly, 'the customer completes the product. He has got to be involved in the creation of the product.' Once again, Amazon.com has become a modern classic, with its customer contributed book reviews. Amazon.com's customers are, effectively, helping it to create its product, for free. The same goes for Internet service providers and their chat forums.[10]

All the new breeds of community of interest meanwhile depend on the member's contribution of time, information and enthusiasm if they are to flourish. This is true of virtually all forms of passion brand. Pressure groups, community groups, charities, religious groups and sports groups in particular all depend on volunteer activists, voluntary donations and a strong sense of emotional affiliation. The clear, cold calculation of economic benefit implied by the arm's length trading relationship spells death to them. Like the online communities of interest, auctions and buying clubs, they also depend on their 'customers' to help produce the product.

The football team's fans are as much a part of the football match as the players on the field. Just imagine a football match being played in a cold, silent, empty stadium. It would be a cold, empty product. What makes the match such an exciting experience is the oohs! and aahs!, the cheering and the booing – the energy and emotional input – of the fans. To a large degree, the fans' behaviour as well as that of the players creates the football experience.

But even examples like these underestimate the full potential of creating value together. The best examples (so far) come from business-to-business, but the fundamental principles are universal. In outsourcing, one firm welcomes another firm inside its operations to take on a particular task or function and the two work together to achieve a desired result such as total cost reduction. In partnership sourcing, supplier and customer join each other in an extremely close working relationship to minimize costs and drive innovation forward. Typically, successful partnerships involve high levels of information sharing and openness (including openness about costs and margins), a blurring of operational boundaries, a joint commitment to reduced costs, shared or joint new product development, and shared goals and performance targets. This theme of 'mutual process reengineering' is central to the future success of solution agents.[11]

Both outsourcing and partnership sourcing are cases of what Fred Wiersema calls 'customer intimacy', where 'customer satisfaction' is replaced by: 'down-in-the-trenches solidarity, the exchange of useful information, and the cooperative pursuit of results'.[12] You could say that this idea, applied to the consumer arena, sums up the consumer agent business model.

We haven't yet discussed the third main form of agent – the transformation guide or agent – in detail, but 'Join Me' is crucial here too. Transformation guides, as consultants Joseph Pine and James Gilmore call them, add value not by selling a product or even by providing a solution, but by helping their clients to achieve a valued goal: to be more successful, healthier, happier and wealthier. They are quintessential 'Join Me' businesses. The product in question is the customer himself, and as Pine and Gilmore point out, 'Transformations cannot be extracted, made, delivered, or even staged; they can only be guided. All transformations occur within the very being of the customer and so must be made by the customer.'[13]

Mutual process reengineering

But as well as being an important co-producer 'the consumer' can also be a crucial source of operational savings. In fact, one of the key benefits of the 'Join Me' approach is the mutual advantages that can flow when two parties work together to change what they do, to help each other reach common objectives in cheaper, quicker, simpler ways. Forget business process reengineering, *mutual* process reengineering is where it's at.

'Join Me' strategies recruit customers as 'investors', promising to maximise their returns.

Back in the 1960s, the self service revolution in retailing made shopping easier and quicker for the consumer. It also transformed the retailer's own cost base, because the retailer no longer had to employ shop assistants to pick items off the shelves for customers.

Then the superstore came along. It incorporated the idea of self-service but went on to make shopping even easier, simpler and cheaper. It helped consumers at many stages in their processes. It was a centralized information point – a place where you could search and find out about products you might want or need. Because it offered a much wider range of products, it tackled organization and coordination costs. You didn't have to traipse from store to store looking for an item; they were all there under one roof – the one-stop shop. By creating customer car parks it helped customers reduce time and hassle carrying their shopping on public transport or to distant car parks.

Centralizing shopping into large, out-of-town sites therefore offered big benefits to the consumer. But it also offered big benefits to the retailer. Larger out-of-town sites were not only cheaper to buy and build, but cheaper to replenish. This helped reduce supply chain costs, while simplifying range management and concentrating buying power. It was a glorious win-win, which made shopping easier, quicker and cheaper for the consumer, and made shop management simpler and cheaper for the retailer.

Likewise with customer service: web-based help pages which let consumers and customers access company data to solve problems for themselves can save companies vast amounts of money in terms of technical support and customer service personnel. As Michael Dell remarks, the use of Internet help pages to provide customers with the help they need 'frees our support technicians to work on higher-value activities. Between sales and support, we average five website visits for every phone call at a cost savings of $8 per call.'[14]

Cisco Systems goes so far as to make everything it knows that's wrong with its product publicly available via its website. Customers just tap direct into Cisco's systems to get the answers they need. Similarly, when Dell was faced with the need to make its computers more environmentally friendly, it redesigned its chassis to eliminate adhesives and paints as well as screws, nuts and bolts and replace them by clips and sliding trays. This made the chassis not only cheaper for Dell to make, but easier for customers to get inside to service. 'This made for time savings that translated into lower costs for both companies,' notes Dell. 'An idea that solves our customer's problem – and enhances our bottom line – is a genuine example of win-win for everyone.'[15]

Mutual process reengineering is, therefore, all about changing not what the customer *buys*, but what he *does*, to mutual benefit. Comments Sandra Vandermerwe, successful business leaders nowadays 'look beyond improving existing ideas, products and services. Instead they look for "new ways of doing things" ... [that] get results to customers'. As Kevin Kelly of *Wired* has noted, this may ultimately result in 'the company that is staffed only by customers'.[16]

Marketing partnerships

Call it what you will – 'viral' marketing, word of mouth, brand ambassadors – but the fact is, in the emerging environment customers are becoming brands' most important media channel. The acid test of whether a product or service passes muster is whether its own customers are prepared to vote for it. Indeed, in the emerging marketing environment, there is almost something suspect about a company that has to rely on paid-for advertising to promote its wares. Thus *Cluetrain Manifesto* co-author David Weinberger remarks that within the next five years the point will be reached where: 'delivering a marketing message will make your company look arrogant and manipulative. And it will look like you are hiding behind your message, afraid to engage in the real market conversation with real customers.'[17] Exaggerated? Perhaps. But it illustrates the trend. Any brand that fails to persuade its customers to join it in promoting it is failing on two crucial counts: credibility and cost effectiveness.

That's because customer recommendations are not only a lot more effective than most traditional media advertising, they are also a lot cheaper. When the UK's First Direct twenty-four hour telephone-based banking service first launched, for example, over 50 per cent of its new customers were generated by word of mouth recommendations. That meant its customer acquisition costs were close to half those of its competitors. Now, of course, marketers are increasingly trying to embed viral properties such as pass-it-on and member-get-member incentives in their marketing and promotional schemes. Through services like Hotmail.com consumers spread marketers' messages for them.

Permission marketing is yet another 'Join Me' approach. Real permission marketing (as opposed to promotions driven direct marketing) involves customers opting-in, joining the marketer's marketing programme. Opt-in e-mails, on pre-specified subject areas, are now causing great excitement in some circles. The bottom line: if the consumer is willing to actively join the marketing process – to volunteer to be marketed to – he is more likely to listen to the messages he receives. This is one of the areas where infomediaries promise to add enormous amounts of value.

Different forms of 'Join Me'

So what do the main forms of 'Join Me' strategy look like? The first is the 'learning relationship' as described by Don Peppers and Martha Rogers in their many books. In a *learning relationship*, more and more information is exchanged between buyer and seller over time, allowing both sides to teach each other how to add the most value, and get the most value, from the relationship. The more the customer tells the supplier about his needs and preferences, for example, the more closely the supplier can personalize and customize his offerings.

Learning relationships take two main forms. The first is between a customer and a valued specialist supplier – a supplier of a product or service that is important to that customer in terms of time, money and emotional investment. Dell's mass customization model of computer manufacturing is a good example. The second is a more general learning relationship where the marketer learns more and more about his client's general preferences over time, and seeks to meet and respond to them in an increasingly fine-tuned manner. This lends itself most clearly to the infomediary and buying agent, which source a growing range of information, goods or services for their clients.

A second key form of 'Join Me' relationship is one based on *'mutual process reengineering'* – the consumer equivalents of outsourcing and partnership sourcing programmes – where supplier and client work closely together to reduce mutual costs and add value. The various breeds of solution agent are perfectly poised to seize the high-ground here.

The third key form of the 'Join Me' relationship is the various species of *club and community* – which by definition are made up of members, rather than 'consumers'. Brands which manage to build communities around them may be one form: Harley-Davidson is a now classic example. Passion brands are another key form. They live and breathe members, supporters, fans, subscribers, believers and so on.

The key to all of them, however, is that the price of getting customers to 'Join Me' is rewarding them for the investment of their valuable assets, just as any investor would expect to earn a return on his investment. 'Join Me' therefore points towards a world where marketing strategies are designed to maximize the return on investment not only for the seller, *but for the customer too*. It's about constructing new (and better) forms of win-win. As relationship marketing expert Martin Christopher remarks: 'The emerging re-definition of marketing is about being primarily concerned with the establishing of mutually profitable relationships between the firm and its customers.'[18]

The hallmarks of the 'Join Me' enterprise

'Join Me' relationships are not necessarily nice, cosy things. Often they are the opposite – extremely tough. But they do allow more value to be created by facilitating exchange along many dimensions – money, information, time, mutual process reengineering and com-mitment – rather than just one, of money for goods.

But multi-dimensional exchange has an odd effect. While one-dimensional exchange can be easily contained, multi-dimensional exchanges tend to seep into everything the business does. To be successful, the 'Join Me' philosophy has to penetrate everything: operations, information systems, culture and values, ways of work-ing, recruitment policies and communications strategies.

Likely prominent characteristics of the 'Join Me' brand include the following:

- ▓ *a win-win philosophy*. The only sustainable basis of a long term and relatively intimate relationship is mutual benefit.
- ▓ *explicit mutuality*. For a 'Join Me' appeal to work, the win-win nature of the deal must be immediately obvious, so that the joiner can clearly see 'what's in it for me'.
- ▓ *transparency*. Not only the benefits, but also the costs must be clear: 'what I have to do to fulfil my side of the bargain'. Also, in order to generate trust, the other side's costs and benefits need to be clear – or at least accessible should the joiner want to scrutinize them. No secrets, in other words. Secrets kill trust.
- ▓ *multi-dimensionality* To generate maximum value, the mutual exchange needs to reach past a pure exchange of money for goods or services into areas such as information exchange and inputs of time, work or resource.
- ▓ *negotiability*. It takes two sides to make a relationship, and in a complex multi-dimensional relationship such as this, trade-

offs are likely and choices need to be made. A solution assembler, for example, might provide a menu of options for customers to choose from.

::: *connectedness.* For the 'Join Me' operator one-way, media-based communications are not enough. Ongoing, direct interaction is the norm.

::: *being aligned.* In 'Buy Me' marketing the incentives of both sides tend to conflict: buyers want to buy cheap, sellers want to sell dear. Aligned goals and objectives such as working together to reduce total costs are needed if the 'Join Me' approach is not to break down.

::: *a 'Join Me!' appeal.* For the 'Buy Me' marketer, the focus of marketing communications is the qualities and benefits of the product or service itself: why it is worthwhile parting with your hard-earned cash to pay for it. For the 'Join Me' marketer, the focus of marketing communications shifts towards explaining 'the benefits of membership', many of which include reassurance about the nature of the people and the organization the customer is committing himself to. The communications focus therefore shifts from the product's attributes to the organization's attributes: to 'the sort of people we are'.

::: *a 'Join Me!' culture.* A corporate culture that sees the organization's primary role as extracting the maximum possible revenues and margins out of markets (i.e. customers) that exist 'out there' is ill-suited to the 'Join Me' approach.

A new take on 'trust'

Looking at these hallmarks of the 'Join Me' enterprise underlines a point I made earlier about the shifting focus of trust. 'Join Me' strategies rest on the foundations of trust. But what sort of trust? As lean thinkers James Womack and Dan Jones warn:

> No one would have suggested that the geopolitical cold war could have been halted if only the two sides had suddenly decided to 'trust' each other. Yet one routinely hears that suppliers and their customers among a value stream can somehow end the industrial cold war through generous application of mutual 'trust', a term which seems to have no operational meaning.[19]

Industrial age marketing has created these cold wars between suppliers and customers, and cold war relationships take time to thaw. Writing in a business-to-business context, Womack and Jones suggest that 'states of war can only be ended when all of the parties willingly negotiate a set of principles to guide their *joint behaviour* and then devise a mechanism for mutual verification that everyone is abiding by the principles'.

You need 'an operational definition of fair behaviour', they continue. Its core principles are likely to include the following:

▓ value must be defined jointly along with a target cost
▓ all parties must make an adequate return on their investment
▓ they must work together to identify and eliminate waste, in order to meet their cost and return targets
▓ transparency – they have the right to examine every activity in the value stream.

Jointly analyzing every action needed to develop, order and produce an item or service makes every firm's costs transparent. There is no privacy. Thus the question of how much money (profit) each firm along the value stream is going to make on a specific product is unavoidable.[20]

This sort of approach is anathema to the traditional industrial age marketer – but it is central to the agency concept. It creates a new and slippery slope of competition.

'Join Me's' slippery slope

There is a snag with 'Join Me' strategies. A major snag. We've already seen that value for time and value for attention are emerging as two key drivers of value. The last thing most consumers want to do is to invest enormous amounts of time and energy into a million and one 'relationships'. 'Join Me' only works for a few, specially valuable relationships dealing with the most important areas of my life. 'Join Me' marketing therefore points to the emergence a two tier marketplace. At the top end lies a small handful of superbrands which have the capability of achieving the high degree of value-adding 'customer intimacy' required by the 'Join Me' approach.

Those that fail to reach a critical threshold – who fail to persuade their customers to join them – find that they are substantially weakened. The customer may still buy their product, but access to the key information age resources of information, trust and commitment is lacking. With that the brand's vitality is sapped. It moves ever more firmly to the fringes of the customer's life.

With 'Join Me', the world of brands begins to split irrevocably into insiders – those whom I let into my life, to create value in my life – and outsiders whom I deal with on a firmly arms' length basis. As this split occurs, outsider brands are likely to be treated in an even more instrumental, even more remote fashion than today. Consumers may turn to buying agents to source them on emerging spot markets, for example: purely on the basis of going price.

Such a split hasn't happened yet. Currently the great mass are in the middle, working on the great data slug trail, to extend and deepen their relationship with customers. Those that succeed in this quest may be able to catapult themselves into the prized position of 'insider', or at least to resist the centrifugal forces applied to the outsider brand. But the message remains. 'Join Me' is becoming a key to competitive edge. The (few) winners will earn a highly privileged place on the 'inside' of the consumer's life. But the 'Join Me' philosophy doesn't only apply to the organization's appeal to the consumer. It affects the whole organization in all key relationships.

embrace 'contract-plus'

> *The purpose of business is to create value and share it with your partners. If you share it effectively they will stick around.*   Frederick Reichheld[1]

> *Networks of social relationships create social capital, which is absolutely critical in this new economy. An ethic of trust and collaboration is as important in the new economy as individualism and self-interest.*
> Charles Leadbeater[2]

THE LAWYER'S NIGHTMARE

As we've just seen, 'Join Me' marketing sounds nice and cosy but in reality its damned difficult. It requires acute sensitivity, painstaking persistence and resolute determination and, probably, an internal cultural revolution. Things like transparency don't come easy to many companies. And our last chapter was only talking about customers, whereas in reality, if it's going to work it has to work with all key 'stakeholders'.

Formally speaking every market transaction represents a contract. One side agrees to hand over a certain amount of X, in exchange for Y. Contracts form the foundation of all commercial relationships. But if you want a 'Join Me' style of relationship with someone, contracts aren't much help. No matter how exhaustive and demanding a contract is, there will always be something else – something extra – that the other party could give, if they so wanted: a piece of information or insight, a bit of extra effort or sacrifice, forgiving a mistake, or a good word in your favour to a third party.

Legal contracts establish the agreed minimum requirements that are necessary for a transaction to proceed. But competition is not about meeting minimum requirements. It is about being the best. And to be the best, you need to get the best out of the people you work with, such as employees, suppliers or alliance partners. You need to get them to go beyond the contract to 'contract-plus'. Yet, by definition, anybody who signs a contract and keeps to the terms specified in it cannot be in breach of it. So you cannot *demand* this of them. You cannot sue them or sack them for failing to give more than the contract specifies. Notes Sandra Vandermerwe: 'The very resources and assets that the modern enterprise needs to generate increasing returns are not owned by it and are beyond its control.' You either *persuade* the owners of these resources to *volunteer* them, or you don't get them.[3]

The question, of course, is how? Suggestion: don't ask a lawyer. A lawyer will want both parties to sign a contract. And the chances are that the very attempt to enshrine ever more demands in a formal contract will sow the seeds of mistrust – 'why do they want me to sign that?' – and get the other party running a mile. The answer is that it's a marketing challenge – a Right Side Up marketing challenge.

Employee contract-plus

For most firms 'contract-plus' is now critical when it comes to employees. The faster we hurtle into the information age, the more companies depend on employees to volunteer things: knowledge and skills; creativity, innovation and initiative; empathy and service.

In the information age it is an absolute competitive necessity to get the best out of people: to create an abundance of what organizational theorist Charles Handy calls 'e factors' such as energy, enthusiasm, effort, excitement and excellence. Organizations can 'make magic', he suggests, when they engage the professionalism, pride and passion of their people.[4]

No wonder there has been such a tidal wave of interest in issues such as staff motivation, culture change and leadership. Companies are now investing vast sums in internal communications and marketing programmes, designed to enthuse and motivate their staff to give their all: to 'live' the brand, to be brand ambassadors. And they have naturally turned to marketers to help them in this task. Much of this marketing input has been self defeating, however.

Traditionally, marketers have been expert mask makers. It has been the marketer's task to generate an attractive mask to present to outside audiences to attract them towards the brand; to change their attitudes and behaviour. The same approach, applied internally, simply brings the mask inside the organization. The *real* objectives and values of the organization – the ones held by those with the power – have not changed one iota. But in order to achieve these same objectives, new internal selling messages are designed to change internal audiences' attitudes and behaviour; to get 'buy in'.

> *Today, competitive edge rests on what people volunteer over and above their formal contracts.*

However, just as consumers have learned to peer behind the marketers' carefully constructed veils of brands, to inspect the people behind them, so have employees. Except quicker, because they have access to more, and better, information. They quickly discover the often enormous gaps between mask rhetoric – the espoused values and objectives – and the reality. Result: the precise opposite to the one intended: increased disaffection and cynicism.

According to research conducted by internal marketing consultancy MCA with Mori in the UK in early 1999, for example, bad treatment of customers by staff is the biggest turn-off factor among customers, with one in six saying it has put them off purchasing a company's product or service. The research also found that only a quarter of employees were strongly committed to helping their organization succeed, and that 'low levels of commitment and understanding are endemic across all levels of staff' (including managerial levels). Says MCA Chairman Kevin Thomson, 'Customers are experiencing the side-effects of low levels of staff buy-in.'

Getting 'buy-in' from the many relatively poorly paid and not-so-skilled front-line service staff who are expected to lie (or act) may be particularly difficult. But surely it should be easier among professional, knowledge workers? Not necessarily. Research indicates that levels of disaffection and discontent tend to be pretty constant across all levels of an organization. And besides, knowledge workers whose skills are in demand have even less reason to be 'loyal' to any particular organization – just look at the exodus of talent from blue-chip firms and management consultants to dot-coms during the height of dot-com fever. As Peter Drucker notes:

> What motivates – especially knowledge workers – is what motivates volunteers. Volunteers, we know, have to get more satisfaction from their work than paid employees precisely because they do not get a paycheck. They need, above all, challenge. They need to know the organization's mission and to believe in it. They need continuous training. They need to see results.
>
> Implicit in this is that employees have to be managed as associates, partners – and not in name only. The definition of a partnership is that all partners are equal. It is also the definition of a partnership that partners cannot be ordered. They have to be persuaded. Increasingly, therefore, the management of people is a marketing job. And in marketing one does not begin with the question, 'what do we want?' One begins with the question 'what does the other party want? What are its values? What are its goals? What does it consider results?[6]

The crucial words here are 'and not in name only'. As we have seen, industrial age marketing is interested in understanding what the other party wants only in so far as this understanding can be used to help the marketing corporation pursue its own goals: to close the sale. The new breeds of agent break with this approach by aligning themselves with the purposes of the customer.

The point of understanding employees' values and goals is not simply to construct messages and programmes which use these values and goals as a better means to achieve exactly the same ends. The point is to answer the 'what's in it for me?' question by changing what the organization does to start meeting employees' values and goals. In other words, to bring 'agency' into the organization. Says Drucker: 'This is neither Theory X nor Theory Y nor any other specific theory of managing people. It goes beyond this and involves aligning the employees' goals with those of the organization – and vice versa.' Strategists Gary Hamel and C. K. Prahalad agree that strategic intent is 'as much about the creation of meaning for employees as the establishment of a direction'.[7]

Contract-plus with business partners

The one area where contract-plus is most accepted – in theory at least – is in business-to-business supply relationships. Here it was that hard-nosed, ruthless, profit-maximizing companies began to realize that arm's length adversarial relationships between buyers and sellers are simply, inefficient. Far more value can be squeezed out of the interactions between the two parties if they share information and ideas and adjust and coordinate the things they do to help each other work better.

One study of the car industry, by Richard Lamming, Professor of Purchasing and Supply at the University of Bath, notes that it in its early days 'craft manufacturers had something special, something of great value that was lost during the development and dominance of mass production. That special something was collaboration: between workforce and management, between labour and capital, and between vehicle assembler and component supplier.' This collaboration was killed, however, by 'the jealous demarcation of duties and covetous ownership of the value chain so stereotypical of mass production'. And it's only over the last few decades that companies have begun the search for ways to recreate that 'something special'.[8]

That 'something special' has taken many forms. By working together to coordinate supply and demand better and move towards 'just in time' deliveries business partners have freed up working capital and reduced material handling costs; by sharing information they have been able to cut costs; by sharing ideas and insight they have accelerated and deepened technical advances; by sharing know-how they have improved quality and reduced waste and got more things right first time. All of these advances have been of mutual benefit. Once one set of competitors have access to these advantages, they force the pace for others.

But achieving these changes proved extremely difficult. As Richard Lamming suggests, the results should really be classified under the heading 'psychology' rather than engineering or supply chain management. Lean supply 'is about a fundamental, very difficult, strategic attitudinal shift – as much a challenge for the hearts and minds of manufacturers as for technical skills'.[9]

In fact, researchers studying the 'lean' revolution in the car industry repeatedly came back to issues such as trust and 'moral trading' as much as 'efficiency' or 'cost'. Theories of 'voice' versus 'exit' in relationships were first developed in this area, for example. So were notions of interdependence, of timespans for reciprocity, of 'goodwill trust' versus 'competence trust'. Thus, for example, one study of the electronics industry distinguished between arm's length contract relations and obligational contract relations where 'traders feel that mutual indebtedness or obligatedness at any time is a normal state of affairs which sustains a relationship'.[10]

Not surprisingly, contract-plus – exchanging more than money for goods: ideas, information, resources etc for mutual benefit – didn't come easily. Many companies used the slogans of supply chain partnerships to practise partner*shaft:* using the new openness to screw their suppliers down even harder, for example. But they have also discovered that the real thing works better than the pretence. And that it changes the philosophy at the heart of marketing.

As Lamming notes, in traditional business-to-business buyer-seller relationships, suppliers would apply all their efforts 'to the pursuit of price increases and beguiling the customer'. Lean supply, on the other hand, focuses on 'reducing costs, and therefore prices, each year ... it turns established thinking on its head.'[11]

Contract-plus and the community

Contract-plus, or 'Join Me' marketing, doesn't only apply to customers, or to employees, or to business and alliance partners. If fits organizations' relationships with 'the community' and the environment too.

Sometimes, executives like to say the corporation needs to earn its 'licence to operate'. But the whole concept is niggardly. It is contract-only thinking: only do as much as you have to, to get the licence to operate 'signed'. The big opportunity, as cause-related marketing expert Sue Adkins points out, is to move beyond 'compliance' towards 'compliance-plus'.[12] Thus, as part of its effort to become 'a valued world citizen' Coca-Cola wants to offer its resources to do good. For example, CEO Douglas Daft has offered to deploy Coca-Cola's formidable distribution network in India to take polio vaccines into rural areas. According to Harvard Business School Professor Rosabeth Moss Kanter, leading-edge companies are discovering that 'applying their energies to solving the chronic problems of the social sector powerfully stimulates their own business development ... they are moving beyond corporate social responsibility to corporate social innovation.'[13]

The benefits of such 'compliance-plus' approaches are perhaps clearest in environmental arenas. Alongside intellectual capital, emotional capital and social capital (as well as, of course, financial capital) companies can also tap what Amory Lovins of the Rocky Mountain Institute calls 'natural capital': the resources of the natural world. Moving beyond a wealth extraction mentality to nature, towards a contract-plus mentality – which focuses on protecting the biosphere rather than merely exploiting it – can yield 'startling benefits for today's shareholders and future generations'.[14]

Wrestling with fog

The benefits of applying a contract-plus marketing mentality are potentially huge, therefore. But it's also extremely unsettling. For a start, Martin Christopher observes, 'The idea of sharing mutual goals and sharing some of the risks, in order to participate in the rewards, is a little nerve rattling for managers who are used to working in an adversarial basis'. Worse, in contract-plus relationships, it's difficult to pinpoint exactly the scale of those risks and rewards.[15]

The whole point about a contract is that it is definite. As social policy thinker Francis Fukuyama points out: 'In market exchange, goods are exchanged simultaneously and buyers and sellers keep accurate tabs on the rate of exchange.' But relationships don't work in the same way. Indeed, any attempt to keep an accurate tab on the exact amount of value exchanged in an ongoing relationship would probably destroy that relationship. As Fukuyama notes: 'In the case of reciprocal altruism [as he calls it], the exchange is time-shifted; one party can give a benefit without expecting any immediate return and does not expect to be exactly compensated.'[16]

Kevin Kelly agrees: 'Industrial production was easy to measure. One could ascertain a clear numerical answer. Relationships, on the other hand, are indefinite, fuzzy, imprecise, complex, innumerate, slippery and multifaceted.'[17] For a generation of managers, especially accountants, brought up on the slogan 'what gets measured gets managed', that's difficult.

A new role for brands

It's also difficult for marketers, who have to rethink what, as well as who, brands are for. Brands started out representing offers to consumers. But with 'contract-plus' they take on a massive new responsibility: to become recruiting agents persuading all the providers of key assets such as custom, labour, intellect and information, raw materials and finance to 'join our wealth creating network rather than that of our rivals'. And as we've seen, by necessity, the appeal has to be grounded on the basis of superior win-win: 'This is who we are. This is what we stand for. This is what we are trying to achieve. This is how we intend to achieve it. Join us and give more, because that way, you will get more.' In this way marketing moves beyond the crafting of effective 'selling' messages – to the communication of 'being' messages.

This is most obviously the case for people-based brands such as consultants. As Helen Shaw, Global Human Resources Director for Arthur Andersen, comments:

The brand has to excite our people so that they can excite other people: our clients. And one thing we know about humans is that they cannot wear a mask for any length of time. So the starting point of our brand has to be the reality of what Arthur Andersen is and what its aspirations are. We have to find out what the unique attributes and characteristics of our people are. And we can only assist in the articulation of those unique attributes and qualities. That is the beginning of our brand proposition.[18]

As organizations compete ever harder for the best people – the most enthusiastic, the most skilled, the most creative and innovative – so the role of marketing as builder of such recruitment brands grows ever more important. And the role of the brand itself begins to evolve. It's no longer packaging and communicating value which has *already* been created, it is helping to organize the value chain or network itself so that superior value can be created *in the future*. It becomes one of the means by which critical resources of intellectual, information, social and emotional capital (as well as physical and financial capital) are *acquired* rather than packaged and sold. The brand becomes not only what consumers and employees 'buy', but what they *invest* in ... to get a good return. Strong brands literally help the organization create more value because they help recruit those most able (and willing) to contribute the most.

> *Brand don't only package value, they recruit value creators by making the win-wins explicit.*

This sort of brand is not just broadcasting messages to external audiences, it encourages 'outside in' messages and questions. And as this happens, managing the brand and managing the internal culture and values of the organization become one and the same. The brand becomes less of a 'unique selling point' and more of what consultant Chris Macrae calls a 'unique organizing purpose: a purpose around which the entire business organizes itself, including all its relationships with other parties'.[19] Likewise, Simon Knox, professor of brand marketing at Cranfield School of Management, and Stan Maklan, a consultant with CSC Index, talk about the brand as a 'unique organization value proposition' or UOVP, which acts as the cable that binds the separate streams or 'wires' of value creation together. 'The UOVP integrates a company's core business processes into a visible set of credentials that add value throughout the supply chain.'[20]

'Join Me' and contract-plus therefore demand that marketers not only help sell offers, but help to create brands as magnets of extra value from all the parties the enterprise most needs. As Michael Dell remarks, 'At Dell, we are trying to build an organization where we can achieve integration across all our functions. Integration with our customers, with our people, and with our suppliers are each good in and of themselves. The model really cranks, however, when you integrate all three.'[21] IBM board member Geoff Papows agrees: 'A growing need to work closely, cooperatively and collaboratively with customers, suppliers, partners and other allies will become the defining factor of enterprise innovation.'[22]

But working closely, cooperatively and collaboratively with customers, suppliers, partners and other allies – building relationships with them – is a very different kettle of fish to trying to trade with them. In fact, an instrumental, arm's-length trading mentality can be positively toxic when it comes to building win-win relationships. Somewhere, *values*, as well as *value*, have to enter the equation.

PART 4

the new quality revolution

From quality products to quality time

'Quality' is a seller-centric notion. It's about the quality of the seller's product or service, not the quality of the buyer's life.

Right Side Up marketing is not only about helping buyers to buy, and creating value 'in my life', it's about maximizing 'my experiential profit': the 'quality of my life'.

For marketers, agents and sellers alike, that's a whole new ball game. In Part 4 we investigate the rules of this new game

the new quality revolution

> *The crucial dimensions of scarcity in human life are not economic but existential. They are related to our needs for leisure and contemplation, peace of mind, love, community and self-realization.*   Fritjof Capra[1]

> *Human beings have always sought out new and exciting experiences to learn and grow, develop and improve, mend and reform. But as the world progresses further into the experience economy much that was previously obtained through noneconomic activity will increasingly be found in the domain of commerce. That represents a significant change. It means that what we once sought for free, we now pay a fee.*
>
> Joseph Pine and James Gilmore[2]

> *We are living in a material world, and I am a material girl.*
>
> Madonna, *Material Girl*

FROM QUALITY PRODUCTS TO QUALITY TIME

Brands first emerged on the back of promises about quality: the quality of the materials used to make a product, and the product's unique 'qualities' or attributes. Nowadays, we all squeal if a product or service proves to be substandard in some way. More recently, a second quality revolution has rolled through the commercial world, shifting the quality focus from *product* quality to *process* quality: getting things 'right first time'. Quality processes help tackle the trade-off between price and quality which has taxed marketers' minds for decades. By developing quality processes companies have found that often they can offer both better quality products or services *and* lower prices.

> *The new frontiers of quality relate not to sellers' offers but to 'my quality of life'.*

Both of these notions of quality are vital. We could never do without them. But they are also producer-centric, and they are not the end of the evolutionary line. In advanced industrial societies at least, we are lucky enough for Fritjof Capra's observation above to be mostly true. The real points of scarcity in our lives are 'not economic but existential'. As we worry less about sustenance we can afford to worry more about self-realization and fulfilment. And as we seek out more chances to 'grow, develop and improve, mend and reform', as Pine and Gilmore put it in the second quote, what we increasingly want to 'buy' is not so much quality products and services driven by quality processes but a better quality *of life*. The one is merely a means to the other. This is the next frontier for marketing: 'selling' enriched value for time, selling 'happiness', as it were.

Quality time has many aspects. Quality time is *time well spent*. Given the opportunity, most people would dearly like to reduce the time and effort they spend on routine chores – or life 'administration'. Which of course accounts for emerging breeds such as buying agents and solution agents. But being a master of life administration doesn't necessarily make you happy. The main point in being a master of life administration is to free up money, time and energy to maximize investment in the things that make life 'worth living'. For all their incredible importance, buying agents and solution agents are just a springboard to this destination, not the destination itself.

Quality time is *sensual, 3D time*. It's very easy to get mesmerized by the dot-com revolution: the share prices, the breathtaking pace of technological development and the exciting new business models. Virtual reality is all very exciting, but for us humans, a virtual life is exactly that – virtual. It is two dimensional. Not real. As Madonna pointed out in her song, we humans are material beings living in a material – not a virtual – world.

Brands that live only in virtual space miss out on whole realms of potential brand experience that can only be generated within a full-blooded, sensual, three dimensional world. No matter how all-pervasive the Internet may become, brands that create valued, three dimensional, tactile sensory experiences will remain as attractive and important as they ever were, whether it's a cool, refreshing drink of Coca-Cola or a thrilling ride at a Disney theme park. Indeed, the more our lives are dominated by the artefacts of the information age, chances are, the more we will yearn to indulge our physical senses. As David Atter, Sales and Marketing Director at Beeb.com, the BBC's online commercial arm, remarks: 'People need high touch to counter high tech. The more high tech the world becomes the more we need high touch to counterbalance it.'[3]

Brands which can touch people – literally – have enormous potential. Management guru Tom Peters recently noted that the rise of a digitally connected globalized economy – in which it takes just one eighth of a second for an electronic message to travel from one side of the world to the other – means there is a death of distance. New low cost competitors from Asia or Latin America may soon be banging on your customers' doors, Peters thundered. 'Your worst nightmare of a competitor is now only one-eighth of a second away!'

To which Kevin Kelly replied: 'That's the bad news. The good news is that those geographically far away competitors will never be any closer than an eighth of a second. And for many things in life, that is too far away. A kiss for instance. Or playing sports. Or getting to know flowers.' These are 'quality' experiences where both senses of the Q word come into play: quality as 'good' versus 'bad', and quality as in unique attributes and characteristics. The quality experiences Kelly is referring to are indeed unique and special and there's nothing the information age, or the so-called 'death of distance' can do to touch them.[4]

Indeed, according to some economists, the really fast growing sectors in modern economies are the ones where being local and in touch is paramount. For example, a whole range of activities – such as nursing, getting a bus or train to work, teaching, going to a restaurant, building, getting a baby sitter or plumber – simply don't lend themselves to global economies of scale, notes economist Paul Krugman. Currently, the biggest growth area in terms of employment is in the 'kinds of activities that we can't program a computer or robot to do for us, that require the human touch, [that] also typically require direct human contact . . . That's why most people in Los Angeles produce services for local consumption, as do most people in New York, London, and Paris.'[5]

Quality time demands such sensual, 3D, real-time, quality experiences, but they are not enough. Pure sensual indulgence can still be emotionally unsatisfying. Quality time demands yet more. It demands *engagement*. Research by psychologists such as the University of Chicago's Mihaly Csikentmihalyi suggests that when individuals get so engaged in an activity – whether physical or mental – that they 'lose themselves' within it, this is when they feel most contented, or 'happy'.

> The types of activities which people all over the world consistently report as most rewarding – which make them feel best – involve a clear objective, a need for concentration so intense that no attention is left over, a lack of interruptions and distractions, clear and immediate feedback on progress towards the objective and a sense of challenge – the perception that one's skills arc adequate to cope with the task at hand.'[6]

There are an enormous range of activities that can fulfil these characteristics. Some of them are 'digitalizable' products like a good book or film. Others are social: the emotional engagement of unfolding human relationships. Yet others are physical: from the joy of the craftsman in his craft to the obsessions of the golf player. Either way, the information age is not going to change this fundamental human characteristic. Indeed, information age products and services will flourish to the extent and degree that they help address it. Selling 'opportunities for engagement' is already a huge business. It is what has powered the growth of the entertainment and leisure industries for decades. Learning is another form of engagement – and another growth industry. And to the degree that the number of ways that it's possible to engage the human mind and body are infinite compared to, say, the number of ways that it's possible to quench a physiological need such as thirst, the growth potential of every and all 'human engagement' industry is also infinite.

Yet another aspect of quality time is *achievement*, or a sense of purpose. Humans are goal driven animals. They plan their days, setting themselves tasks both trivial – such as getting to work on time – and fundamentally existential: achieving the goals they feel will make their life worth living. Stanford University researchers James Collins and Jerry Porras note that one of the characteristics of successful 'visionary' companies is that they set themselves what Collins and Porras call 'big hairy audacious goals'. That's probably true of individuals too. Increasingly, people are outsourcing less existentially important tasks to solution and platform brands to free up time to help them achieve the goals they see as important. But often they need help: encouragement, advice, expertise. This is the potentially huge arena of opportunity for new breeds of 'transformation agent', whose core brand promise is that they will help their clients achieve the goals they have set themselves.[7]

The final aspect of quality of life is *a sense of meaning:* being at ease with our place in the world; feeling a part of something bigger than our small, individual lives; wanting to leave the world a better place than we found it, and so on. This is where a proliferating number of 'passion brands' big and small are flourishing and will continue to flourish. If these brands sell products or services at all, it's only as an adjunct. Their real 'product' is the meaning of life itself.

Time well spent, 3D sensual experience and social interaction, mental and physical engagement, achieving goals, discovering a sense of meaning: industrial age marketing has hardly touched these vast expanses of human need – the existential rather than economic side of life. Nor do the agents we have discussed so far. Buying agents focus mainly on value for money. Solution agents focus mainly on *saving* time. But helping to save time is not the same as helping to enrich it.

The highest and most popular professional qualification in

business is the Master of Business Administration. The term is a relic of a bygone age. The word 'master' implies control and expresses the command-and-control obsessions of the industrial age firm. The focus is on *the business* and its process, not on the customer and his processes. It is inward looking. And the term *administration* implies the orderly processing of things. Only things can be 'administered', not people.

What people are looking for, on the other hand, is something more akin to an OLE! – an orchestrator of life enrichment. It has to be an *orchestrator*, not a master, because it's my life and I have to live it. All you can do is help me along the way. Life, because it revolves around my life, not your business. And *enrichment*, because I want to make the most of my life. It's my existential profit that interests me, not your financial profits. How different would businesses be if their highest qualification was an OLE! rather than an MBA?

beyond brand experience

> The value in a value proposition is the value in the customer's experience, not the value in the product. It is the experience of the customer that must be differentiated.
>
> Michael Lanning[1]

> The history of economic progress consists of charging a fee for what once was free. In the full-fledged experience economy, instead of relying purely on our own wherewithal to experience the new and wondrous, we will increasingly pay companies to stage experiences for us, just as we now pay companies for services we once delivered ourselves, goods we once made ourselves, and commodities we once extracted ourselves.
>
> Joseph Pine and James Gilmore[2]

THE NEW BOTTOM LINE

Experience. This e-word goes a long way to summing up the Right Side Up bottom line: to maximize the financial and existential profitability of 'my life'. By definition, experiences are attributes of my life, not characteristics of your products or services. The value that matters is created in my life, not in your operations and good experiences deliver me high value for time and a good return on attention, as well as value for money.

Experience marketing has been a buzz theme in marketing circles for some time now. But it is treacherous territory, encompassing a wide range of different meanings and implications. There is a big difference, for example, between improving a customer's experience of dealing with a brand by, say, answering the phone efficiently (which is a must for every marketer whether traditional seller or would-be agent) and selling a branded experience such as a Disney ride (which is a specialist business).

> *Experience marketing has been a buzz theme in marketing circles for some time now.*

And there's an equally big difference between providing enjoyable experiences such as a Disney ride and boosting an individual's experiential bottom line by helping them reach an important personal goal or find meaning in their lives. At this point traditional seller-centric entitites begin to fall out of the picture and agents move in.

Meanwhile traditional brands and agents alike face huge operational challenges once they embrace the e-word: brand management as we know it cannot cope with what it takes to be successful at experience marketing, whether it's creating satisfying brand experiences, branded experiences or experiential 'profits' in individuals' lives.

THE LURE OF BRANDED EXPERIENCE

In one sense, marketers have been consummate experience sellers since the year dot. The satisfying 'clunk' of a car door or the lavish finish of a car's interior; the sensuous evocative aroma of a new jar of coffee; the satisfaction of breaking and biting into a thick piece of chocolate; the ability to stretch your legs and lie back comfortably on a flight across the Atlantic – these are all experiences people want and are prepared to pay for. Marketers are acknowledged experts at identifying our yearnings for these experiences, and in delivering them through their products and services.

But there's a problem with this sort of brand experience. The more we automate, the more we let machines do the work, the more commodity-like such offerings become. That's why futurists like Rolf Jensen suggest that, increasingly, the biggest markets will be for feelings rather than tangible products. Tangible products will be sold as adjuncts to these feelings, he says.[3]

Jensen identifies six dreams or story themes which he believes will create the great markets of the future. They are:

- the market for adventures (whether small, medium or large)
- the market for togetherness, friendship and love
- the market for care (both giving and receiving care)
- the who-am-I? market
- the market for peace of mind
- the market for convictions.

Some of today's biggest brands already flourish by selling such 'dreams'. Starbucks didn't become a phenomenon simply because it sold a damn fine cup of coffee. Another reason for its success is that it created a platform for what the Henley Centre calls 'perfect moments': a chance to sit and relax and watch the world go by, which is an extremely precious experience in a world with so many demands on our attention. Ditto Nike. It taps into and helps provide all the emotions that surround sport.

Brands like these sell products which open the door and pave the way to experiences we truly value. There's nothing new here: it's why alcoholic drinks have always been so successful, for example. But it's of growing importance. Indeed, some thinkers say it's changing the very nature of our economy. As consultants Joseph Pine and James Gilmore argue, we are evolving through a progression: from an industrial economy through a service economy into an 'experience economy'.

They illustrate this progress with the example of the birthday cake. Once upon a time, Mum would buy ingredients such as eggs, flour and sugar and make her own cake. Then companies like General Mills and Procter & Gamble started selling branded cake mixes. Then bakeries and retailers started selling pre-made cakes. And now companies like Discovery Zone lay on an entire birthday party, and provide the cake as part of a much bigger experience. Each step up this experiential ladder offers greater value to the buyer; because it is 'more relevant to what he truly wants – in this case, the throwing of a fun and effortless birthday'.[4]

Delight inflation

There's no doubt, creating and staging experiences 'more relevant to what people really want' – rather than simply providing the products or services that serve as a platform for these experiences – has huge marketing potential. Some marketers are so excited by it that they see it as *the* future. One enthusiast has even penned an experiential marketing 'manifesto' paraphrasing Karl Marx's *Communist Manifesto*: 'Customers have nothing to lose but their boredom. They have a world of experiences to win.'[5]

But beware. Selling experiences can easily become a treadmill. In fact, many experiences are more prone to 'commodization' that commodities themselves. That's because they are so prone to the 'been there, done that' factor. Physiological needs such as hunger and thirst need constant replenishment. Coca-Cola knows that no matter how much Coke I drink today, I will still get thirsty tomorrow: demand for the same product – and the same basic experience – is miraculously recreated anew every day.

Similarly demand for most basic solution agent services is intrinsically renewable. I had to manage my finances yesterday, I need to so today, and I will need to do so tomorrow too. But demand for other forms of experience is much less resilient. The first time I see a blockbuster movie it's a thrill. The second time might be fun. But third time round it is likely to be a bore.

In fact, most enjoyable experiences repeated often enough become dull routines. Just look at the fate of themed restaurants, of countless fashion brands and crazes. They are wildly successful for a while. Then the novelty wears off as people begin to think 'been there, done that'. And demand falls off a cliff. Likewise service intended to 'delight' the customer quickly becomes a base expectation. Once we have experienced it, if we don't get it next time round we're disappointed.

'Been there, done that' is the experience marketer's nemesis.

Whereas demand for the same product – for example, Coke – is renewed every day, demand for the same experiences is extremely perishable. It is a victim of delight inflation: the endless need to find a better 'New! Improved!' experience. That's why only a few organizations are cut out to be outstanding branded experience marketers: because inventing and staging 'New! Improved!' experiences is a highly specialized intellectual property business. Like Disney. Like Hollywood.

That's also why many other businesses face an experience marketing dilemma. Take retail. It's often said that retailers should combat shopper boredom by making shopping a high value-for-time activity; by creating 'in-store theatre', staging events, and so on. 'Shoppertainment', they call it. But is this shoppertainment so good that customers are prepared to pay for it in its own right? If not, does it simply add cost to the business? And how much time and energy does the retailer have to invest in new shows and new events – like the theme park operator – to keep the experiences fresh?

Competitive pressures mean there's always a balance to be struck, of course. But the 'been there, done that' factor underlines the essential difference between intellectual property businesses such as entertainment and infrastructure driven businesses such as retail. To survive, intellectual property companies like Disney have to generate a constant stream of new films and new rides – new intellectual property – to keep people coming back. Innovation is what they sell. But even if a retailer puts on some excellent shows, in the end that's not why people go to his store. If his store fails to have the right range, in stock, at the right prices customers won't buy much even if they do visit the store. The one is selling experiences. The other is using experiences to sell and they are not the same thing.

Old wine in new bottles?

Using experiences to sell has two sides. One of these sides takes us right back to the seller-centric marketing flaws we discussed earlier in this book. Marketers have known from the year dot that even the most mundane product has emotional significance. You could say, for example, that one of the reasons mothers care about the soap powders they buy is because of the high value they place on the experience of seeing their darling children looking bright, smart, clean and pretty. And knowing this, marketers have done everything they can to tap into such 'good mother' emotions when promoting their products.

But as we've seen, marketers slide into brand hokum when they start pretending (to themselves or to their customers) that by playing up this emotional, experiential aspect in their marketing communications they are somehow really 'adding value'. It's the consumer who adds this emotional value, not the marketer. Marketers who understand their customers may signal this understanding in their communications. But pretending you can actually *create* this value is a conceit. And what's worse, this conceit is usually driven by a base motive: it's simply an excuse to push up the price.

Jensen, for one, falls into this brand hokum trap. In future, he declares, 'the product will be the appendix, the main purpose of which is to embody the story being told.'[6] For example, 'when any watch will give you the time of day with total accuracy, timepieces must be sold through an appeal to the emotions.' This is very old wine in new bottles. It's 100 per cent seller-centric marketing, where the marketer seizes upon the consumer's dreams, experiences, emotions and feelings simply to use it for his own purposes: to close a sale more effectively.

PASSION PARTNERS

It won't wash, and it won't wash for a good reason. Jensen is right about these dreams. The human desire for adventure, togetherness, care is almost limitless. But the organizations most able to tap and feed these desires are consumer agents who are in it for and with their clients, and who act *for* their clients in helping them to realize the important dreams within their lives.

One of the two main forms of such agent is the community of interest, which brings people together to share an interest in, say, a sport or a hobby and which may not sell experiences as such. By doing so, they help generate 'experiential profits' for people. The really effective communities of interest are not those who restrict themselves to the virtual world of the Internet, but those which use modern information and communication technologies to organize people do real, sensual things in real life.

A mountaineering club, for example, would use an Internet site as the organizing hub of its activities. But the real purpose of a mountaineering club is to have the wind in your face and a hundred foot drop below you. The mountaineering club 'sells' the emotion direct: it is a passion brand. To help it deliver that emotion, it will probably also source mountaineering equipment. The passion drives the commerce, not the other way round. A manufacturer of mountain climbing equipment will naturally evoke a sense of adventure to help sell his products. But when it comes to 'selling' the experience and fulfilling the dream, the mountaineering club is leagues ahead.

Interestingly, in the US, one of the most successful mountaineering equipment 'retailers' is REI – an enthusiasts' cooperative – which has won the trust of its members not only because it shares its profits with them, but because of its enthusiasm for mountaineering. Traditionally, if you wanted to talk to people who were really knowledgeable about mountain climbing and could advise you about the best equipment, REI stores were the place to go. Now REI is using its website to combine commerce, advice and chat as any good community of interest does.

In this market for dreams and experiences, in other words, the people who have a genuine care for these dreams and experiences in their own right – and who generate trust and enthusiasm on this basis – have a definite competitive advantage over those whose main dream lies in using other people's dreams to close sales. The more important the experiential bottom line, the greater the potential of the community of interest and passion brand.

TRANSFORMATION AGENTS

We've seen that there is an important difference between selling experiences and using experiences to sell. There's also a crucial difference between experiences *per se* and the individual's experiential bottom line. Most people like going to see movies and eating out at restaurants. These are enjoyable experiences, which we buy. But there are more important things in life. We have career goals, emotional or relationship goals, financial goals: things we want to achieve in our lives – that make our lives 'worth living'.

But often these things are very difficult to achieve: we cannot achieve them solely through pleasant experiences, we have to work hard at them. We have to invest time, money, emotional and physical energy into them. And we value anyone who can help us along the way. Enter the transformation agent.

The transformation agent doesn't sell enjoyable experiences. But as an OLE – an 'orchestrator of life enrichment' – he does help us reach our goals. And as Pine and Gilmore point out, 'There is no earthly value more concrete, more palpable, or more worthwhile than achieving an aspiration.'[7]

> *Experiences alone are not enough. What people really want is to achieve their goals in life.*

Here lies the heart of a massive new buyer-centric business: the transformation agent's business of helping clients achieve the goals in life that they want to achieve and maximize their overall experiential bottom line. This is the buyer-centric – or human – version of 'New! Improved!': a 'New Improved!' life.

As noted by Pine and Gilmore, the difference between helping people achieve personal 'transformations' and selling experiences is vast. Often the experiences we undergo to achieve our goals are positively unpleasant. We sweat our guts out in a gym in order to lose weight or get fit. We pick over our emotional and relationship problems with a counsellor or psychiatrist. We invest years of our life – and many sleepless nights – studying for professional qualifications. We work ourselves to the bone to pay the mortgage for our dream home. Sellers make things which they sell to us for a profit. By doing these things we 'make' our own lives to improve our own personal bottom line.

So far, however, we have only been able to purchase ingredients of these outcomes, and it's been up to us to use them to reach our goals. We enrol on a course, or we join a gym. The transformation agent goes one step further, however. Using specialist expertise, he guides or coaches us to achieve our goals. He becomes our personal tutor or fitness instructor. The one is a mass produced offering. The other is a personalized service, where the basis of success lies in 'understanding the aspirations of individual consumers and businesses and guiding them to fully realize those aspirations'.[8]

In this sense, the transformation agent is the 'purest' of all the emerging consumer agent models: he is employed by the individual to do that individual's bidding. Transformation agents cannot work on the basis of arm's length instrumental transactions, but only through relationships where there is a rich exchange of information. They require very high levels of trust: trust that the agent is going to use personal, sensitive information *for* me and 'be on my side' and 'act in my interest'. It also requires that the two sides' interests align. One of the foundations of that trust is that the agent is paid by me to help me achieve my objectives, and isn't serving someone else's interests.

But can transformation agents ever be a significant commercial force? Some strands of transformation agency – such as counselling – will always be small and one-on-one. But there are also some huge opportunities for large commercial organizations too. Traditionally, for example, insurance companies have always been the customer's enemy. They do their best to avoid paying up when a claim is made and they need to charge higher premiums to compensate for those claims they do pay. But insurance premiums are driven ever lower because they are commodities: the customer simply searches around for the lowest price. It's a lose-lose relationship.

Now imagine my insurance agent. Instead of trying to work out ways of charging me a higher premium, he looks for ways of *reducing* the premium (and his risk) by helping me make the necessary changes that should mean I never need to make a claim in the first place. He might, for example, taken on the practical task of making sure my home is as secure as possible. He might also visit my home when I'm away on holiday or on a business trip. And if a burglar does break in, or a pipe does burst, he'll make sure someone fixes the doors or the pipes for me. That way, he becomes my friend, not my enemy. The insurance contract becomes just one part of a much more valuable service – which I'm prepared to pay much more for.

Similarly, a health organization could move from treating ailments and diseases to helping patients live healthier lives: 'treating the unpatient'. And personal financial services agents could act for, and with, their clients to manage their financial affairs to reach their financial goals. To be sure, this a premium market. But all the signs are that when it comes to their personal bottom lines, people are prepared to invest enormous sums – especially in other people they can really trust.

BRANDING TURNS INWARDS

Transformation agency doesn't lend itself to seller-centric marketing. But there's one aspect of 'experience marketing' that's crucial for would-be agents and sellers alike. If the customer's experience of dealing with that agent or seller is negative – if the process is a hassle or frustrating – he's unlikely to want to come back for more. It's absolutely vital, therefore, to make my experience of dealing with you as pleasant as possible: to eliminate the negatives and accentuate the positives.

This aspect of brand experience is universal – and is proving to have unexpectedly far reaching effects. Seeing value from the point of view of the customer's experience, rather than the attribute of the product or service can be an eye-opener, as Michael Dell points out. In the computing industry's early days, he remembers, every supplier was focused on what it saw as the big issues: things like product features and state-of-the-art technology. Yet, at the company's weekly Customer Advocate Meetings, where salespeople met with other people from across the company to discuss issues raised that week, a different pattern emerged:

> Almost all the complaints were about what the industry deems 'little things', like whether the power cord was in the box, whether the box was designed for easy access, or whether it was delivered when we said it would be [Dell recalls]. I realized we had to be responsible for anything and everything that affected our customers' experience – especially the little things.[9]

These 'little things' – or 'moments of truth', as some marketers call them – transform our understanding of brands. The brand is no longer the advertising, or the product. The brand emerges from the sum total of real-life interactions between customer and company. Questions like 'Is the order form "friendly" and "helpful"?' and 'Did the order arrive on time?' (i.e. was it 'efficient'?) become acid tests of success for the brand. What the organization says in its marketing communications pales into insignificance compared to what it actually does.

Most large organizations are still wrestling with the sheer scale of the task. To create a consistent brand experience, big service organizations need the same core message to be expressed to millions of customers in countless ways: through marketing communications, through experience of stores or brands, face to face contact with staff, over the phone, via a website, in a selling context or a service context, when the customer is seeking advice or even making a complaint.

Each one is a potential 'moment of truth' where the brand's promise is tested by its reality. Yet, traditionally, few organizations ever thought that their actual operations were essential elements of their marketing communications. When Hewlett-Packard first mapped its seven key customer processes (choosing, ordering, receiving or installing the product, learning about the product, using the product, support during the ownership period and disposal), it discovered what it called a 'staggering maze' of potential moments of truth. But there were hardly any organizational, decision-making or management links back into its brand management processes.

Hewlett-Packard was ahead of the pack in even researching the problem. Many companies are still struggling with the realization that 'brand actions' (as Dave Allen, CEO of consultants EnterpriseIG calls them) are more important than media messages; that 'everything communicates'; and that responsibility for the brand and its communication cannot therefore rest solely with a specialist marketing department. If brand experience is paramount, organizations have to learn how to express their brand values through their behaviour – what they do and how they do it. Human resources and operations move centre stage. As Helen Shaw, Global Human Resources Director at Arthur Andersen, comments: 'The starting point of your brand is your people. The manifestation of your brand is through people. And it's pointless getting excited about your external messages if it falls apart with your people.'[10]

In this way, the experience ladder transforms the marketing challenge. In a product-focused environment, marketing meant communicating the brand's promise and message externally – and there was a big divide between what happened 'inside' the organization and the face it presented to the outside world. In an experience oriented world that divide is no longer viable. The brand is experienced in real-life interactions between customers and organizations, not merely inserted into people's minds via the media to act as some sort of mind-cuckoo.

As Philip Hanson, General Marketing Manager at the Halifax, notes: 'In fast moving consumer [or packaged] goods the product is defined and controlled at the end of a production line. That is very different from the delivery of a service which has to be managed at so many different points of contact with the customer.'[11] Delivering the strategy 'through the people who are actually facing the customers is the biggest challenge. Marketing has to communicate in such a way that it enthuses the whole of the organization – all the people in the network – to deliver the brand experience.' Or as Kevin Thomson, Chairman of MCA, the corporate communications consultancy, comments, 'Brands are being made, delivered, sold, promoted, innovated and improved by internal people.' Business leaders now 'see the reputation and personality of their brands as held in the hands of everyone in the organization. They recognize that the people ARE the brand.'[12]

That's why some business leaders are now convinced that higher staff satisfaction is the only way to deliver superior brand experiences, in which case the first priority of senior management is staff, rather than customer, satisfaction. In this way, the apparently straightforward quest to deliver better brand experience opens up a managerial Pandora's box. Bosses have to stop 'managing' and start leading, motivating and inspiring. They need to overhaul relationships between employer and employed and connect the interests of their employees with those of the firm and its customers. Some companies, of course, have learned to excel in these areas. 'Delighting' the customer with 'legendary service' is the forte of players such as Nordstrom in the US and Richer Sounds in the UK. But overall, rhetoric far outstrips reality.

This challenge is compounded many times over when the 'total' customer experience of a brand depends on the actions of third parties over which the brand's manager has no direct control. This is the situation for a large and growing number of marketers. Packaged goods manufacturers rely on supermarkets for in-store displays to promote their products. Computer companies (except direct sellers like Dell) rely on dealers to sell and service their wares. Car manufacturers rely on car dealers to sell and service their cars.

British Airways says it wants to enhance the customer's experience 'from contemplation (of the flight) to reflection' – from the very first time the client considers making the trip to his on her arrival back home. But this experience is affected by myriad other service providers such as travel agents, airports, hotels, taxis and car hire firms, and so on.

As companies outsource key functions and tasks to specialist providers or form alliances with other companies to round out their offers, this dependence on third parties for the delivery of brand experiences actually increases. But somehow one brand has to learn how to act as the 'system organizer', aligning, orchestrating and motivating a wide range of different parties to deliver the same single 'brand experience'.

Experience marketing is more about motivating people than making offers. It's a different ball game.

Is anybody doing this successfully? One or two companies. Perhaps. Coca-Cola, for example, is effectively a 'system brand' bringing together an entire network of independent bottlers and distributors, all of whom play a crucial part in delivering the Coke experience and the Coke promise. Both the logic of total solutions and brand experience point to the emergence of such system brands.

And system brand or not, in experience marketing the brand has to become far more than a mask which the organization presents to the outside world to help close sales becomes positively counterproductive. Instead the brand has to turn inwards: to become the beacon around which the organization organizes itself – attracting the people who want to achieve its particular goals to work together. And once again 'branding' begins to separate out from 'selling'. The brand stops acting as a pure selling mechanism and starts becoming a means of connecting like minded people together, both within the organization and with outside audiences such as customers and business partners. And there's more where that came from.

broaden the exchange

> *All commerce involves moral choice.*   Jospeh Pine and James Gilmore[1]

MARKETING'S MORAL MAZE

We started this book discussing buying agents, whose appeal to consumers is almost entirely instrumental: make it cheaper, make it easier. We then followed a trajectory – via solution agents, communities of interest and passion brands, and on to transformation agents – where the value of being an expert OLE! comes to the fore.

As we follow this trajectory it transforms the nature of exchange. Industrial age marketing was built to serve, and to operate within, *markets* which are designed for the arm's length, instrumental and one-dimensional exchange of money for goods or services. But as we've seen, the logic of information age marketing – both buyer-centric and seller-centric marketing – is to add new dimensions to this exchange: to trade information and insight as well as money for goods, for example.

Such multi-dimensional exchanges demand new levels of trust (in people, rather than products), and happen best within *relationships* and *communities* rather than traditional markets. But relationships and communities invariably also involve the exchange of *values* as well as *value*. This is the final dimension of the Right Side Up revolution, affecting buyer-centric and seller-centric organizations and brands alike. It puts people – as *people* rather than as 'consumers' or 'employees' or 'investors' – at the heart of commerce.

This linking of values and value is happening for all sorts of reasons. The long-standing post-war 'division of labour' between for-profit and not-for-profit organizations has begun to blur. A retreating 'nanny state' has taught citizens to expect less of governments, and to look for more from the private sector.

As the tools and techniques of branding spread beyond their traditional consumer goods heartlands to all manner of organizations, new forms of 'brand warfare' are appearing. When Friends of the Earth confronted Monsanto over genetically modified foods, for example, this was brand warfare: which brand did the consumer trust most, Friends of the

> *Shared values positively oil the wheels of exchange. They help us pick the right partners.*

Earth or Monsanto? As such brand wars unfold, organizations find themselves competing in a 'single market' for both value and values. Greenpeace wants to sell a cause – a set of beliefs. But if it fails to raise funds, it dies, so it also wants to maximize its share of the consumer's purse. Shell, on the other hand, is not only competing for a share of purse, but for a share of trust and belief. If it fails to win trust and belief in its integrity as an organization, as well as trust in its products, it risks ceding 'brand leadership' over issues like the environment to passion brands such as Greenpeace. Which spells trouble for the future.

Technology is doing its bit too. In the industrial age, notes Kevin Kelly, most technological advances were 'relegated to the inside of a factory . . . [to] cheaper production methods or more specialized materials'. And except for the automobile, the devices these factories produced 'did not penetrate the areas of our lives we have always really cared about: our networks of friendship, writing, painting, cultural arts, relationships, self-identity, civil organizations, the nature of work, the acquisition of wealth and power. But with the steady advent of technology into the networks of communication and transportation,' he points out, 'technology has completely over-whelmed these social areas.'[2]

Globalization fits the same pattern. It is now a commonplace for observers to note that many multinationals are bigger, better resourced and politically more influential than many a nation state. The natural and inevitable result of this development is to ask whether and how these global corporations are using their resources, power and influence for good or evil – and to worry about their apparent lack of accountability to democratically elected bodies. For brands, the price of globalization is social responsibility.

Finally, there's also the fact that material wealth does not equal happiness. As philosopher Roger Scruton points out, 'Pleasure comes with the fulfilment of desire. Happiness comes with the ful-filment of the person.'[3] And happiness has as much to do with finding 'meaning' in life as it has to do with finding pleasure.

ADAM SMITH RIP

For all these reasons, the expectation is growing that brands should adopt and represent *values* as well as value. The trouble is, tra-ditional industrial age markets are deliberately 'value free'. They are *mechanisms* for the efficient exchange of value, and they assume a clear distinction between straightforward instrumental economic transactions and non-instrumental relationships such as those with family and friends.

This Adam Smith-like vision of the market mechanism is incred-ibly powerful. The realization that the 'common good' can be served by the butcher, baker and candlestick maker all pursuing their self-interest in the marketplace was a breakthrough. But it also has a critical limitation: it does not recognize people as people. There are very few pure altruists around. But where people deal with people, they tend to form relationships, affections, bonds, ties of loyalty, feelings of obligation and so on. They naturally enter the spheres of values and morality as well as value.

This is true within businesses. As Kevin Thomson notes, 'Businesses are people and people are shaped as much by their emotions as they are by their intellect.'[4]. As Pine and Gilmore point out, all commercial transactions involve moral choice. To some degree, every sale involves a sharing of values as well as an exchange of value.

Traditionally, marketers' instinct has been to avoid this issue at all cost. Worrying about the morality of something, or the values people hold, complicates things enormously. It's likely to add new layers of cost without compensating streams of revenue, and it will probably divert managers from their real purpose of maximizing shareholder value. Worrying about values and morals gets in the way of the businesses of doing business.

But there is another way of looking at it. Pure instrumentalism and a failure to worry about morals and values is often corrosive to business success, as John Kay, Director of consultancy London Economics, has noted.[5]

Companies that put profit maximization first often fail to achieve their objective, he observes. That's because this goal of profit, or shareholder value maximization, is rather akin to the pursuit of happiness. The pursuit of happiness, he suggests:

> gets in the way of its achievement ... Real happiness depends on interactions with other people. If we treat others in an instrumental and calculating way, they are likely to respond in an instrumental and calculating way. And so we lose the cooperative, caring and loving relationships that are the foundations of true happiness. If your attitude to employees, customers and suppliers is instrumental and calculating, that will be reciprocated in their attitude to you.
>
> There is a real difference between saying to your workers ... 'look after your customers because that is the way we do things here' and telling them 'look after your customers because that way they will buy more'. There is a difference between buying someone a drink because you like them, and buying someone a drink because they might give you something, and people can usually tell the difference.[6]

Indeed, *exchanging and sharing values can be a better way of creating value*. There's a good reason for this, as science writer Matt Ridley explains. 'Value-free' instrumental markets have a habit of eroding trust. As we saw in Chapter 15, it is not instrumentally rational to trust rational people, because instrumentally rational people have no interest in my interests whatsoever. Only in their own. If people really did behave in the instrumentally rational manner that economists talk about, they would have no reason to trust one another, and 'they would be unable to convince each other of their commitment and would never close the deals', suggests Ridley.

By having emotions, on the other hand, we human beings 'alter the rewards of commitment problems, bringing forward to the present distant costs that would not have arisen in the rational calculation'. Emotions such as guilt (which makes cheating painful) and compassion (which elicits reciprocal compassion) actually help us to commit to doing deals which we couldn't otherwise commit to. They actually oil the wheels of exchange. Worrying about someone's values, then, is not an unnecessary complication which gets in the way of rational decision-making. On the contrary, says Ridley, 'The point of moral sentiments . . . is to enable us to pick the right partner to play the game with'.[7]

Another take on the same theme focuses on the value of 'social capital'. 'Social capital' is the 'set of informal values or norms shared by members of a group that permits cooperation between them', suggests social policy author Francis Fukuyama.[8]

Yes, by definition, social capital creates 'a superordinate purpose that distorts the market relationship'.[9] But on the other hand, it's exactly that: a form of capital. If companies and brands want to attract the sorts of partners who want to share more than mutually suspicious instrumental one-dimensional exchanges, embracing *values* as well as value is actually a way of getting ahead of the competition.

For the modern marketer – whether agent or seller – this is a crucial insight. Organizations and brands which are capable of building genuine emotional commitment and social capital have a hugely powerful and valuable asset. This asset helps them to achieve the crucial task of persuading consumers to 'join me in my circle of wealth creation'.

DEMOCRATIZING BRANDS

But this potential comes with a health warning. Like relationship marketing and permission marketing before it, if it's simply picked and used by good old fashioned seller-centric marketers for seller-centric purposes, its value is likely to slip through the perpetrator's fingers. The essence of 'values exchange' is that it must be mutual.

In one sense, the new demands being placed upon brands are rather akin to the democratic revolutions that shook the world from the seventeenth century onwards. Suddenly, for some unaccountable reason, people began to demand an element of control at least power sharing or power devolution – an input into what their governments did. They demanded the vote.

Nowadays, consumers have become aware that every time they purchase an item, they are effectively voting for it. In handing over money, they are effectively condoning or endorsing its actions. And as this realization grows, they are beginning to demand a voice in return for their support. In the political world, democratic movements advanced behind slogans like 'no taxation without representation' – no money without a voice. The same democratic sentiment is now being expressed towards organizations and their brands. As US researcher Hazel Kahan puts it, consumers are beginning to see themselves as citizens not only of countries but of corporations: with certain rights, including the right to have a say in how that organization behaves.

Democratic revolutions transformed the nature of government. Now the same is happening to brands.

The difference is that while the world of politics has had its democratic revolutions, these have hardly begun in the world of commerce, marketing and brands. Traditional marketers like to say 'the customer is king' but actually they think like absolute monarchs. When it comes to his brand, the modern brand manager expects to be given a divine right of control; the right to dictate everything about his brands, including product attributes, design, packaging, brand personality, communication ideas and execution, media strategy, distribution strategy, pricing strategy and so forth. But in a buyer-centric world populated by agents acting for and on behalf the consumer, the consumer expects not only a choice, but a 'say'.

The age of democracy utterly transformed the nature of government: its institutions, its processes, its language, its objectives. Democracy was about governments becoming citizens' agents – doing their bidding, rather than treating them as subjects. Democratizing brands could do the same for the corporation: consumers want corporations to be their agents too.

Marketers have long liked to say they are the consumer's voice within the corporation, but traditionally the scope of this voice has been extremely narrow. The consumer has been listened to, only to the extent and degree that this input can help the company produce a product that sells better. Now the equivalent of elections are needed: processes by which consumer concerns and preferences over *values* as well as value are monitored and responded to. Companies need to listen much harder, about more things. As Glen Peters, futures partner at PricewaterhouseCoopers and author of *Waltzing with Raptors*, puts it, they need to develop 'highly sensitive antennae turned to a wide spectrum of representatives of our emerging global civil society'.[10]

The example of cause related marketing

This developing demand for values 'agency' can be seen in the evolution of cause related marketing. Many companies' initial reaction to the growing consumer demand to broaden the exchange was cynical and short-term: they launched promotions related to a good cause in order to boost sales. But they got short shrift. The only cause related marketing (CRM) programmes with any credibility nowadays are those with genuine, demonstrable win-wins for both cause and brand.[11]

But the nature of this win-win is also changing. In its first incarnations, marketers adopted CRM for typically seller-centric reasons. CRM was one of many devices companies could use to tilt choice in their favour in tie-breaker situations: 'Given that products A and B are to all intents and purposes at price and quality parity,

I would rather buy the product that is doing something for a good cause than not.'

But increasingly, the real issue is not what the cause can do for the brand, but what the brand can do for the cause. As Mike Tuffrey, Editor of *Community Affairs Briefing*, argues, the future 'lies not in using CRM to sell more products through a link with a cause but in social marketing – using the power of marketing to tackle issues directly'.[12]

The next step? To use the organization's resources, power and influence not only to eliminate their negative impact on society (to *stop* polluting the environment, to *stop* abusing human rights) but to actually become 'a force for good'. At one level this already happens. Businesses can and do create benefits for third parties which they never pay for: investing in a plant which triggers economic regeneration in a deprived community, for example. But as Sue Adkins, Head of Cause Related Marketing within the UK's Business in the Community, points out, businesses could do even more if they wanted to. With all their resources and influence 'multi-billion pound multi-national corporations could quite literally change the world'.[13]

Companies that explore this route are becoming a form of social agent for their customers in a very real – though indirect – way. As Michael Willmott of UK researchers the Future Foundation remarks, 'Corporate citizenship is part of the service you offer your customer.'[14] One element, even if it is a relatively small element, of what customers 'buy' is the fact that by buying the company's product or service they are, in their own small way, helping that company (or brand) to make a positive contribution to society. In this way, consumers use their economic 'votes' wisely to achieve their values, as well as value.

UNBUNDLING THE SELLER-CENTRIC BRAND

The rise of *values* exchange as well as value exchange has enormous implications for brands. The traditional brand is a mask designed to attract: to focus the buyer's attention on the positive value of the offer, not on the values of the organization behind the offer. By broadening the exchange with companies, consumers are effectively peeling that mask away.

They are not always delighted by what they find. Brands have been managed to be attractive: to be 'nice'. They have not been managed to be 'good'. But as Roger Scruton observes, 'We are attracted by nice people: but only on the assumption that their niceness is a sign of goodness. When niceness turns out to be a mask, it rather repels than attracts us.' Hence the demand that brands and their producers be good as well as nice.

Overcoming this 'nice versus good' dichotomy is extremely difficult for the seller-centric marketer who lives and breathes closing sales. After all, the only point of being nice was to close the sale. Being good is a completely different kettle of fish.

This dichotomy between the nice and the good is placing the traditional model of the brand as bundle of emotional and functional attributes in a life-threatening pincer movement. As we've seen, marketers started inventing emotional attributes for their brands – by giving them 'personalities' in advertising campaigns, for example – because this was a more effective way of communicating their selling propositions than straightforward, narrowly functional appeals.

But the fact is, these emotions are not real. They are invented. The bundle is artificial. And as the Right Side Up revolution unfolds, new breeds of agent are emerging to address consumers' emotional needs genuinely and directly. We saw two of them in the previous chapter: communities of interest which share and promote a particular passion, and transformation agents. Within the sphere of values, other forms of passion brand such as the pressure group, the charity and the voluntary organization also appeal to, and operate directly on, the emotional plane. Why buy ersatz emotions from an artificial brand personality when you can have the real thing?

If it's narrow instrumental value you want, on the other hand, there is nothing more instrumental than the buying agent. By specializing on either one side or the other – emotion and values or function and instrumentalism – agents threaten to unbundle traditional seller-centric brand strategies, and trump them. Faking it just won't do any more. The rise of buyer-centric marketing with its imperative of creating value 'in my life' means that broadening the exchange to include values as well as value, and this is a must for most sellers and agents alike.

The seller-centric instinct immediately links the issues of ethics, corporate citizenship and social responsibility to whether or not it will help close sales. Even when these issues are not seen as just another 'marketing ploy' to help boost market share, the inevitable argument is that a brand or company with a good reputation is likely to do better in the marketplace than a brand or company with a bad one. That's fine and dandy. But it also misses the point.

Consumers wanting to share their values with organizations couldn't care less whether it helps boost sales or not. That puts the cart before the horse. The demand for things like ethics, corporate citizenship and social responsibility is a demand for agency in the sphere of values: a demand that organizations act 'for' me not only by providing products and services, but by acting with values that I approve of. The heat corporations now feel in this area is the heat of Right Side Up buyer-centricity.

PART 5

right side up in practice

The transition to Right Side Up marketing won't be easy. It's not just a matter of applying new technologies such as the Internet. It also involves inventing new institutions and evolving new mindsets. Would-be agents face a tough time constructing viable business models. Established players face an equally tough time responding to a transformed environment. And putting these three factors together creates a very messy situation. But there is a way through the mess.

liberating marketing

> *As great as the changes in marketing thinking have been until now, future changes in marketing thinking and practice will be even greater. Scholars today are questioning where the core concept underlying marketing should be* exchange *or* relationships *or* networks.
> Philip Kotler[1]

> *The cause of the origin of a thing and its eventual utility, its actual employment in a system of purposes, lie worlds apart: what exists, having somehow come into being, is again and again reinterpreted to new ends.*
> Friedrich Nietzsche[2]

THE END OF MARKETING AS WE KNOW IT?

In *The End of Marketing As We Know It*, former Coca-Cola Chief Marketing Officer Sergio Zyman perfectly sums up the imperatives of seller-centric marketing:

Convincing consumers to buy your products is the only reason a marketer is in business and the only reason that a company should spend any money at all on marketing. Buy my product. Period. If what you are doing now doesn't get consumers to do that, try something else.[3]

Zyman's book is all about getting back to basics. It's a reaction to a time in the 1980s when it seemed that 'image' was the be-all and end-all of marketing. The trouble with those days, he explains, is that this sort of 'brand hokum' marketing (as we called it earlier) was a waste of money. It created what Zyman calls 'virtual consumption' – 'the phenomenon that occurs when customers love your product but don't feel a need to buy it'.

> *Seller-centric marketing isn't the solution any more. It's the problem. It's stifling the new win-wins.*

Whereas, he continues, 'the only thing I care about is real consumption ... Popularity isn't the objective ... marketing has to move these consumers to action.'[4]

Zyman wanted to put brand hokum behind him and to get back to the real thing: good old-fashioned stimulus-response marketing; the consumer as a unit of demand for the marketer's product.

THE NEW WIN-WINS

We started this book noting the incredible power of industrial age win-wins. Marketing was invented to unleash, realize and multiply these win-wins and it did its job brilliantly. Today, these win-wins are subsiding while new, equally powerful information age win-wins beckon. But marketing as we know it isn't helping to realize these new win-wins. In fact, it's obstructing the task. Marketing isn't the solution any more. It's the problem.

The industrial age didn't create all that wealth simply because of a few inventions like the motor car and electricity. It created that wealth by building a complete *system* of mass production, distribution and advertising around them. In doing so, it constructed an interconnecting, mutually supportive web of institutions, concepts and practices: joint stock companies, markets, 'the consumer' seller-centric marketing itself. It needed all these things to unleash its full potential.

The information age won't reach its full potential just because of a few inventions like the Internet. It needs to create a new and different system capable of unleashing the win-win potential inherent in plummeting transaction costs, ever richer content and new flows of information. And to do so it needs its own web of institutions, practices and concepts: joint-info-stock companies or consumer agents, relationships and communities, consumers as information investors and co-producers seeking value 'in my life' – and buyer-centric marketing.

Marketing is the key. As long as we equate marketing with its narrow, emasculated version of helping sellers to sell – rather than with its core function of matching supply to demand, and connecting buyers to sellers – marketing will act as a brake on progress. As we've seen, if we look at marketing in its richer, broader sense of matching and connecting we quickly discover rich new seams of possibility through concepts such as: 'marketing worth buying'; value for time and return on attention; minimizing total purchasing cost and constructing total solutions; marketing that 'reverses the flow' that unleashes the potential of 'Join Me!'.

Only by bringing new technologies, new institutions and new marketing concepts together can we build a new win-win system capable of unleashing this potential.

In liberating marketing from seller-centricity, we also need to liberate brands. Brands were invented as masks to oil the wheels of one-dimensional exchanges of money for goods. But as the Nietzsche quote at the beginning of this chapter points out, the origin of a thing and its eventual utility often lie worlds apart. Brands may have been invented as devices to represent sellers' offers, but they are evolving into something far more important: the means by which different groups of people (including organized consumers and companies) negotiate and renegotiate the mutual exchange of value and values; the means of connecting like-minded people with similar goals together to maximize their joint ability to create, exchange and share wealth.

Actually, there's nothing new here. In his textbook *Principles of Marketing*, for example, Philip Kotler defines marketing as 'a social and managerial process by which individuals and groups obtain what they need and want through creating and exchanging products and value with others.' But as long as 'everyone knew' that marketing and brands were really about helping sellers to sell, such a broader, richer definition was an academic irrelevance. Now it's becoming a life or death matter for organizations, because those who cannot get this process of negotiation right will not survive the Right Side Up transformation.[4]

Old tools, new uses

Does that mean that, as Zyman put it, we face the end of marketing as we know it? Well, yes and no. We've already seen that the end of seller-centric marketing does not mean the end of sellers, or selling.

Likewise, the rise of buyer-centric approaches to the core tasks of matching and connecting does not mean the disappearance of carefully developed marketing tools, techniques and concepts. Yes, an awful lot needs to change and is changing. But we are not talking about a clean sweep. The money, time and expertise invested in developing these tools and techniques will not be wasted as we go Right Side Up: a new buyer-centric era will help unleash their full potential for the first time.

'Buy Me!' advertising that grabs the attention of the would-be buyer and uses it for the seller's purposes may be in (slow) decline. But the skills developed by advertising agencies: the ability to pack enormous amounts of information aimed at particular audiences into tiny amounts of space or time, and to amuse and entertain while communicating and informing: these skills will remain as precious as ever. Agents will need them as much as sellers.

Sellers have also invested vast amounts of time, money and effort learning how to maximize the potential of the database: to glean actionable knowledge from raw data, to discern trends in apparent chaos, to highlight nuggets of value. These skills and technologies are the lifeblood of the twenty-first-century agent business. And what's more, they can speed ahead in an agency environment unhindered by fears about privacy, confidentiality and so on: because the agent is using the customer's information *for* the customer, rather than for a third party.

The same goes for market research. A clever, systematic and

insightful understanding of people's changing needs and attitudes is as vital – arguably even more vital – for consumer agents as it is for traditional offer producers. Indeed market research will be liberated from the 'if the answer is not a soap powder (or a motor car), we don't want to hear it' syndrome that now dominates the industry.

The same goes for the insights that have propelled seller-centric marketing forward. The notion of 'emotional added value', for example, draws on the insight that the classical economist's market exchange – purely instrumental, purely rational – is a fiction. Exchanges always take place between people, and because of this they inevitably have human and social significance: a meaning. Buyer-centric marketing – and new breeds of agent – embrace this insight, and take it further, as we've seen.

Similarly the notion of relationship marketing is based on the fact that more value can be generated by the exchange of both money and information than by the mere exchange of money for goods. Buyer-centric marketing takes this insight as its starting point. The pioneers of one-to-one marketing meanwhile recognized that all relationships are personal and unique, simply because the individuals within them are personal and unique. One-to-one marketing – personalization and customization – is a sine qua non of effective relationship building. Most breeds of agent depend on this insight – and the technologies that make this insight a practical proposition – as their springboard.

The notion of permission marketing meanwhile recognizes that real relationships are only built between sovereign individuals who have an element of choice and control; not in the often phoney, restricted choice presented by the market: soap powder brand A, versus soap powder brand B. It also recognizes that to flourish, the relationship must be focused on win-wins. These insights lie at the heart of Right Side Up.

In other words, the various species of agent – buying agents, solution agents and transformation agents – adopt the insights of 'understand and get close to your customer', of emotional benefit and of database, relationship, one-to-one and permission marketing to liberate these powerful concepts from the manacles of seller-centric marketing; to actually achieve their potential. With buyer-centric marketing, these notions find their true home, for the first time. We are not talking about the 'end' of marketing, but its real beginning.

On the shoulders of giants, once more

The big question, however, is how the old and the new intersect, clash, mix and mingle. And the key point is this: buyer-centric marketers – and consumer agents – are able to do more because they are standing on the shoulders of giants.

You cannot eat, or drive, information. The information age is not a substitute for the industrial age, it is built on its foundations. Agents don't substitute for the thing-wealth created by the industrial age manufacturing and marketing machine; they source it and put it together in new ways to add a new layer of value for their clients. Product brands won't disappear. But a new breed of meta-brands – whose role is to help clients manage their dealings with these other brands – will flourish. It's not instead of, it's on top of.

It's a bit like the human brain – 90 per cent of the brain's activities and functions are to do with organizing and controlling the body's physical needs: keeping the body sustained through food and drink; keeping safe and reacting to danger by being aware of our surroundings and adjusting our actions to the signals we receive; procreation, and so on. We couldn't live without this 90 per cent.

But it's the 10 per cent that really intrigues us. That's where we 'live' our lives: in the conscious bit, where all our emotions, goals, aspirations, dreams and anxieties dwell. The 10 per cent might represent a small, additional layer compared to the bulk of what's going on. But it has become the governing bit; the bit that defines the organism's purposes and sets its direction. This is also true of agents and Right Side Up marketing. They are emerging from the substrata of what went before them.

We think of humanity as beginning with the rise of the 10 per cent of the brain's functions – the part that governs human consciousness – rather than the 90 per cent that does everything else. Similarly we will see the real beginning of marketing – marketing as it was always meant to be – with the emergence of Right Side Up.

are agents viable?

> *The twentieth century business model is to accumulate the trust and the assets of your customers . . . and then proceed to monetize their assets without their permission.*   Mike Saylor, CEO, Microstrategy[1]

ONCE AGAIN, VALUE 'IN MY LIFE'

Traditional industrial age businesses make their money by buying in key inputs such as raw materials and labour, combining them with infrastructure and core internal processes to create an output that people value enough to want to buy. They then go to market to realize this value. Value is created 'in the business' and sold 'in the market'. Agents are different. They create value in their clients' lives: by sourcing 'raw materials' (i.e. products and services) more efficiently and effectively (via buying agents); by streamlining 'internal' (i.e. life management) processes (solution agents); and by helping to realize value (transformation agents and passion brands). It's a very different type of business, and it earns its keep in different ways.

How agents survive

Agents earn their money in five main ways.

1. Direct payments from clients for value created

Wherever one person's work creates value for another, money is likely to change hands. There's nothing new here. People are prepared to pay good money for 'services rendered'; for things that really improve their lives. What is new is the way agents create this value, by acting as a buying agent or in constructing complete solutions in the areas such as personal financial management, home replenishment, home maintenance or personal mobility.

2. Lower operating costs

A key function of multi-dimensional exchange is to exchange value other than money. When an agent asks a consumer to 'Join Me' he is asking a consumer to invest many different assets: by doing work for free – say, inputting data on a website; by helping to create the product itself through chatlines or being a part of the community in a community of interest; by acting as a marketing partner, promoting the agent by physical and electronic word of mouth. And so on. These benefits aren't available to agents exclusively. Seller-centric marketers are racing after them too. But they're crucial to any of tomorrow's would-be low cost operators.

3. Realizing the value created by new economies of scale

Demand aggregators, who combine many individual consumers into single buying units, can wield an enormous amount of power, as every traditional retailer knows only too well. Information collected from consumers, about consumers, for consumers is an enormously valuable asset in the information age, and the agents who are most successful in recruiting consumers to invest this information are well placed to maximize its value in the marketplace.

4. Peeling away the layers of push marketing costs

As we've seen, industrial age marketing was constructed around an information hole, and the 'just in case' push marketing system it developed to compensate for this 'hole in the heart' is enormously wasteful and expensive. Agents who short circuit this cost by letting the consumer say 'here I am, this is what I want' in an organized fashion unleash tremendous amounts of value. This is a win-win glue that binds agents to sellers: agents can actually help sellers revolutionize their costs – which is a service worth paying for.

5. Reappropriating value taken from consumers

This last one is the least obvious but potentially one of the most important. As Microstrategy CEO Mike Saylor points out, the model upon which many great twentieth century businesses were built was 'to accumulate the trust and the assets of your customers through extreme expense on bricks and mortar, inventory, people, and then proceed to monetize their assets without their permission and without their knowledge, in an inefficient way.'

Saylor gives the example of a broadcaster broadcasting Jerry Seinfeld or a *Friends* show on TV. The show is the draw. But 'I sell your eyeballs. Without your knowledge. You don't have any say in who I sell them to.' And the way this asset of attention is sold, he continues, is full of waste because the ads that are shown are only relevant to a tiny proportion of viewers.

We can see similar examples of this 'monetization' of customer assets everywhere. The retailer sells the consumer a product, but aggregates the buying power of many consumers to force down the price he has to pay manufacturers, and maximizes his margins. The insurance company charges a premium to the consumer to cover his risks. He then aggregates these premiums to invest them in the stock and money markets.

Likewise, a bank offers current accounts to consumers who 'invest' their salary in the bank's coffers – at virtually zero interest. The bank then aggregates these many small sums to have access to vast amounts of capital, which it doesn't have to pay for. A magazine company sells subscriptions to readers. What the readers pay for is the magazine. What the magazine company gets – and the readers don't see – is a database: a list which the magazine company duly sells at great profit to all and sundry. And so on.

Then agents come along. And they offer to aggregate the consumer's attention, money, buying power, data – whatever it is – and to sell it on *behalf* of the consumer, in a way that suits the *consumer's* purposes rather than the corporation's purposes. Instead of surreptitiously gathering and monetizing these assets *without* the customer's permission, agents gather and monetize these assets *with* their customer's permission.

That's the agency difference. The agent delivers value for his clients by selling his customer's attention on his behalf; by selling his information on his behalf, by aggregating his buying power, or his savings, etc., on his behalf. In a sense, the agent's job is to reappropriate value existing business models 'steal' from consumers without their knowledge. And he earns a commission for every penny he gets back.

Now, of course, the automatic response of the media owner, retailer, insurance company, bank and magazine publisher is that these revenue streams are just one small part of what they do; that they give the consumer a lot of value in return; and that competition means that the amount of value returned is often so high that they struggle even to make a profit.

> *Agents reappropriate the value traditional business models 'steal' from consumers.*

It may be true. But irrelevant. In fact, that's what makes the agency challenge so disruptive for so many industrial age marketers. Wherever value is appropriated by seller-centric businesses from consumers without their knowledge or consent, agents will make a point of revealing this fact, and offering to add much more value for the consumer by acting for him instead. Why should companies make money selling lists of consumer names and addresses, for example, when organized consumers could sell this information for themselves, and keep control over who it's sold to, for what purposes in the process? Wherever agents succeed in reappropriating value in this way, they help to unravel the opposing business model.

The agency bill

This 'unravelling' is important, because agents will find it hard to gain critical mass if they simply add another layer of activity – and therefore cost – between buyer and seller.

As we've just seen, however, three of the main sources of agency revenue do not come from acting as a new layer, but from replacing existing layers. These layers can reside within customers' operations as well as sellers' operations. Any buying agent worth its salt, for example, will have a price comparison service. As well as helping buyers to find the same items at a lower price (which is worth paying for in its own right) such services also reduce total 'matching and connecting' costs in two ways. First, they help automate a key go-to-market cost for the buyer – the process of searching and comparing prices. Seller-centric marketers have always ignored this cost because they never had to incur it. For the buyer, the ability to slash this cost by automating it is an important plus.

Second, they can reduce sellers' go-to-market costs. The price comparison service effectively funnels buyers to particular sellers thereby reducing their marketing costs. This is so valuable they are often prepared to pay commissions for such referrals.

Table 1 (see over) illustrates how these five streams come together to generate revenues for the consumer agent. Nowadays, when we get a bill from a supplier – say a telecom or energy utility – the bill lists the services we have used and the appropriate charges, and presents us with the sum we now have to pay. It's never much fun getting bills.

With agents, however, getting a bill need not be that unpleasant. If we look at the list in Table 1, some of them are direct payments from client to agent for services rendered. But others are payments for value realized. For example, if the agent sells a lead to sellers ('this client has expressed an interest in skiing holidays'), or has sold aggregated data ('these are the profiles of clients who are interested in skiing holidays') it takes a payment from the seller and passes a proportion of this value back to the original 'information investor'.

Depending on the nature of the agent, payments *to* the client could exceed payments *from* the client. If the agent is a pure infomediary, for example, its entire business revolves around realizing the value of clients' information. Similarly, some buying agents will be able to pass cash back to their clients – while earning a commission for their pains. Bizrate earns a commission from sellers for connecting its clients to them, for example. But instead of 'monetizing this asset without the customer's permission', as Saylor puts, it makes a point of monetizing it *with* permission.

Here's how it explains its policy:

We subtract a $3 processing fee for each BizRater Rebate check that we process. However, before we process a check, members have to

Table 1 Where agents get their income

direct payments for work done/services – *e.g. solution or transformation agency services, such as delivery of goods or personal fitness training advice*

selling information – *payments from the client for information, news etc. collected at the client's request: e.g. specialist news services or product advice*

selling advice – *payments from the client for specialist expertise*

arrangement fees – *special payments for assembling specific solutions for, and on behalf of, clients: e.g. personalized holiday itinerary*

transaction fees – *paid by either seller or buyer, or both, in the course of bulk buys, auctions, reverse auctions, etc.*

commission fees – *paid by sellers for sales closed*

spreads – *on bulk deals: e.g. the difference between price paid in bulk deal and price charged to client*

loyalty contracts – *e.g. instead of ordering a replenishment item weekly, the client agrees to arrange a one year's supply, and the agent gets paid by the supplier for the benefits of this supply contract*

partnership fees – *charged to recommended infrastructure suppliers seeking to provide 'platform' services to clients, such as mobile telephony or credit cards*

selling individual client attention – *e.g. opt-in personalized advertisements*

selling individual leads – *e.g. 'these clients have expressed an interest in your offer'*

selling individually targeted offers – *e.g. opt-in promotions: 'these clients, with this profile, have expressed an interest in receiving offers from suppliers such as you'*

selling advertising – *e.g. highly relevant advertising on tightly focused community of interest sites*

selling aggregated information about an individual – *selling personal and transaction profiles of individuals to selected sellers, with the client's permission*

selling aggregated information about groups of people – *e.g. market research data sold on an aggregated (i.e. anonymous) basis*

selling customer feedback/opinions – *either to other customers or to corporations (e.g. Planetfeedback.com)*

have accrued at least $15 in rebates for the period. In this way, BizRate.com never makes money unless we are sending a much bigger rebate check first.

ALIGNMENT, TRUST, TRANSPARENCY

This statement from Bizrate exemplifies the agent mentality. It's acting for its customers. It's trying to create value for them. At the same time it's making sure it covers its costs and earns its profit. And it's completely above board about how and why the whole set-up represents a win-win. In other words, because it has aligned its interests with those of its clients, it can be transparent about its business model, and it can build its clients' trust around this alignment and transparency.

But what's to stop a would-be agent from slipping over into the industrial age 'asset-appropriation' business itself? The temptation not to pass back rebates, or to recommend a product because the seller is offering much better commission, rather than because it is a better product, is always a significant one. In fact, previous attempts to build agent models have often foundered on this rock. The classic example is the so-called independent financial adviser (IFA). His whole reason for existing was to provide independent, impartial advice in the best interests of the client. But IFAs were, for the most part, 'captured' by sellers through seller commissions. Another classic case of side-switching is the advertising agency. Advertising agents started out selling advertising space on behalf of media owners. They ended up buying it on behalf of advertisers.

The crucial question in each case is not fine intentions and pure motivations but the logic of economic incentives: to whose interests are you most aligned? Seller-centric business models are constructed to align the interests of the people who run the business with the interests of its investors. Investors invest their money in a firm to maximize their returns, and they pay the firm's management to do this for them. The board of directors of the typical company acts as the shareholders' agent. As far as the firm is concerned, the price of capital is agency. If it wants people to invest in it, it has to agree to maximize their returns.

The consumer agent is no different, except that this time it is the consumer investing his assets: crucially, information. For the agent, the price of information is agency. Alignment with the consumer therefore lies at the heart of the agent's business model.

That doesn't mean there aren't pitfalls or difficulties, however. Capitalists often complain about their agents on the board. They often complain that the board is failing to do its job in maximizing returns. They may complain that the board's members are paying themselves too much for doing it. They often want to construct special mechanisms, such as stock options, to make sure that the interests of the board are truly aligned to those of the shareholders.

And if we look at the history of financial reporting and accounting standards we can see that they are the results of an information arms race. The report and accounts are supposed to be a statement of stewardship: the board's stewardship of shareholders' financial investment. But the development of accounting standards has been driven by investors' endless quest for open, honest, factual disclosure of how effectively their company board agents are acting for them, and companies' endless attempts to get round these disclosure rules to sweep problems under the carpet and flatter their own performance.

No doubt the emerging world of agents will face the same issues. But the problem hasn't stopped the corporation as shareholder agent from blossoming to become the dominant form of commercial organization in the world today. Similar debates will not stop agents from gaining critical mass in the information age.

New value metrics

In fact, such debates are now urgently needed. Because if we look at the world of accounting and financial reporting we can see that it too has been entirely seller-centric. Accountants know everything about calculating value from the point of view of the seller but they know hardly anything about calculating value from the point of view of the buyer.

They can tell you everything, down to the finest bit of activity based costing (in sophisticated companies), about the cost of making and selling products, for example. But they never stopped for a second to study consumers' purchasing or solution costs. They have invested enormous sums of money, time and effort in trying to assess the effectiveness of advertising, direct marketing, and so on from the point of view of the seller – where effectiveness is defined as maximizing the returns on the seller's investment. But no one has bothered to measure advertising effectiveness from the consumer's point of view. How helpful is advertising in helping buyers buy? Does the cost of advertising (embedded within the final price of the product) represent good value for money, from the buyer's point of view?

Value for time spent searching and shopping for goods. Value for attention paid to marketing communications. Total purchasing cost (versus narrow product price). Whether a company's marketing is 'worth buying'. There's a whole new set of marketing measurements that still have to be developed. Wily agents will start developing their own 'report and accounts': designed to prove, period by period, just how the agent has provided excellent returns on the consumer's investment.

In the early days, as they struggle to gain critical mass, agents will indeed find it hard to make ends meet. Many things have to fall into place before they become viable. But as they mature, the real question begins to change: with agents snapping at their heels will traditional seller-centric businesses *remain* viable?

If we look back to the five main sources of agent revenue we can see that three of them are positively disruptive to traditional industrial age business models. Realizing new economies of scale by organizing the consumer's buying power, reversing the flow of marketing from push to pull, and reappropriating value 'stolen' from customers all strike right to the heart of today's typical consumer facing business.

And agents don't have to gain too large a share of any particular market before they make their financial presence felt. There's many a modern business – such as retailing – which depends on the first 90 per cent of its income to cover its costs, and only earns its profits on the last 10 per cent. There's also many a modern business which depends on just a small proportion of high value customers for most of its profits. As McKinsey's John Hagel notes, 'Many traditional business models are economically unstable in the face of the loss of even a small fraction of their best business.'[2]

By transforming the ways consumers relate to and interact with these businesses, that is precisely what agents aim to do: seize the best business from old model players. That means traditional seller-centric businesses and marketers will be forced to respond. The question is, how?

evolutionary trajectories

> To scale a higher peak – a potentially greater gain – often means crossing a valley of less fitness first. A clear view of the future should not be mistaken for a short distance.
>
> Kevin Kelly[1]

FIGHT OR FLIGHT?

Faced with the rise of the organized consumer and buyer-centricity, what do traditional players do? Organized consumers and their agents may be transforming the business environment, but numerically speaking they are always likely to remain a small minority. Like the lion on the savannah, their numbers may be tiny compared to the numbers of gazelles, zebras and wildebeest, but they create the environment in which these other beasts must act. Or to put it another way, agents are like that 10 per cent of the human brain that takes it to another level – of consciousness. But this 10 per cent depends on the continued existence of the other 90 per cent, even if it does 'take control'.

So what can traditional players do? They have five main options: fight, flank, go hybrid, co-operate or migrate.

Fighting means refusing to co-operate; putting every obstacle in the way of a would-be consumer agent. To gain credibility, for example, a buying club may need to offer certain high profile brands. But if those brands refuse to supply the buying club they may be able to undermine its credibility, protect the channels they do control – and their own margins.

Flanking means deliberately ramping up all those marketing elements that have the effect of helping buyers to buy: the useful information, the impartial product comparisons, the expert recommendations; plus, of course, minimized purchasing costs and fuller solutions. In this way, certain sellers may make the experience of dealing with them so satisfying that, again, a fully fledged agent finds it difficult to get a look in.

> *Faced with the Right Side Up revolution sellers can resist, adapt or become agents themselves.*

A hybrid strategy mixes good old fashioned selling with agency. A car company selling a car might offer to act as the consumer's agent in sourcing insurance or loans for that car. Alternatively a loan provider may say to potential customers, 'If you buy a car using one of our loans, we will source the car of your choice at the cheapest possible price.' In this way, a player in one industry turns another industry's core offering into a mere promotional tool. In the UK, for example, the Woolwich bank has tried something similar with its Motorbase service: customers taking out a car loan with the Woolwich can source their cars at discounted prices from a fleet operator rather than traditional full-price dealers.

For some companies, however, co-operation may be the best strategy. If a buying club or community of interest can provide you with the end product of your marketing – a customer – much more efficiently than you can using traditional 'push' marketing methods, it may create win-wins all round – for yourself, the agent and the customer – to work together to reduce total go-to-market costs.

The final main option is to migrate. There are many business models that have potential elements of agency within them. The question is, whether to focus on these elements and amplify them (while downplaying traditional seller-centric activities), or vice versa. Retailers already aggregate consumers' buying power, for example. But they don't buy *on behalf of* their customers. They still buy, and then sell. They still work according to a 'push' model. The opportunity to migrate from one model to another is clearly there, however. And the same is true in many other industries, as we'll see.

There is a sixth option – which is not necessarily an option but will nevertheless be adopted by many marketers with a traditional mindset – and that is to adopt an agency *positioning*: *to pretend* you are acting like an agent, but only to close more sales. In the long run, it's not tenable. But in the short term, such tactics can be extremely effective in muddying the waters.

CLIMBING NEW FITNESS PEAKS

Which of the five options is best depends on a number of factors, two of which are crucial. The first is the nature of the business itself. We've seen how in the information age there are four basic types of business: infrastructure providers, intellectual property creators, passion partners and relationship or connecting businesses. Each model lends itself more to one approach than another. Most intellectual property creators are natural sellers. They don't work by sourcing things customers already know they want. They prosper by offering customers things they didn't know they wanted, or didn't know they could have. Their ability to offer something truly special means they retain a powerful position as a seller. Other businesses such as retailers or credit card companies are basically infrastructure-driven businesses, and they may be well placed to use that infrastructure for agency purposes.

The second influencing factor is how embedded you are within the traditional model and how successful you are at it. Take a simple example such as Walkers Snack Foods, which came from nowhere to become the dominant player in the UK's salted snacks market. The way it did this was by using all the classic ingredients of industrial age marketing. It improved its quality; it broadened its distribution; it used improving economies of scale to keep prices low; it introduced new products such as the tortilla chip Doritos; it used promotions and advertising to engage consumers and remind them of its existence and value. Walkers has flourished because it understood the industrial age logic of mass production, distribution and advertising, saw the opportunity to extend this logic further, and pushed down this road as hard as it could. Clearly, it would be crazy for Walkers to change tack now. It has climbed to the top of what biologists call a fitness peak.

Fitness peaks happen when an organism has evolved in such a way that it is optimally aligned to its environment and any further change – say, longer legs or tail, or bigger feet (whatever) – are likely to take it 'down hill'. They would be changes for the worse, not better. A camel, for instance, is close to the fitness peak for deserts. It has feet which splay out to help it walk on shifting sands. It has humps which it uses to store nourishment to survive long periods without food or water.[2]

But environments are always changing – the fitness peak is always moving – so organisms are always having to adjust to stay at the top. Often there's a 'spur' or 'ridge' between the old peak and the new one. In the commercial world, companies often find they need to adjust a product line, invest in a new technology, or change an organizational structure or culture in order to perform better. They realize they are not at the top of their particular fitness peak, and identify the path to that peak.

But sometimes the path to that fitness peak isn't smooth or direct. A deep valley may have opened up between the new fitness peak and the old one. If the desert has grown green and lush, the camel has got to change an awful lot of fundamentals to get to the new fitness peak. Sometimes, the new peak may be very close 'as the crow flies', but the journey by land requires the organism to descend deep into the valley of competitive unfitness before climbing the other side. Which means it will probably perish along the way.

This is how organisms – and companies – get caught on local optima. Within the mountain range as a whole, their particular peak might be low compared to the peaks representing much higher levels of fitness and performance. But even if they have a crystal clear view of these much higher peaks, they still cannot make the journey from one to another. The intervening valleys are just too deep.

Together the information age and the rise of Right Side Up are triggering a veritable earthquake. Yesterday's supremely high altitude peaks are subsiding into the plains, and new peaks are being thrown up all around them. And these peaks are appearing at all points of the compass. The faster your particular peak loses altitude the more vulnerable you become. But choosing which peak to go for (infrastructure provider or passion partner? intellectual property creator or agent?), and finding the ridge or spur that can take you there isn't easy. Let's look at some of these choices in more detail.

MANUFACTURING AND BEYOND

Similar pressures – and possible evolutionary trajectories – apply across most manufacturing industries. Take cars. Yesterday, it seemed entirely natural for a Ford Motor Company to make and sell cars. Tomorrow might look very different. Ford may outsource the actual making of cars to more efficient, dedicated 'own label' suppliers (who make cars for other companies too). The key processes of matching (technological developments to different groups of consumers' desires) and connecting might be separated out from the actual processes of making the car.

This has already begun with some car manufacturers sharing plant and placing different 'badges' on its output; and with some parts suppliers such as Magna International expressing interest in full car assembly. In this scenario the car company moves from being an infrastructure operating business to become an intellectual property business. Already, as Charles Leadbeater notes, 'The term "car manufacturer" is increasingly a misnomer. The "car makers'" main skills are increasingly intangible. They excel at designing and assembling cars, marketing them and arranging consumer finance for car buyers.'[3]

But that's just one scenario. By reversing the flow car manufacturers might be able to transform both the cost structures and value added by their supply chains. Just as Dell mass customizes computers for its customers, the car maker's dream is to mass customize cars, thereby building a direct relationship with the consumer where information as well as money changes hands.

Successfully moving from a make-then-sell mode of operation would cut out massive costs that arise from perpetual mismatches of supply to demand while transforming (and sidelining) the role of the dealer. Under mass customization, dealers would no longer close sales, the car companies would.

At the same time, the rise of buying agents poses a double-edged sword of threat and opportunity to the car manufacturer. Fleet buyers and car hire firms are perfectly placed to evolve towards a buying club role. They already 'bulk buy' cars at very good rates. Why not simply add individual consumer orders on to these bulk buys, closing the sale at a price much lower than traditional retail channels while still being able to keep a handsome margin for their pains? The threat to the car manufacturer is obvious: loss of control and reduced margin. The opportunity, however, is to reengineer the marketing and distribution process, cutting swathes of cost from a legacy system that's now bloated and unwieldy.

> *As we turn Right Side Up old industrial divisions of labour blur, and new ways forward emerge.*

A fourth alternative for Ford would be to evolve towards a new solution superbrand role: one that looks at motoring from the consumer's, rather than the producer's, point of view: assembling everything the motorist needs (vehicles, financing, insurance, servicing and maintenance, traffic navigation etc.) into complete packages. Ford CEO Jacque Nasser's redefinition of the Ford Motor Company as a 'leading consumer company that provides automotive products and services through world class brands' gives a hint in that direction.

A fifth alternative would be to become the globe's leading overcapacity rationalizer, buying up rivals to eliminate overcapacity, stretching existing economies of scale in car design and assembly even further on a global scale, to keep on adding extra value for the consumer at lower cost.

Become a super-efficient infrastructure operator, shift to an emphasis on intellectual property (design and marketing), reengineer marketing processes through an accommodation with buying agents, evolve towards a solution agency role, or create an information-rich flow-reversing relationship with the customer? Each one of these is a possible evolutionary trajectory for the car manufacturer. But they represent very different futures – different directions of evolution. Choices have to be made.

The packaged goods heartlands

But what about packaged goods, the industry that invented modern marketing as we know it? Similar choices apply. The big plus for traditional producers is that their products are still needed. If we want to get our clothes clean, we still need soap powders. The downside, however, is that traditional seller-centric marketing strategies face being trumped either by buying agents (which threaten to decimate old brands' margins and influence) or by solution agents (which threaten to reduce them to the status of an invisible ingredient). Who cares what soap powder they use if they provide me with fresh clean clothes, ironed and ready to wear?

One obvious response is to extend the old industrial age win-wins. They may be subsiding, but in many instances they're not completely spent, as the Walkers example shows.

There are still economies of scale/cost benefits to be realized, particularly in the rationalization of overcapacity and in globalization: spreading costs and marketing spends out to create economies of scale at global rather than national or regional level. Many branded goods companies such as Unilever, Procter & Gamble and Philip Morris are culling their 'brand tails' – lesser, underperforming brands – to focus resource on major brands with global potential.

Another important realm of consumer goods is small ticket and impulse items, where what matters above all is presence and immediacy rather than sophisticated information services. Why employ an agent to buy ice-cream for you, when it's hot and you want one now, and there's an ice-cream vendor standing in front of you? As Boston Consulting Group's Philip Evans and Thomas Wurster remark, 'Does anybody need search engines, databases, threaded discussion groups, chat rooms – the whole panoply of comprehensive, objective navigation – to select and buy a pack of bubble gum?'[4]

Besides, many of these brands have the incredible momentum of

100 years of brilliant industrial age marketing behind them. They're 'intimate celebrities', both famous and familiar parts of our lives at the same time, which is an incredibly powerful position to be in.[5] For those with deep pockets, excellent products and brands, and superb infrastructure, simply extending and deepening the win-wins they already know may be the best course. Buying agents and solution agents will want to do business with them.

Nevertheless, those industrial age win-wins *are* sinking, and the pressure from the new imperatives of buyer-centric marketing – such as making your marketing worth buying and providing value for time and attention – is inexorable. So another way forward is to embrace specific elements of the Right Side Up marketing recipe book.

One company that is meeting this challenge head on is Procter & Gamble. With its heavy investment in research and development (including areas like pharmaceuticals), Procter & Gamble has set its sights on becoming 'a technology company' rather than a mere consumer goods producer: it is trying to evolve towards the rising information age peak of intellectual property. As chairman John Pepper said recently:

> There will be a far greater premium on leading-edge product technology. Brands that fall into the trap of merely *shifting* value with 'me-too' line extensions will quickly fall behind the market leaders that *create* value with fundamentally better, new products. In fact, a hallmark of tomorrow's leading brands will be their ability not just to improve existing products but to create entirely new product categories with innovative technologies.

Meanwhile, with initiatives like Reflect.com, Procter & Gamble is experimenting with the potential of 'reverse the flow' mass customization. Unilever, on the other hand, has begun tiny but brave experiments in the realms of solution agency, with its MyHome.co.uk clothes and home cleaning service. Yet others, such as Nestlé, are realizing the crucial importance of food solutions and investing heavily in this market, along with experiments such as Nescafé branded coffee houses which take the two dimensional product brand into the creation of three dimensional experiences.

Coca-Cola has long been decades ahead of its peers in understanding key issues such as value for time. Its strategy of being 'within an arm's reach of desire' fits perfectly with the themes of value for time and of creating value 'in my life'. It doesn't expect consumers to go searching for it. It goes to where consumers want to be. Through its sponsorship programmes, it is also seeking to embed itself as an essential ingredient in a crucially important new form of intellectual property – global events like the Olympic Games and soccer World Cup that bring people together in a shared fascination.

Meanwhile, there are huge opportunities for consumer goods companies to rationalize their go-to-market processes; to work with retailers and agents to reduce the costs of the go-to-market process. Initiatives such as the Efficient Consumer Response represent a start down this road.

Nevertheless, the overall trend is clear: mass produced consumer goods are fast losing their former role as pinnacles of incremental value creation to become a part of infrastructure – something consumers simply expect to be provided cheaply and efficiently. And most of these companies' share prices have begun to reflect that.

Retailers

The double edge of opportunity and threat is perhaps even greater for the traditional retailer. The threat side is that retailing is embedded in seller-centric marketing: retailers are basically distribution channels for sellers, and their business is constructed around the aggregation and distribution of physical goods.

The buying agent threat to this traditional business model is mortal: it literally tears the business into two. By reversing the flow and collecting and aggregating information and demand from the consumer, buying agents threaten to add much more value on the matching and connecting front (better choice at lower prices). This way, they get to 'own' the relationship and the information resource it creates. Meanwhile, specialist third party logistics providers can fill the breach to tackle the fulfilment side. 'E-tailing' is not a real threat to retailing. But the buying agent is.

Yet, at the same time, many retailers are perfectly poised to make the next evolutionary step and become fully fledged superbrand buying agents themselves. In fact, many of the things they have done over the years to increase the efficiency of their existing business model may, in retrospect, be seen as mere preparations for the day when they discovered their true role and future.

It's worth charting a few of the major steps in this trajectory. Back in the fifties and sixties retailers were traders and distribution channels for manufacturers. Retailers purchased manufacturers' stock and then tried to sell that stock to consumers. Having virtually zero access to information themselves – without EPOS data, all that happened at the checkout was that money changed hands for goods – retailers were almost completely reliant on manufacturers for information. Manufacturers used them as sales channels. Retailers were firmly a part of the push, stimulus-response marketing system.

Agents are catalysts. You don't need to trigger large scale competitive upheaval.

Then a few things began to change. The rise of EPOS data meant that retailers got a much better handle on what sold and what didn't sell. They began to understand the market better than manufacturers. With information and knowledge came power. At the same time, retail concentration created increased buying power and therefore negotiating muscle. Retailers began to extricate themselves from the role of mere sales channel to become an independent intermediary, playing one manufacturer off against the other, to maximize their own profits.

The next crucial step was the development of sense-and-respond operational systems. Retailers began to realize that buying in bulk, and then trying to sell this bulk, creates all sorts of costs (such as storage and marketing), and that these costs could be radically reduced by moving towards just-in-time replenishment systems. Instead of buying stock from manufacturers and then trying to sell it, they began to build EPOS-driven systems that would enable them to order what the consumer was buying. They had begun to reverse the flow.

But this was still on a mass, anonymous scale. Orders transmitted, often daily through computer automated ordering systems, represented aggregated demand information. Next came recognition of the individual. Starting with loyalty cards with connected basket data to names and addresses – and moving on, crucially, to

Internet ordering, retailers began the long evolution from mass marketers to one-to-one marketing. And with the development of home delivery services they began to change their business model – from one where consumers organized their lives around the shop and shopping, to one where they organized their operations around the consumer's life: to create value 'in my life'.

With these operational and infrastructure developments the most advanced retailers now stand poised at the edge of the next leap into buying agent status: aggregating consumer data and demand to help them, as buyers, to buy.

Making this leap won't be easy, however. Shifting from a business model where property is the key asset to one where customer relationships are the key asset is massively risky. Moving to a buying agent stance is just as big a culture change. And the learning curve required by the move towards an agency model is very steep.

Buying agency is not the only way forward for the retailer, of course. Improving shoppers' value for time by moving into 'shoppertainment' is an intellectual property based route – one whose potential has already been proved in a few showcases such as the Niketown retail concept. Some specialist retailers will evolve towards what the Henley Centre calls 'passion partners', exploring a fascination with a particular area with their customers. Realizing new economies of scale, on a regional and global basis, is a perfectly viable infrastructure-based strategy currently being pursued by companies such as Wal-Mart. If your infrastructure efficiencies are strides ahead of what any would-be buying agent can achieve, then as a traditional player you can still beat off the buying agent unbundling threat. On the other hand, there are many ways in which buying agents could trump these efficiencies by adding value 'in my life'. Just like the car companies, retailers have many potential ways forward, and they lead in very different directions.

THE MEDIA

The same is true for the media. The one thing that traditional media excels at doing is bringing lots of people together to share important public events, whether it's TV drama that's got everyone talking, or coverage of celebrity events such as World Cup football matches. That's not going to go away. In fact, it's one way traditional media owners can extend and deepen their existing business model: as long as there are sellers to sell (or agents to create clients), advertising in these forums will remain immensely powerful and immensely expensive. To the extent and degree that this 'blockbuster' entertainment function is needed existing media companies can continue ploughing their existing furrow. Making an event out of a new film, or book. Organizing events around it, so that it becomes a thing people do, talk about, take part in. Going to see a new film when everyone is talking about it – when it's fresh and new – is very different to seeing it on video a year later. There's nothing new here. It's a natural for this business.

But underneath this extremely high profile activity, in the bowels of the business, most traditional media owners are being attacked, simultaneously, on three fronts.

First, digital distribution. As we saw in Chapter 8, a high proportion of what consumers pay for when they buy a traditional media product such as a newspaper or CD is the physical information carrier – the newsprint or CD itself. And media owners' source of power rests on their control of this distribution mechanism. With digital distribution, those cost and power structures – and therefore revenue streams – begin to dissolve.

Second, media owners' core business – the provision of information – is being commoditized. 'News' is now everywhere, we face information overload, and original sources of news, such as Reuters, are finding ways to bypass traditional news distributors by going online and providing services to Internet portals like AOL. And special intellectual property – information that people really value – is, by definition, a rare thing: the great blockbuster movie or novel, for example.

As Jay Walker, founder of Walker Digital Corporation lab – an Internet business model incubator that spawned Priceline.com – comments: 'There are only four ways to create value in the new economy, and they're really simple: information, entertainment, convenience and savings.' The trouble with information *per se* is that 'there's almost no business there ... it gets reduced to a very low, almost commodity level [and] if information is your product you can't control its redistribution on a network'. The trouble with entertainment, on the other hand, is that real entertainment – the entertainment that consumers are prepared to pay good money for – 'is very expensive to create ... it's very hard to entertain in our society'.[6]

Slowly but surely, in other words, with a few special exceptions the core value of the media's product is subsiding. The third challenge is that the glue that made the media so powerful in the information age – advertising funding – is being unbundled by agents. Once-rich sources of classified advertising revenues are migrating to new Internet-based virtual exchanges and communities of interest. Infomediaries are moving in on the connecting-buyers-to-sellers business by reversing the flow. Instead of sellers sending messages to potential buyers, infomediaries (in their various forms) send messages from potential buyers to potential sellers, thereby fundamentally reengineering both the costs and the mechanics of the advertising process.

Sliced this way and that, what viable evolutionary trajectories are there for traditional media? We've seen one: the blockbuster creation and distribution approach. A second intellectual property-based approach is to move from advertising funding to subscription funding, such as Pay TV; a route which lends itself (in some cases) to a community of interest model.

Classified ad driven publications and programmes (especially those on digital TV) have a similar evolutionary path: to become community of interest builders. They can create their own marketplace for special interest groups, combining chat, opinion sharing, advice, news about new product developments, discussion and debate about pros and cons of aspects of the industry, plus efficient transactions, plus perhaps reverse auction or buying club functions.

As making money out of making and distributing copies – books, films, CDs, software – declines, publishers will discover that another aspect of their business – the role of information filter or editor – is rising rapidly in value and importance. Using technologies such as those developed by Microstrategy with strategy.com, media companies have the opportunity to evolve towards an information agent role: filtering and seeking out the information that I want. With their much vaunted editorial independence, news companies are well placed to move into the 'impartial information adviser' agency role. Currently, however, they are classic top-down 'push' business models, and to fulfil this agency function they need to reverse the flow – to be able to connect the information the customer wants to the information sources they have.

Like their counterparts in the holy trinity of the industrial age marketing system, therefore, media companies face a number of possible ways forward including:

▓ more of the same, extending existing strengths through 'block-busterization'
▓ evolving towards a community of interest building role, which combines the provision and sharing of information with advertising and transactions
▓ becoming the consumer's trusted information agent
▓ becoming an ingredient supplier to other services (such as providing news feeds to portals)

THE NEW CONVERGENCE

Manufacturing, retailing and the media. These were the holy trinity that were brought together by industrial age win-wins to form a single, formidable marketing system. Now those win-wins are dissolving and these once-familiar business beasts are evolving in different directions. So much so that soon we will realize that, like 'the consumer', these categories of 'manufacturer', 'retailer' and 'media' are fading industrial age terms.

But even as these different entities fan out across the new information age landscape, seeking out the new fitness peaks, they are tending to converge on the same pinnacles of value. Take just one example: the home maintenance solution agent. Utilities, financial services outfits such as insurance companies, retailers and start-ups like HomePro.com could all stake their claim on the same 'opportunity space'. The key battles are no longer between different players *within* producer-defined 'industries' for 'market share' but between players from many different industries – all drawn towards a new centre of gravity of consumer value: the new high ground of value 'in my life'.

Seller-centric marketers often like to see this in terms of 'brand extension': they see everything in the world through the eyes of their brand first, the customer second. Technology-minded people point to how converging technology is creating these pressures. Both have their truths. But the real driving force is the demands of buyer-centric consumer value.

If I can buy a product by pointing a mobile phone at a bar code, then why shouldn't my telecom provider become a bank? If so, he may want to use an existing bank's infrastructure to provide this service: he may want to 'ingredientize' or 'own labelize' the bank's offering. The bank, however, may have different ideas. It may want to evolve towards a personal financial agent role, with the mobile phone as a key part of this one-to-one interactive service. For the companies concerned, these are major strategic issues. But these strategic issues are now defined by the dictates of buyer-centricity: minimized purchasing cost and total solutions.

As traditional sellers grope towards agency services, ignoring and transcending old industry boundaries thus becomes the norm. To replace stolen and broken items for their clients, many insurance companies buy direct from suppliers, thereby avoiding the retailer mark-up. But why limit this to replacing stolen or broken items. Why not expand this into a fully-fledged buying service for customers? In which case, you are treading on traditional retailers' toes.

And why don't credit card companies use their incredible ability to aggregate consumer information evolve to become buying clubs on a vast scale? Instead of simply paying for big ticket items with your credit card, *order* the item you want and let the credit card company aggregate demand. Via a website, for example, the card company could solicit interest each month from all its customers planning to buy cars, electrical goods, holidays, airline tickets, and so on.

If they don't move in such a direction, then a different type of financial demand aggregator will slice their business up: the personal financial agent who aggregates the debts and savings of millions of clients and 'plays' the money markets for them, placing debts over night, each night in the lowest interest lender – and placing savings, over night, each night with the highest paying borrowers. By the end of the year 2000, Microstrategy chief Mike Saylor hoped to have aggregated $50 billion worth of consumer equity for just such an operation. The agency mindset changes everything.

HYBRID CAPITALISM

The dissolution of old industry boundaries is accelerated by the fact that moving to a hybrid agent role can be an excellent way to cannibalize another company's business. A share trading operation like Ameritrade, for example, does not have a credit card business. But if it can act as agent, arbitraging its customers' credit for them in order to increase their loyalty to it as a brand, then it's a win-win for Ameritrade and its clients. A likely response from a credit card company? To offer free or zero margin sharing trading as a 'promotional incentive' for its clients.

As buyer-centric marketing takes over, sellers will 'happily commoditize each other's business to protect their own individual businesses from commodization', predicts Boston Consulting Group's Philip Evans. A TV manufacturer, for example, sets himself up as a specialist home theatre navigator, providing comprehensive and objective information about all the video and audio products made by other manufacturers which consumers might want to source to get the best final result. Within this overall service it 'almost invisibly' presents its own products in 'a favourably biased light'. In response, of course, the sellers of video and audio products provide objective information about TVs.

In this way, by offering navigation services that solve customers' problems instead of pushing products, and by providing impartial comprehensive information about the products they do *not* sell, suppliers can take on the mantle of agency in *most* of what they do.

Visionaries like Microstrategy's Mike Saylor see huge potential in such activities. He's busy signing up as many partners as possible to syndicate his strategy.com technologies, which provide the platform for personalized services of this sort. Companies using the strategy.com platform will use agency services – affecting *other* people's businesses – to shore up customer loyalty to their own business, Saylor predicts:

> You have 99 channels [potential agency services]. One of them you are not going to offer. The credit card guy is not going to offer credit card arbitrage. So when the finance guy offers credit card arbitrage, the credit card guy offers personal health advice, or else he's going

to get killed. So the point is they are all attacking each other. And we are selling the weapons.[7]

The emergence of such hybrids underlines the pressures that are now building on traditional seller-centric marketing strategies. We still live in a seller-centric marketing world. But as the information age, agents and buyer-centric marketing gain critical mass that will change in three ways. First, we will see 'pure' agent models emerge – such as HomePro.com. Second, existing players will migrate towards an agent role. Third, as with the examples cited by Evans and Saylor, sellers will increasingly have to incorporate buyer-centric elements into their marketing strategies. And the exact nature of the approach taken by the marketer concerned will become an issue in it own right.

Airlines have already faced this issue. Ideally, what they would like to do is to slash their transaction costs, cut out travel agents (and their commission) and 'build relationships' with their customers (i.e. gather information about them) by selling tickets direct over the Internet. But this approach is entirely seller-centric. Buyers want to be able to shop around; to find the best deal; to make easy comparisons between flight times and offers. So to forestall the rise of online travel brokers who do this job for consumers, in both the US and Europe competing airlines are getting together to create an unbiased site which achieves some of their transaction cost and commission objectives, while also giving the consumer some of the ease and objectivity he or she wants. The tussle between seller-centric and buyer-centric strategies – and entities – continues.

Likewise in white goods, where Whirlpool has invested in a website called Brandwise which provides detailed, independent, objective assessments of the strengths and weaknesses of different brands of washing machine and refrigerator, plus chat rooms where previous owners discuss the merits of various models. Now Brandwise is moving from being an information-only site to closing transactions – and questions are being asked about its true allegiance. As one Net-posted article asked: 'Just how unbiased can the reviews be, given that among its financial backers is Whirlpool, one of the largest appliance makers in the world?'[8]

As more and more companies begin visualizing their business in terms of finding products for their customers as opposed to finding customers for their products they are trying to wrestle with this issue of what it means to represent a customer's interests, comments one-to-one marketing pioneer Don Peppers. 'I don't know what the real resolution is,' he admits honestly.

Closely related is the whole debate about firms' objectives. Can a company whose prime purpose is to maximize shareholder value really be on the side of its customers?

A clever answer is that if the company's business model is agency – if it makes its money by being the best and most effective agent around – then of course it can. The issue gets a little more complicated if, instead of seeing the financial stakeholders as being the 'owners' of the company, the consumer's investment of valuable information (and time) is recognized as being an investment that deserves a return.

Companies are already facing similar issues with another group of stakeholders: employees. We now live in a world where, often, the company's most valuable asset resides in the heads of people who walk out its doors every night we need to rethink our notions of 'capital'. As *Fortune* writer Tom Stewart points out, companies needed to raise funds to build factories, utilities, whatever. Offering shares of the company to stockholders turned out to be a good mechanism to do that. But increasingly, one does not need those large machines. Or one rents them. Instead, the real investments in the company are made by people who have invested in developing their own human and intellectual capital. They are a kind of capitalist. Their investment is their talent. Says Stewart, 'That raises a fundamental question for the company: why are we here? And who are our real investors? The answer is that a company's real investment is in bringing these smart people together. We are moving towards a sort of hybrid capitalism. There are the people who put up the capital to buy the desks, and manage the cash flow etc. And there are other people who put up the intellectual capital the company works with.'[9]

This raises a further question. We started out in this book noting how the joint-stock company helped to unleash and power the industrial age. But the joint-stock company was just one of many radical institutional innovations and ideas such as the extension of democracy, the creation of local government, the birth of modern savings and insurance schemes, and the development of a professional civil service which helped unleash the full potential of the industrial age.[10] The information age is based on a revolution in technology.

But its true potential will only be unleashed by equally radical institutional innovations and ideas. The joint-info-stock company, or agent, is one of them. And they encourage the spread of new ideas about business. 'To fully address the infomediary opportunity you have to adopt the customer's side,' observes McKinsey's John Hagel. This is a 'fundamental mindset shift that is a very challenging issue for many large companies. I am reasonably optimistic that some companies can make that shift. But there is no doubt that it is probably one of the most challenging and wrenching changes that a large company would have to go through in order to address this opportunity.'[11]

Right Side Up marketing does indeed represent a fundamental mindset shift. The issues it raises are indeed very challenging – and 'wrenching'. But the opportunity is also much too big to ignore.

notes

Chapter 1 Introduction

1. Philip Kotler, *Kotler on Marketing*, Free Press, 1999, p205

Chapter 2 The agency revolution

1. Theodore Levitt, *The Marketing Imagination*, Free Press, 1983
2. Interview with Mike Saylor, 10 May 2000
3. Interview with Barry Hill, 14 June 2000
4. Interview with Philip Evans, 12 April 1999

Chapter 3 On the shoulders of giants

1. Seth Godin, *Permission Marketing*, Simon & Schuster, 1999, p55
2. Douglass C. North, *Institutions, Institutional Change and Economic Performance*, Cambridge University Press, 1990, p12

Chapter 4 The great incubus

1. Stuart Kauffman, *At Home in the Universe*, Viking, 1995, p27
2. Interview with Niall Fitzgerald, Unilever Co-Chairman, *Market Leader*, Autumn 1998
3. Stuart Kauffman, *At Home in the Universe*, p14
4. Differentation is particularly tough for industrial age marketers because they create value through the production of standardized offers. But while offers naturally congregate around fitness peaks, customers don't. Customers are 'naturally' different to one another. They don't need to struggle to be different. They *are* different. For industrial age and information age marketers the imperatives are quite different, therefore. While 'differentiation' is an endless issue for the industrial age marketer who sells sameness; the ability to achieve cost-effective standardization (to minimize the costs of complexity) is an ever present issue for the customer-centric information age marketer who lives and breathes customization.
5. Glen Cox, *New Product Introduction – Successful Innovation/ Failure: A fragile boundary*, ACNielsen/Ernst & Young, 1999
6. Information Resources Inc, 1999 Pacesetters Study
7. Michael Dell, *Direct from Dell*, HarperCollins Business, 1999, p141
8. Niall Fitzgerald, *Market Leader* interview, Autumn 1998
9. Seth Godin, *Permission Marketing*, p38
10. If you haven't read Peter Senge on 'the beer order game', do. It's brilliant. See Peter Senge, *The Fifth Discipline*, Century Business, 1990
11. James Womack and Daniel Jones, *Lean Thinking*, Simon & Schuster, 1996, p87
12. Marketing old hands now complain about this changing atmosphere. Veteran Hugh Davidson, author of the *Offensive Marketing* books, protests that the marketing profession has been taken over by 'markeaucrats'. (See Hugh Davidson, *Even more Offensive Marketing*, Penguin, 1997, p51.) Peter Dart, of the Added Value company, complains that 80 per cent of marketers' time is now spent on presentations and administration and that the 20 per cent that's left is 'boring, rooted in the past'. Marketing people, he complains, have become 'kind of, well, constipated . . . in industries where marketing has traditionally been important for decades, which are showing great signs of utter stagnation.' (Peter Dart, 'In My Opinion', *Business Life*, June 1997)

13. Robert Wehling, Senior Vice President, Procter & Gamble, in an internal memo to all regional managers, June 1995
14. Peter Sealey, 'How e-commerce will trump brand management', *Harvard Business Review*, July–August 1999, p171
15. John Brand and Ian Davis, 'Marketing's Mid-life Crisis', *McKinsey Quarterly*, 1993, No. 2
16. Peter Senge, *The Fifth Discipline*, p50

Chapter 5 Wanted: 'New! Improved!' marketing

1. Don Peppers and Martha Rogers, *The One-to-One Future*, Currency Doubleday, 1993, p54
2. Interview, Philip Evans
3. Interview, James Milojkovic
4. For a more detailed discussion of this point, see Alan Mitchell, 'Out of the Shadows', *Journal of Marketing Management*, 1999, Vol. 15, pp25–42
4. Adrian Slywotzky and David Morrison, *Profit Zone*, John Wiley, 1997

Chapter 6 Two false dawns

1. Sergio Zyman, *The End of Marketing As We Know It*, HarperCollins Business, 1999, pxv
2. Interview with Martha Rogers, 9 March 2000
3. Susan Fournier, Susan Dobscha and David Glen Mick, 'Preventing the premature death of relationship marketing', *Harvard Business Review*, Jan–Feb 1998
4. Martha Rogers, writing in Frederick Newell, *loyalty.com*, McGraw Hill, 2000, pxv
5. Seth Godin, *Permission Marketing*, p137
6. Ibid., p43
7. Ibid., p158
8. Ibid., pp44–8
9. James Twitchell, *Lead Us into Temptation*, Columbia University Press, 1999, p192
10. Simon Knox and Stan Maklan, *Competing on Value*, FT Pitman, 1998, p19

11. Vance Packard, *The Hidden Persuaders*, David McKay, 1957; revised edition, Pelican, 1981

12. James Twitchell, *Lead Us into Temptation*, Columbia University Press, p177

13. quoted in Helen Jones, *Advertising Effectiveness*, Financial Times Retail and Consumer, 1998

14. Speech to Paine Webber's annual media conference in New York, December 1999

Note: An alternative explanation of comments like these is that they are just sophisticated sales pitches. These are advertising industry executives coming up with a new and better way of selling advertising to their clients. To the extent that claims about the nemesis of product or service differentiation are exaggerated, this may be true. Some marketers draw upon writings by Ted Levitt to support their case, especially a ground-breaking essay where Levitt pointed out that a core functional benefit such as bread from a baker, or loans from a bank, quickly becomes a mere 'entry ticket' because, to enter that particular business, every competitor must offer that benefit. So competition spreads out across a series of additional features – presented by Levitt as a series of concentric rings from the core product, to the 'expected' product, to the 'potential' product. These marketers draw the conclusion that the real and final frontier of competition must lie at the outer circle – like the outer wave spreading from a stone thrown into a pond – and that as areas like core product, service, credit terms are matched by competitors, this final frontier must, necessarily, be the intangible added values of brand imagery, associations, emotional attributes etc.

In fact, the whole point of Levitt's essay was to point out that differentiation can, and does, take place anywhere, within any of these rings, all the time. Competitors are always trying to out do each other down in whatever respect they can, so the target of competition is always moving. The point is, not to be able to invent an ever-lasting 'unique selling point' but to be expert at creating a whole series of them, over time. That is why Levitt called his essay 'Marketing Success Through Differentiation – of Anything' in Theodore Levitt, *The Marketing Imagination*

Chapter 7 Trapped!

1. Peter Senge, *The Fifth Discipline*, p44
2. Theodore Levitt, *The Marketing Imagination*
3. Ibid., p153
4. Ibid., p162
5. Ibid., p154
6. Peter Drucker, 'Management's New Paradigms', *Forbes*, 5 October 1998
7. Sergio Zyman, *The End of Marketing As We Know It*, p232

Chapter 8 At last! An escape route!

1. Stephen Haeckel, *The Future of Interactive Marketing*, Harvard Business Review, November–December 1996
2. From an interview in *Strategy + Business*, Booz, Allen and Hamilton, Issue 2, 2000
3. For more examples, see James Twitchell, *Lead Us into Temptation*, Columbia University Press, 1999, p33
4. see for example, Thomas Stewart, *Intellectual Capital*, Nicholas Brealey, 1996
5. Allan Leighton, quoted in Reuters interview, 13.12.99

Chapter 9. Who is marketing for?

1. Don Peppers, interview, 9 March 2000
2. Sergio Zyman, *The End of Marketing As We Know It*, p232
3. Indrajit Sinha, 'Cost transparency: The Net's real threat to prices and brands', *Harvard Business Review*, March–April 2000, p44
4. Philip Kotler and Gary Armstrong, *Principles of Marketing*, 7th edition, Prentice Hall, 1996, pp12–13
5. From an interview, 12 April 1999

Chapter 10 Would your customers buy your marketing?

1. Barry Hill, interview
2. R. H. Coase, *The Firm, the Market and the Law*, University of Chicago Press, 1988, p6
3. Berryman, Harrington et al, 'Electronic Commerce: three emerging strategies', *McKinsey Quarterly*, 1998, No. 1
4. Douglass C. North, *Institutions, Institutional Change and Economic Performance*, p28
5. Patrick Butler et al, 'A revolution in interaction', *McKinsey Quarterly*, 1997, No. 1
6. see *Business Week*, 'At Ford, e-commerce is job 1', 28 February 2000
7. Interview with Niall Fitzgerald, *Market Leader*, Autumn 1999
8. Berryman, Harrington et al, 'Electronic Commerce: three emerging strategies'

Chapter 11 Do you provide return on attention?

1. Seth Godin, *Permission Marketing*, p93
2. www.cluetrain.com
3. quoted in Kevin Kelly, *New Rules for the New Economy*, Fourth Estate, 1998, p59
4. Seth Godin, *Permission Marketing*, p25
5. Ibid., p48
6. WPP Annual Report and Accounts, 1999
7. Quoted in Alan Mitchell, *Brand Strategies in the Information Age*, FT Retail and Consumer, 1997
8. David Weinberger, 'Why everyone hates marketing', *Journal of Brand Management*, Vol. 7, No. 4, March 2000, p292
9. Mike Saylor, interview, 10 May 2000
10. John Hagel and Marc Singer, *Net Worth*, Harvard Business School Press, 1999, p232
11. Regis McKenna, interview, 14 June 1999

Chapter 12 How valuable is your offer?

1. Robert Reich, *The Work of Nations*, Simon & Schuster, 1991
2. *Business Week*, 27 March 2000

3. Geoffrey Colvin, 'How to fix GM: Sell it to Toyota', *Fortune*, 6 March 2000

4. quoted in Tim Burt, 'Winds of change start to blow', *FTAuto* survey, 16 September 1999

5. Kevin Kelly, *New Rules for the New Economy*, p199

6. Adrian Slywotzky and David Morrison, *Profit Zone*, p40

7. Not all connector businesses are agents. Agents are only one form of connector business. And it would be a mistake to see, say, a telecom company as a connector business. Telcoms provide the infrastructure for connector businesses: what they sell is the technology that makes the connections; connector businesses sell the fruits, or content, of these connections.

8. Tom Stewart, interview, December 1998

9. Kevin Kelly, *New Rules for the New Economy*, p147

10. Joseph Pine and James Gilmore, *The Experience Economy*, Harvard Business School Press, 1999

Chapter 13 Can *you still deliver value?*

1. Kevin Kelly, *New Rules for the New Economy*, p112

2. Garth Hallberg, *All Customers Are Not Created Equal*, John Wiley, 1995

3. Richard Koch, *The 80/20 Principle*, Nicholas Brealey, 1998

4. Brian Wolff, *Customer Specific Marketing*, Cadmus Publishing, 1996

5. Garth Hallberg, *All Customers Are Not Created Equal*

6. John Hagel and Marc Singer, *Net Worth*, p224

7. Ibid., p210

8. With a repeat purchase of around 45 per cent more than a half of all car buyers would rather do business with a stranger than with the people they know.

9. Philip Evans, *How Deconstruction Drives Deaveraging*, Boston Consulting Group Perspective pamphlet, 1998

Chapter 14 Do you offer 'value for time'?

1. For example, the Henley Centre reports that in 1991 51 per cent of UK consumers agreed with the statement 'I never seem to have

enough time to get things done', while by 1998 that proportion had jumped to 63 per cent. Among full time workers, the figure was 73 per cent, and amongst single working parents, 79 per cent. (Henley Centre, *Planning for Consumer Change*, 1999)

2. Gallup poll, September 1998, quoted in Henley Centre, *Planning for Consumer Change*, Issues book, p9.
3. Joseph Pine and James Gilmore, *The Experience Economy*, p67
4. Roland Berger & Partners, *How to implement consumer enthusiasm*, ECR Europe, 1999

Chapter 15 Why should people trust you?

1. Martin Hollis, *Trust within Reason*, Cambridge, 1998
2. Philip Stephens, 'A question of trust', *Financial Times*, 19 February 1999
3. Matt Ridley, *The Origins of Virtue*, Viking, 1996, p250
4. Douglass C. North, *Institutions, Institutional Change and Economic Performance*, p33
5. Francis Fukuyama, *Trust: the social virtues and the creation of prosperity*, Free Press, 1995
6. Nirmalya Kumar, 'The power of trust in manufacturer-retailer relationships', *Harvard Business Review*, November–December 1996
7. David Weinberger, 'Why everyone hates marketing', p293
8. Widely publicized research by the Henley Centre in the UK seems to show, for example, that well-known consumer brands are often more trusted than many venerable institutions. But this research needs to be treated with caution. First, polling very high on the trust stakes hasn't stopped brands like Kellogg losing swathes of market share to rivals such as own label. Clearly, trust doesn't count for much if you are not perceived as still delivering value for money.

   And if you recast the research just slightly you can end up with very different results. Some of the highest scorers in the Henley Centre research are multinationals. But when consumers are asked if they trust 'multinationals' in general, trust levels plummet. And when the Future Foundation asked a similar set of questions about *people*, as opposed to *institutions*, they came up with a very different picture. The 1999 research by Mori showed that 70 per cent or more of the British public said they trusted doctors, teachers, TV news readers, judges and clergymen to tell the truth. These trust levels had actually *risen* over the previous decade, not fallen. On the other hand, business leaders – including, presumably, business leaders behind the brands which consumers trust so much – got short shrift, with barely 20 per cent of consumers saying they trusted them to tell the truth.

9. Philip Stephens, 'A question of trust'

Chapter 16 Who are brands for?

1. John Hagel, *Harvard Business Review* online discussion forum
2. Michael Lanning, *Delivering Profitable Value,* Capstone, 1998, p3
3. John Hagel, *Harvard Business Review* online discussion forum
4. Interview with John Hagel, April 1999
5. David Weinberger, 'Why everyone hates marketing', p291
6. see, for example, Dave Allen, 'The ACID test', *Journal of Brand Management,* Vol. 7, No. 4, p257; John Hagel and Marc Singer, *Net Worth,* pp230–1
7. Don Peppers, letter to *Harvard Business Review,* May–June 1999
8. Bob Tyrrell, 'The new service ethos, a post-brand future – and how to avoid it', *Market Leader,* Autumn 1998
9. Interview with A. G. Lafley, June 2000

Chapter 17 Create total solutions

1. Adrian Slywotzky and David Morrison. *Profit Zone,* Wiley, 1997
2. The Store's Maureen Johnson in a presentation to ECR Europe Conference, Paris, 1999; and Howard Southern and Maureen Johnson, *Consumer Value in the Future,* WPP The Store, 1999
3. Regis McKenna, *Real Time,* p38
4. Kevin Kelly, *Out of Control: the new biology of machines,* Fourth Estate, 1994, p27
5. Peter Drucker, 'Management's New Paradigms', p169
6. Fred Wiersema, *Customer Intimacy,* Knowledge Exchange, 1996, pp6–7
7. Adrian Slywotzky and David Morrison, *Profit Zone,* p37
8. Michael Dell, *Direct from Dell,* p161

9. Adrian Slywotzky and David Morrison, *Profit Zone*, pp83–5
10. Sandra Vandermerwe, *Customer Captialism*, Nicholas Brealey, 1999
11. Philip Evans and Thomas Wurster, *Blown to Bits*, Harvard Business School Press, 1999, p96
12. John Hagel and Marc Singer, *Net Worth*, p235
13. Sandra Vandermerwe, *Customer Capitalism*, p76

Chapter 18 Minimize total purchasing costs

1. Adrian Slywotzky and David Morrison, *Profit Zone*
2. Patricia Seybold, *customers.com*, Times Business, 1998, pp11–15
3. Ibid.

Chapter 19 Reverse the flow

1. Stephan Haeckel, *Adaptive Enterprise*, Harvard Business School Press, 1999, p6
2. James Womack and Dan Jones, *Lean Thinking*, p24
3. Don Peppers and Martha Rogers, *The One-to-One Future*, p266
4. Michael Dell, *Direct from Dell*, p142
5. *Business Week*, 28 February 2000
6. Stephan Haeckel, *Adaptive Enterprise*, pxviii
7. See, for example, Alan Mitchell, *Efficient Consumer Response, a new paradigm for the Europe consumer goods industry*, FT Management Reports, 1997
8. Martin Christopher, *Marketing Logistics*, Butterworth Heinemann, 1997, p1
9. Regis McKenna, *Real Time*, p6
10. Interview with Regis McKenna, 12 April 1999
11. Kevin Kelly, *New Rules for the New Economy*, p21
12. quoted in Alan Mitchell, *Efficient Consumer Response*
13. McKenna, *Real Time*, p42

Chapter 20 Think 'Join Me!'

1. Charles Leadbeater, *Living on Thin Air*, Viking, 1999, p25
2. Stan Davis and Christopher Meyer, *Blur: the speed of change in the connected economy*, Perseus Books, 1998, p55
3. Don Pepper and Martha Rogers, *The One-to-One Future*, p57
4. An interview with Jay Walker, *Strategy + Business*, Booz, Allen & Hamilton, Issue 19, Second Quarter 2000
5. Sandra Vandermerwe, *Customer Capitalism*, p121
6. Stephan Haeckel, Director of Strategic Studies, IBM, in a letter to *Sloan Management Review*, Vol. 41, No., Fall 1999
7. Michael Dell, *Direct from Dell*, pp166, 158
8. Ibid., p140
9. Regis McKenna, *Real Time*, p43
10. Speech to the International Advertising Association, 7 June 2000
11. See James Womack and Daniel Jones, *Lean Thinking*, and Richard Lamming, *Beyond Partnership*
12. Fred Wiersema, *Customer Intimacy*, p7
13. Joseph Pine and James Gilmore, *The Experience Economy*, p183
14. Michael Dell, *Direct from Dell*, p147
15. Ibid., p163
16. Kevin Kelly, *Out of Control: the new biology of machines*, p39
17. David Weinberger, 'Why everyone hates marketing', p293
18. Martin Christopher, Adrian Payne and David Ballantyne, *Relationship Marketing*, Butterworth Heinemann, 1991 vii
19. James Womack and Daniel Jones, p275
20. Ibid., p276

Chapter 21 Embrace 'contract-plus'

1. Frederick Reichheld, Bain and Company, Institute of Direct Marketing symposium, 12 May 1999
2. Charles Leadbeater, *Living on Thin Air*, p11
3. Sandra Vandermerwe, *Customer Capitalism*, p214
4. Charles Handy, *The Empty Raincoat*, Arrow Books, 1995, pp158 and 197
5. MCA/MORI research, 1999
6. Peter Drucker, 'Management's New Paradigms
7. Ibid., p166

8. Richard Lamming, *Beyond Partnership*, Prentice Hall, 1993, p238
9. Ibid., pxvii
10. M. Sako, quoted in ibid., p144
11. Ibid., pp209, 172
12. Sue Adkins, *Cause Related Marketing*, Butterworth Heinemann, 1999, p45
13. See Rosabeth Moss Kanter, 'From Spare Change to Real Change', *Harvard Business Review*, May–June 1999, p124
14. 'A Road Map for Natural Capitalism', *Harvard Business Review*, May-June 1999
15. Martin Christopher, Adrian Payne and David Ballantyne, *Relationship Marketing*, p61
16. Francis Fukuyama, *The Great Disruption*, Free Press/Profile Books, 1999, p174
17. Kevin Kelly, *New Rules for the New Economy*, p137
18. Quoted in *Issues*, the magazine of Enterprise IG, May 1999
19. Chris Macrae, *The Brand Chartering Handbook*, Addison-Wesley, 1996
20. Simon Knox and Stan Maklan, *Competing on Value*, Financial Times Pitman, 1998
21. Michael Dell, *Direct from Dell*, p222
22. Geoff Papows, *Enterprise.com*, Nichoas Brealey, 1999, p10

Chapter 22 *The new quality revolution*

1. Fritjof Capra, quoting Walter Weisskopf in *The Turning Point*, Flamingo, 1982, p440
2. Joseph Pine and James Gilmore, *The Experience Economy*, p163
3. see also John Naisbitt, *High Tech High Touch: technology and our search for meaning*, Nicholas Brealey, 1999
4. Kevin Kelly, *New Rules for the New Economy*, p94
5. Paul Krugman, *Pop Internationalism*, MIT Press, 1996
6. James Womack and Daniel Jones, *Lean Thinking*, p65
7. James Collins and Jerry Porras, *Built to Last*, Century, 1996

Chapter 23 Beyond brand experience

1. Michael Lanning, *Delivering Profitable Value*, p79
2. Joseph Pine and James Gilmore, *The Experience Economy*, p67
3. Rolf Jensen, *The Dream Society*, McGraw Hill, 1999, p4
4. Joseph Pine and James Gilmore, *The Experience Economy*, Harvard Business School Press, 1999, p22
5. Bernd Schmitt, *Experiential Marketing: How to get customers to sense, feel, think, act and relate to your company and brands*, Free Press, 1999
6. Rolf Jensen, *The Dream Society*, p53
7. Joseph Pine and James Gilmore, *The Experience Economy*, p190. This section's notion of the transformation agent draws heavily on Pine and Gilmore's discussion here of the market for 'transformations'.
8. Ibid., p173
9. Michael Dell, *Direct from Dell*, p207
10. Interview, January 1999
11. Interview, December 1998
12. Kevin Thomson, *Emotional Capital*, p37
13. See for example, Anthony Rucci, Steven Kirn, and Richard Quinn, 'The employee-customer profit chain at Sear', *Harvard Business Review*, January–February 1998

Chapter 24 Broaden the exchange

1. Joseph Pine and James Gilmore, *The Experience Economy*, p183
2. Kevin Kelly, *New Rules for the New Economy*, p32
3. Roger Scruton, 'Do the Right Thing', *The Good Life*, Demos, London 1998
4. Kevin Thomson, *Emotional Capital*, 1998
5. John Kay, *Foundations of Corporate Success*, Oxford University Press, 1993
6. John Kay, 'The oblique approach', *Financial Times*, 28 October 1998
7. Matt Ridley, *The Origins of Virtue*, pp135–8
8. Francis Fukuyama, *The Great Disruption*, p16
9. Ibid., p200
10. Glen Peters, *Waltzing with Raptors*, John Wiley, 1999. Quote from

Glen Peters, 'Why nice guys finish first', *Financial Times*, 7 December 1999

11. see Sue Adkins, *Cause Related Marketing*
12. quoted in ibid., p13
13. Ibid., p7
14. Talk to the Marketing Forum, 1999

Chapter 25 Liberating marketing

1. Philip Kotler, *Kotler on Marketing, pxiv*
2. *quoted in Daniel C. Dennett, Darwin's Dangerous Idea*, Penguin, 1995, p465
3. Sergio Zyman, *The End of Marketing As We Know It*, p5
4. Philip Kotler and Gary Armstrong, *Principles of Marketing*, p6

Chapter 26 Are agents viable?

1. Interview, 10 May 2000
2. John Hagel and Marc Singer, *Net Worth*, p224

Chapter 27 Evolutionary trajectories

1. Kevin Kelly, *New Rules for the New Economy*, p92
2. For more on fitness peaks, see Stuart Kauffman, *At Home in the Universe*, and Stuart Kauffman, *The Origins of Order*, Oxford University Press, 1993
3. Charles Leadbeater, *Living on Thin Air*, pp37–8
4. Philip Evans and Thomas Wurster, *Blown to Bits*, p138
5. Charles Leadbeater, *Living on Thin Air*, p21
6. An interview with Jay Walker by Randall Rothenberg, *Strategy + Business*, Issue 2, 2000
7. Interview, 10 May 2000
8. wirednew.com/new/business
9. Interview, November 1998
10. Charles Leadbeater, *Living on Thin Air*, pviii
11. Interview, 6 April 1999

index